JERRY BAKER'S
Lawn Book

JERRY BAKER'S
Lawn Book

Jerry Baker

BALLANTINE BOOKS • NEW YORK

Library of Congress Catalog Card Number: 86-91705

ISBN: 0-345-34094-9

Cover photo by Charles Schridde
Cover design by James R. Harris
Book design by Gene Siegel

Manufactured in the United States of America

First Edition: March 1987

20   19 18 17 16 15 14

To
Ilene
my wife, my life, my love
and
my children
Sue, Diane, Pat, Jeff, and Kassie
my pride and joy and hope

Contents

Acknowledgments

I never get tired of saying thank you to people who lend me a helping hand. In writing this book, I have called upon many of my friends to help me provide the ideas and techniques that can make your adventure into the green scene more exciting, rewarding, and fun than most of you thought possible.

In some places in this book I may sound like your science teacher, the one you were sure had no heart, pounding away at a basic principle of science until he was sure you had it down pat. Your grass and *I* want you to *act* and *react*—without hesitation—when you observe some change occurring in your lawn or in the weather that controls these changes.

Thanks for my professional education—as it relates to grasses and especially grass seed—go to Ed Fahlstrom, president of Michael-Leonard Seed Company and Mock Seed Company. Ed has taught me all I know and continues to teach me. I am forever indebted to him and to his vice-president, John Magoun, who helps with the education of my friends at Hardrock Horticultural Center at Jackson State Prison.

Thanks also to the Loft Seed Company, which is always promoting the grass seed industry, and to K-Mart Corporation, which makes it possible for me to help you through their top-quality Super K-Gro lawn and garden products.

Thanks to Dr. Eliot C. Roberts, director of the Lawn Institute, who keeps my mailbox full of the latest information and changing trends in grass growing. Dr. Roberts does not know how to say no when anyone asks for help or information on grasses.

Thanks to Dr. Jack Murray of the USDA at the Beltsville Agricultural Research Center for all of his efforts in getting me information on the cool-season grasses.

Thanks to the USDA and Cooperative Extension Service for their cooperation with their lists of the publications available to you, the homeowner.

And thanks to Nelson sprinklers, Rainbird, Acme Garden Chemicals, and to John Botsford (president of Idea Mower Company, Ferndale, Michigan), who makes me keep trying new innovations in turf equipment.

Thanks again to Carole Compton, my manuscript typist, who makes this readable, and to Grace Smith, who keeps all of the irons in the fire sorted out.

Lastly, thanks to the American Seed Trade Association, which is fighting for the American home gardeners' rights to fairness and understanding in grass seed packaging and the simplification of labels. They are dedicated to the standardization of seed labels throughout the country and removal of the confusing kind-and-count labels.

Foreword

An editor recently told me that the mention of lawnwork "turns people off." I asked her if she had a lawn to look after, and whether she enjoyed it. "Oh," she said, "I am only twenty-seven, single, and live on the nineteenth floor of an apartment building." I forgave her her ignorance. On the other hand, eighty-one million Americans have lawns of varying sizes and qualities. What nearly all of them have in common is their desire to have the greenest grass on their side of the fence. Oh! I grant you that the degree of enthusiasm varies greatly from person to person, but it adds up to $2.263 billion annual sales of lawn fertilizers and weed killers (not to mention the millions spent on mowers, chemicals, and other lawn tools and equipment). Hold it, I'm not done yet. Now, add the billion or so dollars that industrial landscapers and fertilizer applicators take in. I would say that's a far cry from "turned off."

Lawn care itself is a love-hate relationship. We love the results, but hate the work. And the incredible variety of fertilizers, weeds, chemicals, bugs, diseases, mowing and watering techniques can be pretty confusing. But, even though lawn care can be frustrating and bewildering, that's a far cry from "turned off."

Getting the wrong answers to the right questions from poorly trained garden-shop help often starts your Saturday off on the wrong foot. I grant you that the three numbers on a bag of fertilizer can turn out to be the odds on your lawn living or dying. The super-duper weed killer that makes your weeds grow, not go, does try your patience, but that's still a far cry from "turned off."

What it all amounts to is you want answers and techniques that work *for* you, not *against* you, and that's what this green-grass-growing guide book is all about! I'll tell you what you need to know, when you need to know it, and how to use it once you've got it. The advice here is fast, safe, economical, and fun.

Let's get one thing straight, right now. No matter how odd, funny, silly, or even crazy my suggestions may sound, try them! You will be absolutely amazed at the results. The savings in money and effort will flabbergast you.

So, let's get growing so that we can do some crowing when the greenest grass really does end up on our side of the fence.

Let the turf turn you on, not off.

1

Grasses and Grass Types
Hound Dogs in the Bullpen and Rebels in the Outfield

Give Credit Where Credit Is Due

Most of you take grass for granted, considering it just a pleasant green mass that enhances your personal environment. Let me give you a few facts that may inspire you to have greater respect for your green scene:

- An acre of grass is the equivalent of a seventy-ton air conditioner—returning over 2,400 gallons of water to the atmosphere on a warm, sunny day.
- A twenty-five-square-foot patch of grass supplies enough oxygen to support an adult.
- Grass takes in carbon dioxide, sulphur dioxide, ozone, hydrogen fluoride, and peroxyacetyl nitrate—the worst group of atmospheric pollutants—and returns the true breath of life: pure oxygen.
- The grass and trees along the interstate highway system alone manufacture enough oxygen to support 22 million people.
- Of all the plants, grasses are the most important to man. All of our breadstuffs (corn, wheat, oats, barley, rye, rice, and sugarcane) are grasses.

Count the Grass Plants in Your Lawn

How many plants do you have to grow to be considered a farmer? According to the Lawn Institute, many gardeners grow more grass plants in their lawn than a farmer grows cornstalks in his field. Thirty-five million lawn grass plants to the acre, or about three million for the average four-thousand-square-foot lawn, make up a good dense turf. That's quite a population!

With these little bits of trivia tucked into your memory, let's grow on to prove that we all really do have a green thumb. Your lawn is a *great* place to start.

The subtitle of this chapter probably makes it sound like I've written a novel about a southern family feud instead of a lawn care book. Hounddog and Rebel are just two of the dozens upon dozens of grass seed varieties that are available to you. Derby, Blazer, Citation, Delray, Baron, Monopoly, Rugby, and Touchdown are a few others that may end up gracing your lawn. There are over three hundred different varieties of grass seed for sale in the United States and Canada, and more are being developed every year.

Grass varieties are as different as people or pets. The quality, looks, and stamina of all three are determined by their "bloodlines." Grass seed breeders look for the best and strongest traits in many types of grasses—from "cour" (a grass) all the way down to the fine-textured bent grasses—crossing and recrossing the different types, trying to develop grasses that will make lawn care a pleasure.

Patent Pending Goes to Seed

A "Breeder's Rights" law, which protects the seed varieties and vegetable clones that are developed by individual breeders, was passed in 1971. As soon as this protection was available, dozens of new lawn grass varieties were released. Every year since then, new and improved grasses have been made available to the homeowner.

Many Are Called, But Few Are Chosen

This truism suits the many new lawn grass cultivars that are so popular these days. The hundreds of inbreds and polycrosses that are bred each year are carefully scrutinized for the superior attributes that could establish them in the market. Some are loaded with glamour, but nevertheless fail, often for simple reasons like not being able to resist a commonplace disease. Others display little initial glitter but eventually gain popularity for want of any serious faults.

Wherever and however it is evaluated, any new cultivar must display certain basic favorable characteristics, or the effort of bringing it to market would not be worth it.

It will, for example, have been well screened for tolerance against the more commonplace diseases. It will be lower-growing, and thus denser at normal mowing heights, than is common grass. And, of course, it will have shown satisfactory hardiness and adaptability over a sizable market area.

Typically, it takes several years to evaluate a prospective cultivar and then years more to build up a supply of foundation seed with which to start field plantings. Even if the cultivar survives this far and grower interest beings to pick up, it will be two *more* years before the field plantings yield economical quantities of marketable seed—and the seed's developers get their first chance to recoup their investment!

With such a closely supervised progression of stages to develop a commercial product, almost any proprietary lawn grass will inevitably be an improvement over common grass. Not surprisingly, though, relatively few grasses are "chosen."

The Lawn Institute

Since it would be impossible for grass seed packagers to test and keep up with the claims of each of these new varieties, they rely on the *Lawn Institute* to keep things straight.

The Lawn Institute was formed in 1955 as a nonprofit corporation to encourage and assist in, through research and public education, the improvement of lawns, turf, and grasslands.

The Institute cooperates with the major lawn-research and education centers throughout the United States, Canada, and other countries that are members of the International Turfgrass Society. In addition to sponsoring research and publication, the Institute also monitors the results of lawn and turf research.

The Institute also maintains a close association with the American Seed Trade Association, the American Society of Agronomy, the American Society for Horticultural Science, and the Soil Conservation Society of America.

As a result, the Institute can provide invaluable information on the best grasses, the best chemical products, the best equipment, and the best techniques for planting and maintaining lawns and turf. This information is available to garden writers, broadcasters, consultants, classroom instructors, cooperative extension specialists and agents, and the general public.

Evaluation of Grass and Lawn Maintenance Products

The Institute's Variety Review Board evaluates and registers proprietary grass cultivars submitted by grass breeders. A "Seal of Approval" is available for these proprietary products. Lawn maintenance products may also be granted a "Seal of Approval," upon compliance with Institute standards and procedures.

Even Grass Gets an Annual Award

In addition to its many other jobs, each year the Lawn Institute's Variety Review Board selects several of the top varieties for special recognition. This helps you and me and the seed packagers narrow down our choice of grass seeds from the more than three hundred varieties available. The Lawn Institute will also help you find just the right variety of grass seed for your area. Send a stamped, self-addressed, business-size envelope to:

The Lawn Institute
P.O. Box 108
Pleasant Hill, Tennessee   38578

with a request for the current year's "Grass Seed Recognition List" and for the variety recommended for your area.

Getting to Know Your Grass Seed

Dr. Robert Schery, a retired director of the Lawn Institute, describes lawns as the basic "floor" for your garden. It's possible to make a great "ha-do" out of selecting just the right texture, color, height, and density of grass as a background or basis for your complete green scene.

Let me tell you, folks, if it's variety you want, then you've got an incredible range of grass varieties to choose from. Some are coarse and for rough purposes only. Others are fine-textured and produce a turf that is truly like velvet. Some are for warm climes only, and some will grow as far north as grass will grow. Some need much care, others almost none.

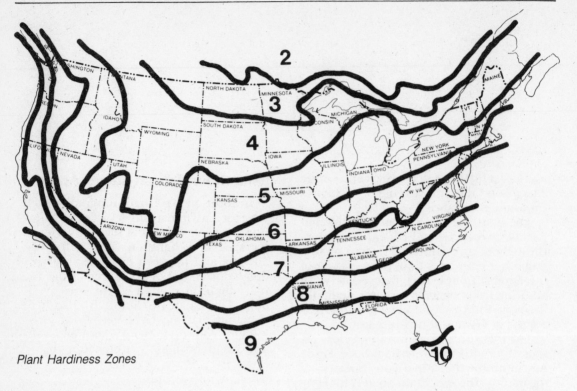

Plant Hardiness Zones

Turf Grass Selection

To establish a satisfactory, permanent lawn you'll have to select properly adapted turf grass species and cultivars. If the grasses you've selected are not adaptable to your environment, level of maintenance, or use, you'll end up with an inferior lawn or a lawn that never establishes itself.

The purpose of this chapter is to help you fit the right grass to the right garden—and gardener. I've included descriptions (see pages 5–25) of the most popular varieties, along with advice on where they'll grow best, and on their proper care and feeding.

Snowbird and Sunbelt Seeds Know the Difference

Let's take a look at just where the different types of grass are most comfortable.

In general, most northern grasses (if treated properly) can adapt to growth in the intermediate zone. Of the southern types, only a few Bermudas and zoysias can be used very far northward.

Refer to both the plant hardiness zone map and the lawn grass preference tables that follow to find the best varieties for your little corner of the world. These Lawn Institute recommendations will show you how to use your grass seed friend's talents best.

Keep Your Eyes on Mixed Company

It's important to remember that turf grasses are more often planted as seed blends and mixtures than as cultures of just one variety.

A seed *blend* is a combination of two or more cultivars of the same species, such as the Adelphi and Baron Kentucky cultivars of bluegrass. A blend is usually suited to a broader range of soils, environments, and cultural intensities than is a stand of a single cultivar. In addition, blending generally reduces the incidence of lawn diseases.

A seed *mixture* is made up of two or more different turf grass species. The chief advantage of a mixture is that each species will be better adapted to certain environmental conditions than will the others.

For example, a perennial ryegrass will often be included in a bluegrass-fescue seed mixture, even though the ryegrass may not be as broadly hardy as the other species. It will help make lawn cover quickly, even though it may not persist in extreme climates.

Shade, sandy soils, poorly drained soils, or low maintenance are conditions that require specific turf grass mixtures.

Sowing seed blends or mixtures is a good way to spread the risks over several seed types and to end up with a lawn that's more adaptable to your local conditions. Your lawn may include a wide range of soil and environmental conditions, and mixtures and/or blends can help deal with these varied conditions.

Grasses State by State	Kentucky Bluegrass	Fine Fescue	Bent Grass	Tall Fescue	Ryegrass	Bermuda Grass	Zoysia	Dichondra	St. Augustine Grass	Centipede Grass	Carpet Grass	Bahia Grass
Alabama				x		x	x			x		
Alaska	x	x		x	x							
Arizona	x	x	x	x	x	x	x			x		
Arkansas						x	x		x	x	x	
California	x	x	x	x	x	x	x	x	x	x		
Colorado	x	x	x	x	x							
Connecticut	x	x	x	x	x							
Delaware	x	x	x	x	x							
District of Columbia	x	x	x	x	x	x	x					
Florida					x	x	x		x	x	x	x
Georgia				x		x	x		x	x	x	
Hawaii												
Idaho	x	x	x	x	x							
Illinois	x	x	x	x	x	x	x					

Grasses
State by State

	Kentucky Bluegrass	Fine Fescue	Bent Grass	Tall Fescue	Ryegrass	Bermuda Grass	Zoysia	Dichondra	St. Augustine Grass	Centipede Grass	Carpet Grass	Bahia Grass
Indiana	X	X	X	X	X	X	X					
Iowa	X	X	X	X	X							
Kansas	X	X	X	X	X	X	X					
Kentucky	X	X	X	X	X	X	X					
Louisiana						X	X		X	X	X	
Missouri	X	X	X	X	X	X	X		X			
Montana	X	X	X	X	X							
Nebraska	X	X	X	X	X							
Nevada	X	X	X	X	X	X	X			X		
New Hampshire	X	X	X	X	X							
New Jersey	X	X	X	X	X							
New Mexico	X	X	X	X	X	X	X			X		
New York	X	X	X	X	X							
North Carolina	X	X	X	X	X	X	X			X		
North Dakota	X	X	X	X	X							
Ohio	X	X	X	X	X							
Oklahoma	X	X	X	X	X	X	X			X		
Oregon	X	X	X	X	X							
Pennsylvania	X	X	X	X	X							
Rhode Island	X	X	X	X	X							
South Carolina	X	X	X	X	X	X	X			X		
South Dakota	X	X	X	X	X							
Tennessee	X	X	X	X	X	X	X			X		
Texas	X	X	X	X	X	X	X		X	X	X	
Utah	X	X	X	X	X	X	X			X		
Vermont	X	X	X	X	X							
Virginia	X	X	X	X	X	X	X			X		
Washington	X	X	X	X	X							
West Virginia	X	X	X	X	X							
Wisconsin	X	X	X	X	X							
Wyoming	X	X	X	X	X							
Puerto Rico					X	X	X		X	X	X	X
Virgin Islands					X	X	X		X	X	X	X

The situation is simpler in the South. There the improved cultivars are generally planted alone as vegetative starts since they are not sexually inbred and don't come true from seed. Vegetative starts include sprigs, which are small pieces of sod or grass plant stems; plugs, which are small circular pieces of turf cut out of sod; and sod.

Typical Seed Label

FINE-TEXTURED GRASSES	Germination
29% Baron Kentucky Bluegrass	90%
29% Adelphi Kentucky Bluegrass	90%
20% Jamestown Red Fescue	85%
COARSE KINDS	
20% Perennial Ryegrass	80%
OTHER INGREDIENTS	
0.0% Crop seed	
1.5% Inert matter	
0.5% Weed seed	

Seed packages must list what kinds of seeds and other materials are in the mix. Look for cultivars that grow well in your area—and for very low percentages of weed seed and inert matter.

SELECTING THE APPROPRIATE TURF GRASS BLENDS AND MIXTURES

The chart at the bottom of the page will give you an idea of how some popular seed mixtures and blends will grow in your state.

SEED PACKAGE LABELING

The seed label is a good buyer's guide to purchasing quality seed. Check the label to determine the species or cultivars in the package. Also, check the percentage of (a) pure seed; (b) other crop seed; (c) weed seed; and (d) inert matter. The price of a seed package is usually determined by its varietal composition, germination, and purity. The current market supply of the grasses included in the mix is another important cost factor.

Fortunately, if you purchase your lawn seed mixture from a reliable source, you are likely to get good-quality seed—blended by experienced seed experts—which combines the proper varieties for your area. Beware, however, of bargain blends, which are often offered for less than a dollar per pound. These are very likely to contain a high percentage of coarse grasses, less well-cleaned seed, and *weed* seeds. A low-priced, rapid-lawn-establishing seed mixture is a poor buy if it contains large portions of temporary and weedy perennial grasses unsuitable for a permanent, quality lawn.

	Bahia Grass	Hulled Bermuda	Unhulled Bermuda	Perennial Rye	Annual Rye	Tall Fescue	Kentucky Blue	Derby Perennial Rye	All Fescue Mix	Custom	Parkway	Bluegrass Mix	Campus Green	Super K-Gro Spot Seeder	Super K-Gro Game Time	Super K-Gro Shady	Super K-Gro Showplace
Alabama		o	o	o	o	*		o	*	*			o	o	o	o	o
Arizona	*	*	o	o	o	o	o	o	o	o	o	o	o	o	o	o	o
Arkansas	o	o	o	o	o	o	*	o	o	o	o	*	*	o	o	o	o
N. California				o	o	*	o	o	*	*		o	o	*	*	*	*
S. California	*	*	o	o	o	*	o	o	*	*		o	o	*	*	*	*
Colorado				o	o	o	*	*	o	o	*	*	*	*	*	*	*

* Highly recommended   o Recommended   N Not available

	Bahia Grass	Hulled Bermuda	Unhulled Bermuda	Perennial Rye	Annual Rye	Tall Fescue	Kentucky Blue	Derby Perennial Rye	All Fescue Mix	Custom	Parkway	Bluegrass Mix	Campus Green	Super K-Gro Spot Seeder	Super K-Gro Game Time	Super K-Gro Shady	Super K-Gro Showplace
Connecticut				o	o	o	*	*	o	o	*	*	*	*	*	*	*
Delaware				o	o	o	o	*	o	o	o	o	*	*	*	*	*
Florida	o	*	*	o	o	o			o				o	o	o	o	o
Georgia		o	o	o	o	*			o	*	*		o	o	o	o	o
Idaho				o	o	o	*	*	o	o	*	*	*	*	*	*	*
Illinois				o	o	o	*	*	o	o	*	*	*	*	*	*	*
Indiana				o	o	o	*	*	o	o	*	*	*	*	*	*	*
Iowa				o	o	o	*	*	o	o	*	*	*	*	*	*	*
Kansas				o	o	*	o	*	*	*	*	o	*	*	*	*	*
Kentucky				o	o	o	*	*	o	o	*	*	*	*	*	*	*
Louisiana		*	*	o	o	o			o	o			o	o	o	o	o
Maine				o	o	o	*	*	o	o	*	*	*	*	*	*	*
Maryland				o	o	*	o	*	*	*	o	o	*	*	o		*
Massachusetts				o	o	o	*	*	o	o	*	*	*	*	*	*	*
Michigan				o	o	o	*	*	o	o	*	*	*	*	*	*	*
Minnesota				o	o	o	*	*	o	o	*	*	*	*	*	*	*
Mississippi		*	*	o	o	o			o	o			o	o	o	o	o
Missouri				o	o	*	*	*	*	*	o		*	*	*	*	*
Montana				o	o	o	*	*	N	N	N	*	o	o	*	*	*
Nebraska				o	o	*	*	*	*	*	*		*	*	*	*	*
Nevada		o	o	o	o	*	o	*	o	*	o	o	*	*	o	o	o
New Hampshire				o	o	o	*	*	o	o	*	*	*	*	*	*	*
New Jersey				o	o	o	o	*	o	o	*	o	*	*	*	*	*
New Mexico		o	o	o	o	*	o	o	*	o	o	o	*	o	o	o	o
New York				o	o	o	*	*	o	o	*	*	*	*	*	*	*
North Carolina				o	o	*	o	*	*	*	o	o	*	*	*	*	*
North Dakota				o	o	o	*	*	o	o	*	*	*	*	*	*	*
Ohio				o	o	o	*	*	o	o	*	*	*	*	*	*	*
Oklahoma		o	o	o	o	o	o	*	o	o	o	o	*	*	*	*	*
Oregon				*	*	o	o	*	o	o	o	o	*	*	*	*	*
Pennsylvania				o	o	o	*	*	o	o	*	*	*	*	*	*	*
Rhode Island				o	o	o	*	*	o	o	*	*	*	*	*	*	*
South Carolina		o	o	o	o	*			o	*	*		o	o	o	o	o
South Dakota				o	o	o	*	*	o	o	*	*	*	*	*	*	*
Tennessee		o	o	o	o	*	o	*	*	*	o	o	*	*	*	*	*
Texas		*	*	o	o	o		o	o	o			o	o	o	o	o
Utah				o	o	o	o	*	o	o	o	o	*	*	*	*	*
Vermont				o	o	o	*	*	o	o	*	*	*	*	*	*	*

* Highly recommended   o Recommended   N Not available

	Bahia Grass	Hulled Bermuda	Unhulled Bermuda	Perennial Rye	Annual Rye	Tall Fescue	Kentucky Blue	Derby Perennial Rye	All Fescue Mix	Custom	Parkway	Bluegrass Mix	Campus Green	Super K-Gro Spot Seeder	Super K-Gro Game Time	Super K-Gro Shady	Super K-Gro Showplace
Virginia				o	o	*	o	*	*	*	o	o	*	*	*	*	*
Washington				o	o	o	*	*	o	o	*	*	*	*	*	*	*
West Virginia				o	o	o	o	*	o	o	o	o	*	*	*	*	*
Wisconsin				o	o	o	*	*	o	o		*	*	*	*	*	*
Wyoming				o	o	o	*	*	N	N	N	*	*	*	*	*	*

* Highly recommended	o Recommended	N Not available

YOU HAD BETTER KNOW HOW MUCH TO BUY

Most homeowners purchase and plant far too much grass seed. Then, when the grass surprises them and sprouts, there is hardly enough room for each little seed to be born, let alone grow. If you were to use a mechanical seed drill, which professionals use to plant sod fields and playfields, your seed would be set ¼ inch apart. If you hand-planted your seeds following this ¼ inch spacing, you would have a super lawn within a month. The following table shows some helpful facts that will help you give your grass room to grow.

YOU MUST GET DOWN TO THE GRASS ROOTS

If you expect to grow a lawn that makes people take a second look, you have to choose the right grass varieties for your climate, soil, pocketbook, time, and health. The information we've just gone over should certainly give you a growing head start—with little reason to worry about the results.

	Days to Germinate	Seeds per Pound (in thousands)	Seeding per 1,000 Square Feet	Life	Texture	General Utility	Effectiveness in Shaded Areas
Kentucky Bluegrass	28	2,400	3 lb.	Permanent	Fine	Best	Poor
Merion Bluegrass	28	3,500	2 lb.	Permanent	Fine	Best	No
Chewings Fescue	21	450	8 lb.	Permanent	Very Fine	Good	Good
Creeping Red Fescue	21	400	8 lb.	Permanent	Very Fine	Good	Good
Creeping Bent Grass	28	6,000	3 lb.	Permanent	Very Fine	Fair	No
Poa Trivialis (Rough Bluegrass)	28	2,200	4 lb.	Permanent	Fine	Fair	Best
Tall Fescues	10	375	8 lb.	Permanent	Coarse	Poor	Fair
Meadow Fescue	8	250	10 lb.	Permanent	Coarse	Fair	Good

	Days to Germinate	Seeds per Pound (in thousands)	Seeding per 1,000 Square Feet	Life	Texture	General Utility	Effectiveness in Shaded Areas
Red Top	6	4,100	3 lb.	3 Years	Coarse	Poor	No
Perennial Ryegrass	8	210	10 lb.	3 Years	Coarse	Fair	Fair
Annual Ryegrass	8	225	10 lb.	1 Year	Coarse	Poor	Fair
White Clover	10	700	6 lb.	Permanent	Coarse	Good	Fair

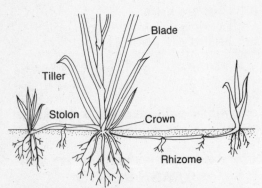

Grass plants spread through below-ground or above ground runners.

AGROPYRON

Botanical Name: Agropyron sp. (includes *A. critatum* and *A. smithii*, which are fairway and western wheatgrasses)

Remarks: Agropyron is used for rough areas, such as roadsides, that are inhospitable to the better turf grasses.

General Characteristics: Agropyron is fairly open (for relatively thin cover) and has extensive rooting that helps it tolerate drought conditions.

Habitat: Agropyron prefers semiarid, cool, sunny plains. The fairway species, at least, is very cold-hardy (into Hardiness Zones 2–3).

Source: Seed is available (but not for select turf types). Agropyron spreads by underground stems (rhizomes).

Care: Agropyron is undemanding. It requires only occasional fertilizing.

Mowing: Mow Agropyron to 2–3 inches high.

BAHIA GRASS

Botanical Name: Paspalpum notatum

Remarks: Bahia grass is one of the more economical southern grasses and makes establishing an inexpensive lawn possible in the Deep South. It was first used as a pasture grass; only recently has its value as an ornamental lawn grass been recognized. It's not as elegant as the improved Bermudas and zoysias (because of its coarse texture), but it can be attractive if properly cared for.

Bahia grasses are native to tropical America and were most likely introduced to Texas from Cuba. (The word *Bahia* refers to a state in Brazil.) As indicated by their names—Argentine and Paraguay—other selections have come from South America.

General Characteristics: Bahia grass is fairly coarse, has dark, hairy leaves, and produces deep, vigorous roots. It is more erect and open-growing than other southern species, with less foliage—and is therefore more likely to become weed infested. It is quite tolerant of shade—the best of all the warm-season grasses.

Habitat: Bahia grass is widely tolerant, enduring poor, sandy habitats such as roadsides, and can be started from seed. It will grow in the sun or in partial shade. It is well adapted to the southern Atlantic and Gulf coastal plains and is widely used in Florida and the Deep South. It is planted in coastal environments as far north as the Carolinas.

Varieties: The Pensacola, Paraguay, and Argentine varieties have finer leaves.

Argentine has soft, hairy leaves. It is somewhat coarse, and is well adapted to southern Florida. This selection is often used for lawns because it produces fewer seedheads and is easier to mow than Pensacola, which is often used for roadsides.

Common Bahia grass is very coarse and often winter-kills at temperatures below 20 degrees F. It is not generally recommended for lawns.

Paraguay has hairy leaves with a dull sheen. It is slow to germinate and is a heavy seedhead producer. Otherwise, it is much like the Pensacola variety. Paraguay does not seed well in the humid Southeast. It is produced in Texas.

Paraguayan 22 Bahia grass (also known as Tifton) is coarser than Paraguay, and more like the Argentine variety.

Pensacola is the best germinating variety. It is fine-leaved and glossy, hardy, cold-tolerant to 5 degrees F (maintaining its color during the winter), and pest-resistant.

Seaside paspalum is fine-textured, has few seedheads, and is drought-tolerant. It was developed as a low-maintenance, salt-tolerant lawn grass that is vegetatively propagated as Adalyd grass.

Tifhi is a Pensacola hybrid but is denser and leafier.

Wilmington is similar to Pensacola, with a fine texture, dark-green leaves, and fewer seedheads. It is more cold-tolerant and is propagated vegetatively.

Source: Bahia grass is available as seed or from vegetative starts (sprigs, plugs, or sod). It spreads by aboveground runners (stolons) and underground stems (rhizomes). Seed production for the improved Bahia grass types is in the developmental stage. A ready supply of the finer-leaved Wilmington variety (a poor seed producer), for example, is not yet available.

Care: Bahia grass requires less attention than other southern species (except for centipede grass), but looks better when adequately tended. It is highly tolerant of neglect and poor conditions, such as soil infertility, drought, moist soil, and acid and alkaline soils. It is also resistant to lawn diseases, chinch bugs, and other lawn insects.

Bahia grass seed has a waxy coat that slows the penetration of moisture. It is therefore slow to germinate unless treated. High rates of seeding (10 pounds per 1,000 square feet) will help establish a good stand quickly. Two or three pounds of seed will develop a turf over time.

A seed mixture that contains fine fescues as well as Bahia grass will develop a turf cover more quickly. As the Bahia grass fills in, the fine fescues will fade out. Bahia grass is also used as an overseed into thin stands to help develop a thicker lawn.

Spring plantings are best, but Bahia grass seed sown in the fall will overwinter in the soil. This permits it to be used in "all season" seed mixtures. Southern seed mixtures may include Bahia grass, zoysia grass, Bermuda grass, and centipede grass. If winter grasses are added, the mixture may be seeded at any time of the year.

Seedheads are particularly conspicuous in the spring and can reduce the quality of the turf. You can limit seedhead formation by omitting or delaying early spring fertilization or by using a growth retardant.

Bahia grass responds well to fertilizer applications made in March and September—along with additional slow-release nitrogen applied during the summer (only). Two to 4 pounds of nitrogen per season is usually adequate.

Avoid arsonate, simazine, and atrazine weed killers. Bahia grass is tolerant of 2,4-D herbicides, but, like crabgrass, it is injured by methyl arsonate.

Mowing: Bahia grass is generally mowed intermediate to tall (1½ to 2½ inches high). It has an intermediate (or fairly thick) growth. Very close mowing favors weeds. Bahia grass foliage is fairly "stringy" and you'll need a sharp mower for a clean cut.

BERMUDA GRASS

Botanical Name: Cynodon dactylon (and its hybrids)

Remarks: Bermuda grass is attractive and fine-textured with a deep color. The special selections and hybrids are finer-textured and better-looking and are recommended for better lawns. The vigor of Bermuda grass helps make a thick lawn in a hurry. It also helps crowd out weeds and brings about rapid recuperation from any blemish.

General Characteristics: Bermuda grass is a vigorous warm-season grass that spreads by rhizomes. It can become an aggressive pest when used to border flower beds and in lawns where bluegrass is preferred.

Bermuda grass forms thatch readily. It is not highly susceptible to disease or insects. It is moderately resistant to drought, salt air, and wear, but is not frost-tolerant. Frost damage will slow its growth, the grass will turn off-color, and eventually turn brown. Fortunately, it recovers quickly with the return of warm weather. When exposed to extreme cold, the less winter-hardy Bermuda grasses will be winter-killed.

Dormant Bermuda grasses that are overseeded with fine fescues or perennial ryegrasses retain a uniform green throughout the winter months. The winter grasses will also help keep weeds out.

Habitat: Bermuda grass demands full sun and cannot stand shade. It does best on neutral, fertile soils and when provided with proper care. It is tolerant of varying soil conditions.

Bermuda grass grows especially well in the upper South, from middle Georgia to eastern Oklahoma (Hardiness Zones 7–8), where there is much "wild" volunteer growth, and throughout the lower elevations of the Southwest. In southern Florida and along the humid Gulf Coast (Zone 9), Bermuda grasses are well adapted, but other warm-season grasses are often easier to care for.

Varieties: Bermuda grasses originated in the warmer regions of Europe, Asia, and Africa. The names *Bermuda* and *Ba-*

hama suggest that Atlantic islands were their westward route of migration.

Unselected common Bermuda grass is propagated from seed. It is attractive if well taken care of, although somewhat more open and coarser than other Bermuda grasses.

Sunturf was introduced from South Africa. It produces few seedheads, is denser and more attractive than common Bermuda grass, is reasonably tolerant of cold, and remains green a little later in the fall. Its runners stay mostly aboveground, so it is easier to control at garden borders. Sunturf is susceptible to rust disease. It is propagated vegetatively.

The Tifton varieties are mostly sterile, triploid hybrids between common and Africa Bermuda grasses. They are usually attractively dense and fine-textured, with few detracting seedheads. They require a high level of maintenance. The new Tifdwarf variety is very low-growing.

Tifgreen (also known as Tifton 328) is widely used for golf course greens. It is an excellent fine-textured grass that is tolerant of low clipping, disease, and cold, but is sensitive to 2,4-D. It is propagated vegetatively.

Tiflawn (also known as Tifton 57) is used for lawns and athletic turf. It is tough; very vigorous; deep-green-colored; resistant to insects, disease, and drought; and moderately cold-tolerant. It is propagated vegetatively.

Tifway (also known as Tifton 419) is fine-textured and deep-colored. It resists cold discoloration. Its stiffer consistency makes it desirable for use on golf course fairways. It spreads rapidly and is propagated vegetatively.

U-3 is more dense and fairly winter-hardy, surviving as far north as Missouri (although it will suffer from diseases such as spring dead spot), but will winter-kill at low temperatures. It wears well, is drought-tolerant, spreads more slowly, and is susceptible to spring dead spot.

Other Bermuda grass varieties are Ormond (for the Southeast), Everglades (Southeast), Texturf 10 (Southwest), and Tiffine (Southeast).

Source: Common Bermuda grass is available as seed. It spreads vigorously by runners and rhizomes, tends to thatch, and sprouts more rapidly from hulled seed. The named cultivars are planted as vegetative starts (sprigs, plugs, or stolons) procured from turf grass nurseries.

Dehulled common Bermuda grass seed germinates quickly. It is highly variable, but more economical to propagate and maintain. Two to 3 pounds of Bermuda grass seed per 1,000 square feet are adequate. Unhulled seed is often planted at the higher rate.

Select varieties of Bermuda grass are propagated from living starts—sprigs or stolons—and are more costly to propagate and maintain. These are scattered at the rate of from one to six bushels per 1,000 square feet, topdressed, and watered. Plugs may be planted from 6 to 12 inches apart. The closer together the plantings are, the more rapidly they will develop.

Care: Bermuda grasses have high maintenance requirements. They are an aggressive, fast-growing group—with relatively high water and fertilizer needs—that demands regular attention: monthly feeding, twice-weekly mowing, and regular weed control.

One application of fertilizer per month is desirable. Bermuda grass lawns need about 1 pound of nitrogen per 1,000 square feet, but a complete fertilizer applied to meet soil-test recommendations is best.

Irrigation should be dictated by soil and climatic conditions. Hot, dry weather or sandy, coastal-plain soils will increase the need for watering.

Diseases and Pests: Most Bermuda grasses are tolerant of selective herbicides, fungicides, and insecticides. Any slight discoloration that occurs shouldn't last long.

Simazine and atrazine are safe when applied on dormant Bermuda grasses. Dalapon, Vapam, and methyl bromide may be used to clean out Bermuda grass where it is not wanted. (A clean kill of all grasses should be expected.) Glyphosate (Roundup) will also kill Bermuda grass under renovation conditions.

In the Southeast, sting and lance nematodes may weaken Bermuda grass roots. A nematocide will help improve turf quality. In the Southwest, the *Eriophyid* mite can be controlled with diazinon and fertilizer. Throughout the transition zone spring dead spot can cause blemishes that are difficult to heal. A combination of fungicides and insecticides can help prevent this dieback.

Mowing: Mow Bermuda grasses at low to moderate heights. Common Bermuda grass is generally mowed 1½ inches tall, while some of the elegant gold-green hybrids (such as Tifgreen and Tifdwarf) are mowed as low as ¼ inch high. Bermuda grass grows rapidly and needs frequent mowing.

BUFFALO GRASS

Botanical Name: Buchloë dactyloides
Remarks: Buffalo grass is native to and used in plains from northern Texas to Nebraska where irrigation (that could support better cover) is not possible.

General Characteristics: Buffalo grass is soft, open-growing, and grayish green, with slow vertical growth. There are separate male and female plants.

Habitat: Buffalo grass is adapted to drylands without irrigation. It likes the sun and endures drought and compact soils better than competing grasses. It grows best in Hardiness Zones 5–7

Source: Limited seed or vegetable starts are available. Buffalo grass spreads by stolons.

Care: Buffalo grass needs little or no care. Like other southern grasses, it is dormant in cold weather.

Mowing: Mow to 1 to 1½ inches high; buffalo grass is often left unmowed for roadsides.

CANADA BLUEGRASS

Botanical Name: Poa compress
Remarks: Canada bluegrass is used only in low-quality "maintenance" situations.
General Characteristics: Canada blue-

grass is broadly tolerant. It gives an open, sparse turf with short grayish green rhizomes and arching stems.

Habitat: Canada bluegrass colonizes poor soil, but competes poorly on fertile land. (Better species are available for good habitats.) It stands shade well and is hardy into Zones 2–3.

Source: Some seed is available, usually by special order.

Mowing: Canada bluegrass grows best at 3–4 inches high, but is often *not* mowed when used to cover poor land.

Care: Canada bluegrass requires little care.

CARPET GRASS

Botanical Name: Axonopus affinis

Remarks: Carpet grass is seldom planted except on difficult wet sites where the growth of other species is limited.

General Characteristics: Similar to St. Augustine, but without the "half-twist" to the leaves. Carpet grass has an intermediate growth. It will grow many seedheads.

Habitat: Carpet grass is adapted to wet soils, often volunteering in boggy situations. It grows best in sun or partial shade and in Hardiness Zones 9 and 10.

Source: Carpet grass is started from seed or vegetative starts.

Care: Carpet grass requires minimum care. It is seldom planted on better sites, so it must endure the tribulations of a boggy habitat.

Mowing: Mow carpet grass at a medium height: 1–2 inches high.

CENTIPEDE GRASS

Botanical Name: Eremochloa ophiuroides

Remarks: Centipede grass is an excellent "poor man's" intermediate lawn grass. The quality of centipede grass lawns is generally lower than that of the finer-textured Bermuda grasses and zoysia grasses.

General Characteristics: Centipede grass is perhaps the best low-maintenance, warm-season grass. It is a relatively undemanding, medium-textured grass that is somewhat temperamental about fertility, soil conditions, and some soil pests (for example, ground pearl).

Centipede grass develops slowly into an aggressive, weed-free turf that requires little attention. It produces little thatch and is therefore not subject to scalping or other mechanical injuries. The seedheads are usually low and inconspicuous.

It is low-growing, seldom reaching higher than a few inches tall when uncut. It is more shade-tolerant than Bermuda grass, but even so, it is not useful in the shade except in a high, open shade (under old pine trees, for example).

Centipede grass is generally disease-resistant, but it does not recover from injury as quickly as Bermuda grass and is not as wear-resistant as zoysia grass. (It is not recommended for athletic turf or play fields.)

Centipede grass endures drought quite well. It may turn brown from lack of water, but greens up quickly with rain. During most summers, irrigation will be required to keep it unformly green.

Habitat: Centipede grass is mainly suited to the coastal plain in the southern part of Zone 8 and northern part of Zone 9. It grows best in sun or moderate shade. It is also well adapted to the infertile, sandy soils of the coastal plain, but is sometimes temperamental there.

Centipede grass can survive in the upper South, but is not as well adapted as Bermuda grass and zoysia grass and is discolored by frost. It is not tolerant of salt sprays and thus does not do well by the seaside. It is well adapted to the coastal plain, from North Carolina south through northern Florida, and on west into Mississippi. It does not grow as well west of the Mississippi, as these more arid regions are characterized by increasing soil alkalinity.

Centipede grass prefers acid soils. (An application of iron is sometimes required to restore grass color on alkaline soil.) Where iron is available and proper nutrient balances have been maintained, centipede grass can be grown on soils with pH's above 7.0. It will grow better on well drained soils than on water logged soils.

Varieties: Centipede grass is also known as Chinese lawn grass—and originated in the Far East. *Eremochloa ophiuriodes* is a small genus of the bluestem *Andropogon* tribe. It consists of a handful of species native to southeastern Asia and the East Indies.

Few selections of centipede grass have been evaluated. The different strains of centipede grass are distinguished by stem color—either red or green.

Source: Centipede grass seed is available, but the grass is slow to establish, and little is seen the first year (crabgrass usually covers). During the second year it will shoulder out the crabgrass to make a good if not luxurious turf.

The seed is in limited supply, and expensive. ($15.00 per pound is common.) There are some 500,000 seeds per pound. Seeding rates vary from a few ounces to a pound per 1,000 square feet. The denser the seeding is, the more rapidly the lawn will establish itself.

Vegetative starts are available from nurseries in the form of sprigs or plugs. These should be planted in rows a foot apart—with individual starts 6 to 12 inches apart. Sprigs should be planted 1 to 2 inches deep, with moist green foliage left aboveground. These can be planted in a well-prepared bed or within an existing poor lawn. Spring planting provides the best possible start.

Centipede grass spreads by stolons, with short internodes. The stolons root at the joints and cause the development of a sound turf. A good leaf canopy also develops.

Care: Centipede grass needs little attention. It is at its best with little or no maintenance other than mowing.

It resents generous fertilization, since this forces growth. A single application of lawn fertilizer each spring will provide enough nutrients for most conditions.

The grass's initial response to the fertilizer will usually fade rapidly.

Centipede grass often turns chlorotic due to nutrient imbalances (especially in soils that are not acid). Apply iron sulfate or iron chelate to help control leaf yellowing or chlorosis. (Use only at the rates recommended on the product.) Adding more nitrogen will make the chlorotic condition worse.

Centipede grass spread (by stolons) at flower and other garden borders is relatively easy to control. Edging once a year will usually do the trick.

Diseases and Pests: The thick turf that centipede grass develops usually keeps out weeds, and weed killers aren't needed. Most herbicides can be used safely, but avoid arsonate weed killers. Ground pearl is the main insect pest—causing dwarfing of the roots and thinning of the turf. Controlling ground pearl is difficult. Nematocides may improve the appearance of centipede grass if it is infested with nematodes.

Mowing: Mow centipede grass at a medium height, 1–2 inches tall. It grows fairly slowly, and mowing every 10 to 20 days is usually sufficient. The open texture of the turf makes mowing with light equipment easy.

COLONIAL BENT GRASS

Botanical Name: Agrostis tenuis
Remarks: The colonial bent grasses provide elegant turfs that require care within the capabilities of most homeowners, but do require consistent mowing.

General Characteristics: These grasses are fairly erect, but spread by aboveground stolons rather than by rhizomes. They are finer-textured than bluegrass, fescue, and ryegrass, with foliage that tends to concentrate near the tips of the stems.

Habitat: Colonial bent grass does best in climates that are at least seasonally moist, such as the West Coast north from San Francisco, the region leeward of the Great Lakes, and in the misty highlands of New England. They can tolerate acid soil and like sun or partial shade. They grow best in Hardiness Zones 4–6. The colonial bent grasses are hardy, but not at their best, in Zones 1–3. (They are especially subject to snowmold.)

Source: Colonial bent grass is easily started from seed. Highland is the workhorse cultivar and is available in high-quality seed.

Care: Other than the need for frequent mowing, colonial bent grass has no special requirements. To be at its best, it should probably be given more consistent care than bluegrass.

Mowing: It is usually best to mow these grasses at ¾ to 1 inch high and to mow frequently (at least twice per week). Infrequent mowing removes too much tip foliage at one time, resulting in stubble and sometimes death.

CREEPING BENT GRASS

Botanical Name: Agrostis stolonifera

Remarks: Creeping bentgrass is an unusually elegant grass, but requires consistent and abundant care—including regular thatch thinning. Its proper care is probably beyond the capabilities of the homeowner.

General Characteristics: These grasses are more prostrate than colonial bent grasses, and the abundant stolons build up mat.

Habitat: Creeping bentgrasses do best in moist, fertile locations that receive constant care. They grow best in Hardiness Zones 1–3 and 4–6.

Source: Seed is available for a few varieties (such as Emerald and Penncross); vegetative starts (stolons) are available for the majority of the varieties.

Care: Top turf of golf green quality requires constant attention to disease control, fertilization, watering, weed prevention, and so on. An occasional topdressing with weed-free soil (⅛–¼ inch thick) is very helpful in preventing thatch.

Mowing: Mow these grasses low (¼ inch or less high for golf greens) and frequently (every second day is preferable).

KENTUCKY BLUEGRASS

Botanical Name: Poa pratensis

Remarks: Probably the most versatile, widely adapted, recuperative turf grass. Its chief drawback in new plantings is how slowly it sprouts, especially in cool weather. (Mixing in fine fescue or perennial ryegrass will help speed up coverage.)

General Characteristics: Kentucky bluegrass has a graceful texture and attractive color, with the leaves standing erect. Most varieties are self-reliant, recuperative, and tolerant of pest control chemicals. (Certain cultivars become more temperamental in Zone 6.)

Habitat: Grows best with full sun, but tolerates partial shade. Likes fertile, near-neutral, well-drained soils of good structure, but is broadly adaptable. At its best in Hardiness Zones 1–3 and 4–6. Kentucky bluegrass enjoys partial shade when in Zone 6 and survives best in the shade in the South.

Varieties: Arboretum (from Missouri) and Park (from Minnesota) are selected strains of natural bluegrasses. Park is especially noted for its rapid sprouting. Delta, a Canadian selection, is little different. Merion is a low-growing, dense variety, and an outstanding choice for an elite lawn (in the northern zone only). It does suffer from a number of diseases (but not leaf spot, one of the worst), and requires extra feeding and thatch removal for top performance. Newport is strong in autumn but then peters out. In national ratings, few varieties equal Merion.

Source: Usually planted from seed. Choose blends and mixtures that include the newer disease-resistant cultivars. Spreads by underground stems (rhizomes), with abundant tillers (additional leafy shoots growing from the grass plant stem) in autumn.

Care: Enjoys 4 pounds of nitrogen per 1,000 square feet annually (at least half applied in the autumn), but can do well at half this rate. Gradual-release feeding is best during the summer. Avoid generous spring fertilization in Zone 6. In all zones: Avoid overzealous care during hot weather.

Mowing: Common grass is best mowed rather tall, at least 1½ inches. Newer cultivars bred for lower growth can withstand mowing at an inch tall. Don't let bluegrass get lanky-tall; mow when new growth reaches double the customary mowing height. Mows neatly except during seedhead formation. Increase mowing height by as much as 3 inches in Zone 6.

RED FESCUE

Botanical Name: Festuca rubra. Subspecies *rubra* forms the "spreading" group; subspecies *trichophylla* comprises the "creeping" fescues; subspecies *commutata* embraces the "chewings" types.

Remarks: Good in mixture with Kentucky bluegrass, withstanding the tribulations of dry, sandy, infertile soils and shade. The vigorous seedlings establish new seedings quickly, but it is best mixed with bluegrass, since it spreads slowly. This grass's weakness is hot, moist weather (seldom a problem in the North).

General Characteristics: Fine-leafed, with a rich, dark-green color. Red fescue has narrower, "wirier," and generally denser foliage than bluegrass, but is otherwise similar. Spreading fescues develop rhizomes almost like bluegrass. Their growth is reasonably open; the growth of creeping fescues is intermediate. The chewing fescues are quite dense, with tuftlike clumps exhibiting little rhizoming.

Habitat: Prefers sun or dry shade; better adapted to poor soil and drought than is bluegrass. Does best in Hardiness Zones 1–3 and 4–6. Most useful if mixed with bluegrass and often suffers summer dieback in Zone 6 if planted alone.

Varieties: Improved chewings cultivars such as Highlight, Jamestown, and Koket have better color and lower growth and are the best choices for "show" lawns.

Source: As for Kentucky bluegrass (see page 18).

Care: Similar to bluegrass, except that it's a "light feeder" requiring only half the rates customarily given bluegrass. Endures drought well.

Mowing: Except for a limited number of new cultivars, red fescue should be mowed reasonably tall, 1½ inches or higher. It is somewhat tougher to mow than bluegrass and may show "gray hair" if the mower blade is not sharp.

REDTOP

Botanical Name: Agrostis gigantea

Remarks: Redtop is used mainly for cover along ditches and wasteland. It was once widely employed as a nursegrass in seed mixtures; but it is not desirable as a permanent lawn component.

General Characteristics: Redtop makes a thin turf. It is a robust bent grass that usually gives way to stauncher lawn grasses and will turn coarse where it does persist.

Habitat: Redtop is widely adapted, but is most competitive in cool, wet habitats of low fertility and tolerates acid or inadequately drained soils. It grows best in Hardiness Zones 4–6.

Source: Redtop grows from seed, but with no select cultivars. It is acceptable (in small amounts) as a nursegrass.

Care: It requires little care for the special uses for which it is employed, but profits from abundant moisture.

Mowing: Mow redtop fairly tall, like bluegrass (see page 18).

ROUGH BLUEGRASS

Botanical Name: Poa trivialis
Remarks: Rough bluegrass is a very attractive cover for cool, moist shade, but wears poorly. It is soft, light green in color, fast-sprouting, and spreads aboveground much like bent grass.

General Characteristics: Its prostrate, creeping stolons are more like bent grass than bluegrass. Rough bluegrass is very attractive, but is weak and has shallow roots.

Habitat: Rough bluegrass prefers moist or partial shade and will not grow well in open sun or dry soils. It grows best in Hardiness Zones 4–6.

Source: Seed is available (no select cultivars).

Mowing: Mow rough bluegrass as you would colonial bent grass (see page 17).

Care: In most places rough bluegrass requires irrigation; otherwise it is cared for in the same way as Kentucky bluegrass or bent grass.

RYEGRASS

Botanical Name: Lolium perenne
Remarks: The new "turf-type" ryegrass cultivars are bred for lower growth, better looks, and greater hardiness. Ryegrass will crowd out bluegrass and fescue in seed mixtures if it makes up more than about 20 percent of the mixture (but will yield to them otherwise). It can provide clean, weed-free seed if a nurse species is needed. Ryegrass is often sown alone for quick cover (as on athletic fields) and in mild coastal climates. It is generally not expected to persist, turning coarse during the second year. Norlea varieties are less aggressive and better at letting slower bluegrasses gain a foothold in new lawns.

General Characteristics: Ryegrass is a bunchgrass. It doesn't spread, but thickens by growing additional stems on each grass plant (tillering).

Habitat: Ryegrass does best in mild (maritime) climates, but the newer cultivars are hardy and more broadly adapted. Ryegrasses grow best in the sun. Best in Hardiness Zones 4–6.

Source: Ryegrass is planted from seed and is the quickest-sprouting of the better turf grasses. There are many new and select cultivars. Sow generously (6 pounds per 1,000 square feet) to assure a tight turf.

Care: Ryegrass needs the same care as Kentucky bluegrass, but grows more rapidly and requires more frequent mowing.

Mowing: Mow as you would Kentucky bluegrass (see page 18). Unimproved ryegrass does not mow as neatly as bluegrass, so choose one of the new "turf-type" cultivars.

ST. AUGUSTINE GRASS

Botanical Name: Stenotaphrum secundatum

Remarks: In terms of most growth characteristics, the word for St. Augustine grass is *moderate.* It is neither the best nor the poorest. It is probably the most shade-tolerant of the southern grasses. It's not elegant, but it is popular in coastal areas from the Carolinas to eastern Texas. St. Augustine grass is moderately rapid-growing (but not as fast as Bermuda grass).

General Characteristics: St. Augustine grass leaves are an attractive dark-green color and are blunt at the tips. The leaves occur in groups at the nodes, which overlap the bare internodes. They are coarse-textured, with a loose-leaf characteristic. The leaf blades are wide and smooth except for a cluster of hairs and a constriction and distinctive half-twist where the blade joins the sheath. The stems are thick and flat. The grass is low-lying with few unsightly seedheads.

Habitat: St. Augustine grasses are widely adapted to hot, humid conditions, mucky soil, sun, or shade and are tolerant of salt spray. They are mainly used in humid, coastal climates—growing well near the seashore and in general throughout low-lying coastal plains.

They are often grown northward into Zone 8, although they grow best in Hardiness Zones 9 and 10. St. Augustine grass will be green nearly year-round in southern Florida and only off-color briefly in northern Florida. (It produces excellent sod on the muck.) It will also survive in the higher, drier, colder environments north to the Piedmont and Little Rock and west to Dallas, but will not perform as well further south.

These are the best warm-season grass varieties (except for Bahia grasses) for use in the shade. They are also excellent in the full sun.

Varieties: Stenotaphrum secundatum is native to subtropical America. It is a small genus consisting of three species, two of which are native to southern Asia and a third that originated along the southern Atlantic and Gulf coasts of America. This last variety was originally introduced into Arizona and California.

Common St. Augustine grass and the Roselawn variety are both coarse and relatively open—with a few leafy branches and long internodes. Bitter Blue is relatively dense, low-growing, dark-colored, and well adapted to coastal environments. Floratine is more dense, somewhat more finely textured, and tolerates low mowing.

Floratam, a SAD-virus-resistant type, is the best choice in Texas (where SAD "St. Augustine grass Decline" is widespread). Floratine is a denser variety best for Florida.

Source: St. Augustine grass is generally inexpensive and available as sod or other vegetative starts (sprigs or plugs). It spreads rapidly by runners.

Care: St. Augustine grass is relatively inexpensive to maintain, with only moderate requirements for fertility, irrigation, and so on. However, providing it with the proper cultural care and protecting it from insects and diseases often requires equipment, chemicals, and knowledge beyond that of the home gardener. Lawn care specialists can be a great help.

These grasses are planted in the spring or early summer. The best growing environment is in cultivated, fertilized beds that are watered (consistently) until the roots form. With fertilization, weed control, and a few months of good growing weather, turf can be obtained from starts 1 foot apart.

Spring and fall applications of a complete fertilizer and a summer application of organic nitrogen are usually adequate. Organic nitrogen, which doesn't stimulate growth as much, also helps reduce chinch bug injury. St. Augustine grass will require irrigation during periods of natural rainfall shortages.

St. Augustine grass tends to build up a spongy thatch that separates the foliage from the roots beneath. Vertical cutting or thinning is important, but close clipping and raking in the spring (when recovery is rapid) and removal of clippings throughout the year will help prevent thatch accumulation.

Diseases and Pests: In recent years St. Augustine grass has been badly afflicted by chinch bugs. Infestations throughout the Southeast have moved westward into Texas. Unfortunately, chinch bug populations gradually develop resistance to insecticides. This means that it's necessary to develop new chemicals, which is costly. Generally, however, whichever insecticide is used will also control webworms, armyworms, and other insect pests.

St. Augustine grass is not particularly tolerant of weed killers except for simazine and atrazine, which are used to help eliminate weeds during the lawn's establishment period.

Nematodes cause injury to St. Augustine grasses by damaging the root systems. Use of a nematocide should provide greener, more vigorous grass.

Mowing: Mow St. Augustine grass medium to tall, generally about 2 inches high. Mowing is easy because of the grass's vigorous growth and because its leaves lie low to the ground. Vigorous grass tends to be firmer and stronger and thus allows for a cleaner cut of the blade. St. Augustine grasses may be mowed as low as 1 inch, but will produce a tighter, less weedy turf when clipped at close to 2 inches. Weekly mowing is generally adequate. Lightweight mowers tend to ride high on St. Augustine grasses, elevating the height of the cut and encouraging the formation of thatch.

TALL FESCUE

Botanical Name: Festuca elatior

Remarks: Not an elegant lawn grass, and unattractive in a fine lawn, but useful where nothing else will survive or where only minimum care is possible. It is one of the worst "weeds" in much of the Northeast, where it volunteers in bluegrass lawns—from which it cannot be selectively removed. Tall fescue can become a pest in finer-textured lawns, where it makes coarse clumps.

General Characteristics: A coarse, nonspreading bunchgrass that is deep-rooting and persistent.

Habitat: Tall fescue is broadly adaptable, enduring poor soils that dry in the summer. it grows best in the sun or in some shade. Tall fescue is used primarily for rough acreage and along roads. It is sometimes suggested for athletic fields or hot, dry sites in the upper South, where bluegrasses and fine fescues find the going rough. Tall fescue grows best in Hardiness Zones 6–7.

Source: Tall fescue is grown from seed, usually of the Kentucky 31 or Alta cultivars. It is easily started, with good seedling vigor, but is coarse and clumpy. Plant it heavily; crowding dwarfs the grass and makes it more presentable.

Care: Tall fescue survives with minimum care. Fertilize it from time to time to maintain color.

Mowing: This robust pasture grass should be mowed tall, preferably 3 inches high.

VELVET BENT GRASS

Botanical Name: Agrostis canina

Remarks: Velvet bent grass is probably the most elegant of turf grasses. It is not hard to care for if its demands are met, but it is probably better suited to care by professionals than by the average homeowner.

General Characteristics: Velvet bent grass is similar to creeping bent grass, except that is lower-growing and finer-textured.

Habitat: Again, velvet bent grass is similar to creeping bentgrass, except that it is more "insistent" on acid soil. It grows best in Hardiness Zones 1–3.

Source: Seed is available for the Kingstown variety.

Care: Care for these grasses is like that for the creeping bentgrasses, except that they are not as demanding of fertilization.

Mowing: Cut as low as creeping bentgrass, or even lower (with a special greens-type mower).

ZOYSIA GRASS

Botanical Name: Zoysia matrella

Remarks: Along with Bermuda grass, zoysia grass is the elite southern turf. No grass produces a thicker, more resilient cover.

General Characteristics: Zoysia is much like Bermuda grass, but is slower-growing and "tougher." It will develop thatch and will not tolerate shade. It is very wear-resistant, a tremendous advantage in heavy-use areas. It has good resistance to drought but may need some irrigation.

Zoysia grass has a very short season. It will turn off-color in October, and not green again until April or May. Unfortunately, brown zoysia grass is about as unattractive as brown crabgrass.

Fine-leaved zoysia grasses tend to produce a puffy growth. They do not produce abundant seedheads and are not garden border pests like Bermuda grasses—it's easier to keep them out.

Zoysia grasses do not mix well with other grasses. Cool-season grasses and zoysia grasses are not compatible.

Habitat: Zoysia grasses are warm-season grasses, even though selections like Meyer are hardy in the cool regions of the country.

Zoysia grasses prosper in partial shade as well as in sun. They do best in good soil, limited to near neutral pH (7.0), but are well adapted to widely varying soil conditions. They are best in Hardiness Zones 7–8, although they are also widely used in Zone 9.

Zoysia grasses are widely recommended for use in the transitional zone, where crabgrass and other summer annual weeds have an advantage over cool-season grasses.

The shorter the growing season in a region, the longer the period of dormant foliage. (The number of frost-free days in a location provides a good estimate of growing season.) In the midlatitudes, zoysia grass is dormant from October until April (about 6 months).

Zoysia grasses have some resistance to injury from salt spray and they are useful along the coast.

Varieties: Zoysia grasses are native to eastern Asia and its outlying islands. There are three different types of zoysia grass: wide-leaf *matrella*, medium-leaf *japonica*, and fine-leaf *tenuifolia*.

The *matrellas* are often called Manila grass, a name that refers to types found in the Philippines. The *tenuifolias* are at times referred to as Korean velvet, patio, or flagstone grasses, again an indication of an eastern-Asian origin.

Lawn zoysias may be considered subspecies of *Z. matrella*. As with Bermuda grass, there is sexual crossing, so that zoysia from seed contains at least some coarser plants that are regarded as *Z. japonica*, or Japanese lawn grass.

Flawn zoysia grass is a selection of the *matrella* type that is hardy in the mid-Atlantic states. it is also well adapted to the Southwest. Midwestern zoysia grass is a selection released by Purdue University in Indiana. Meyer zoysia grass ia a dense, hardy selection of the *japonica* type. Emerald is a *tenuifolia* hybrid with *Z. japonica*.

The *matrellas* discolor less readily than the finer-textured *japonicas* in the far South.

Source: Zoysia grass comes from mainly vegetative slow starts, as with the improved Bermuda grasses. Seed is occasionally available (but doesn't come true to type).

Care: Zoysia grass is not as demanding as Bermuda grass but, because of its slow growth, should be well tended, at least until it fills into a tight sod. Once injured by wear, disease, insect, or maintenance error, it is slow to grow back.

Zoysia grasses are planted in spring and early summer to provide the longest growing season possible for establishment.

Plant at 2 pounds of seed per 1,000 square feet. Mix it with other seeded grasses to help provide cover and crowd out weeds. Zoysia grasses may be seeded with cool-season grasses simply by mixing the zoysia grass seed with a name-brand seed blend or mixture.

Sprigs or stems about three nodes in length are planted by covering one end with soil. Plugs are set into the soil. The closer the spacing of sprigs and plugs, the more rapidly the lawn will be established. Six-inch spacing within and between rows is about right.

Uniform watering is of critical importance. A complete lawn fertilizer should be used. Two to 3 pounds of nitrogen per 1,000 square feet per season (once established) and perhaps 6 pounds of nitrogen per 1,000 square feet during sod development are adequate. In time, zoysia grass will develop thatch, which creates the need for higher-intensity fertilizer applications.

Zoysia grasses spread by aboveground runners (stolons) as well as underground stems (rhizomes). This spread is slow. In the far South, it usually takes a full year to develop a tight sod. In the transition zone, it may take 2 to 3 years, depending upon the competition.

Diseases and Pests: Zoysia grasses are susceptible to disease and insect damage and will require the use of herbicides and insecticides. Billbugs are troublesome in many locations, especially in the Deep South. Nematodes may cause injury, and control is difficult.

A well-developed zoysia grass lawn *should* crowd out weeds, so that weed killers are not needed.

Mowing: Generally mow zoysia grasses from 1 to 2 inches tall, although some cultivars can be mowed lower. Zoysia grows slowly, but even so, it is seldom advisable to let mowing go more than 10 days. Zoysia is hard to mow, so a heavy-duty reel machine is recommended.

2

Soils
Muck Raking the Gardener's Way

It all begins with the soil. If you are really interested in a better-than-average lawn, you must first pay attention to the type and quality of soil that makes up the area where you intend to create it.

To most people, soil is just dirt. It just lies there. We walk on it and we track it into the house when it's wet.

In reality, a spoonful of soil is a dynamic chemical potion with billions of molecules of nature's elements and billions of microorganisms in a constant state of chemical and biological change.

A spoonful of soil from any spot on Earth has an individual make-up that is different from the soil at any other place. However, there are some simple, easy-to-understand chemical reactions that happen in all soils. These simple, universal reactions can make a vast difference in how your garden grows.

In this chapter I'm going to give you a brief but necessary lesson in soil science. It may seem unnecessary to you right now, but you will soon understand how important it is if you want your green dream to come true.

Your soil, often referred to as dirt, plays an extremely important role in plant growth. Soil provides grass with food and water and acts as a supporting anchor for the grass's roots. The kind of lawn you achieve will depend on how well you care for your soil. As simple as it may sound, badly managed dirt returns bad grass, while well-managed dirt will give you good grass.

Soil Is Just Dirt Cleaned Up

For the sake of those of you who have not read my previous books, I would like to explain how I use the word *dirt*. The proper and professional way to refer to the natural growing medium is *soil*, but we have been told not to play in the dirt since we were little kids. So I'll use both words from time to time—but they mean the same thing.

The Mechanics of Dirt— Ooops!—Soil

Dirt is made up of four main parts: water, air, organics, and minerals.

Water and air fill the spaces between

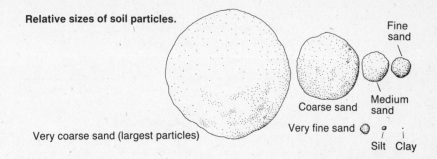

Relative sizes of soil particles.

Fine sand

Coarse sand

Medium sand

Very coarse sand (largest particles)

Very fine sand

Silt   Clay

the solid particles. The organics are decayed plant material, fungi, and bacteria that collect near the soil's surface. Minerals are the remnants of rocks that have been exposed to the elements for thousands upon thousands of years and have combined with certain components of the decaying material found in your particular area.

Thousands of different types of soil are found throughout the world, and nobody can be expected to know them all. In most cases, you can contact the Soil Conservation Service in your county for a soil survey map, which will indicate the soil types found in your general area. This information can be a great help in improving your little patch of the world.

What Have Buckshot and Basketballs Got to Do with Dirt?

Your local dirt is made up of three types of soil particles: sand, silt, and clay. One important difference between these "separates" is the size of the particles that make up the soil. Sand is the largest-size particle, but there are five different standard sand particle sizes. Silt particles are the second largest. Clay particles are the smallest (less than 1/10,000 inch in diameter), which is why clay soil is so thick and heavy.

How Soil Particles Shape Up

It might help you to visualize the relative sizes of the different kinds of soil par-

ticles if I list them, from the largest to the smallest, comparing them to more familiar objects:

Very coarse sand has the largest particles—let's pretend these are as big as a ball 8 feet in diameter. At this scale, coarse sand would be a 4-foot ball, medium sand would be a medicine ball, fine sand would be a basketball, and very fine sand would be a softball. Silt particles, by comparison, would be the size of a golf ball, and clay would be the size of a buckshot.

Playing Around with Particles

You will also hear a lot about soil texture as your knowledge of your lawn increases. *Texture* refers to the relative amount of each type of particle (sand, silt, and clay) in your soil. Sixty percent sand, 20 percent silt, and 20 percent clay, for instance, constitutes sandy loam.

It's important to understand the soil texture of your property if you want to have a healthy, super-looking lawn. The ideal texture for super grass is 50 percent sand, 25 percent silt, and 25 percent clay. However, many a beautiful lawn, golf course, park, or athletic stadium has been grown on soil with a less than ideal mix— as long as careful attention is paid to the lawn's other needs. In fact, it's this kind of challenge that makes the grass game worth playing.

The spaces between soil particles determine the soil's ability to hold or drain water. The spaces between sand particles

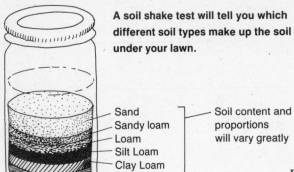

A soil shake test will tell you which different soil types make up the soil under your lawn.

Sand
Sandy loam
Loam
Silt Loam
Clay Loam
Clay

Soil content and proportions will vary greatly

are called macropores, the spaces between clay particles are called micropores. Too many of either kind is bad for your lawn—and must be modified to give the grass plants the most comfortable growing and support system.

Shake Your Dirt!

Before you can make the adjustments necessary for super soil, you'll have to test your soil to find its exact texture.

Add 1 teaspoon of dishwasher detergent (which helps separate the particles) to a quart jar two-thirds full of water. Add soil from your yard until the water is 1 inch from the top of the jar. Replace the top tightly and shake the mixture vigorously for about 5 minutes. Let it sit overnight. The different soil types should separate out into layers, and you can check the percentages.

Another good test for soil composition is a simple touch test. Feel your soil—rub it between your fingers and thumb, or squeeze it. Different soils have different characteristic "feels":

Sand. This is simple. Sand has a gritty feel. When squeezed and released it will "brush up" (pull apart).

Sandy Loam. This is a dirt mixture made up of more than 50 percent sand, with the balance in clay and silt. Sandy loam will feel like a soft velour.

Loam. Here we have a contradiction between the way the soil feels and what it's made up of. Loam is 25 percent to 40 percent sand, but contains enough clay and silt to make it feel both smooth and grainy.

Silt Loam. This consists of over 50 percent silt and feels soft and smooth.

Clay Loam. This is a child's delight. The soil is made up of more than 30 percent but less than 50 percent clay, with the balance made up of silt and sand. Clay loam can be formed or shaped.

Clay. If you have 50 percent or more clay in your shake test, or if you can cut, shape, or carve your soil, you have clay.

Don't Be Afraid to Change or Challenge

I have seen many homeowners take one look at their finished, graded lot and almost cry. Often, they're looking at soil made up of big, dry, chunks of clay hauled in from a nearby sewer or expressway site and dumped and graded—just enough to pass inspection—with no thought given to its ability to produce grass or house trees, shrubs, and plants. Today, most well-managed jurisdictions require builders to return 6 to 8 inches of sandy loam to the finished grade. If I were you, I would scream, scold, and swear loud enough to get this done.

If this doesn't work, let's just make the bad dirt good ourselves!

First, take the shake test (above) to determine what you are faced with—what

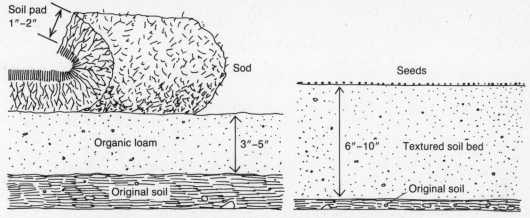

New seed needs a much deeper prepared soil bed than sod does.

percentages of which particles you need to add to achieve a perfect soil mix. Next, decide which method of lawn repair will fit your soil, budget, and temperament best.

Above all, don't rush! I know it's embarrassing to have a mud pit or sandy desert around your house, but if you just take the time to evaluate and modify it properly, the results will be terrific!

Starting from Scratch Is Easier

Please don't despair, even if you are convinced that the soil you're looking at is a real sow's ear. We can make it into a silk purse. In most cases it will take more elbow grease and common sense than greenbacks or heavy equipment.

Call all of your friends, relatives, local parks and recreation departments, and anyone else that may have grass clippings, leaves, sawdust, compost, or any other organic material that they can spare.

If your problem is too much clay in your soil, then you should also look for the contents of deserted sandboxes or surplus "sharp" sand. If too much sand is your problem, you might try trading some of your sand for the extra clay some other guy got stuck with.

Seed or Sod?

You'll have less work to do if you use sod, because you don't have to improve the soil texture as deeply as for seed. Sod, as a rule, comes with its own 1- to 2-inch-deep soil pad, so adding another 3 to 5 inches of firm, well-drained organic loam should do the trick. Seed, on the other hand, requires a more deeply textured soil bed, from 6 to 8 inches deep—and 10 inches deep would make me, and the seed, even happier. Stolons and plugs prefer the same type, texture, and depth of soil as seed.

I must caution you at this point not to let your enthusiasm for modifying the soil get the best of you. Don't overtexture the dirt bed to the point where you end up with an organic bog. Remember, you want the turf (grass), not the textured bed, to feel like a carpet when you walk on it. Don't laugh! I've seen it happen. I once lost a pair of shoes in the middle of a friend's lawn when I sank into the mud base below.

Full Modification Can Cost a Fortune

For most homeowners, fully modifying the existing soil texture is prohibitively expensive. "Full modification" means

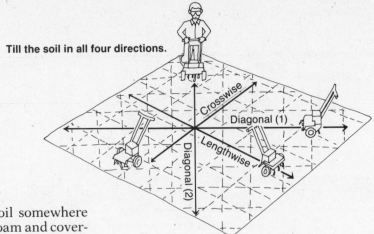

Till the soil in all four directions.

hauling in a mixture of soil somewhere between loam and sandy loam and covering the undesirable soil below to a depth of 12 inches. As a rule, only small areas should be fully modified.

Semimodification Isn't as Drastic as Starting from Scratch

I have heard garden center staff tell folks simply to till sand into peat if they want to do something less drastic than full modification to their dirt. The sand is supposed to separate the clay particles and make the soil more porous. Folks, that's a lot of malarkey! It can make the clay problem even worse. You must add a great deal of organic matter—peat moss, old decayed manure, sawdust, compost, and shredded leaves, evenly tilled into the soil—if you want more porous soil.

After adding organic materials, green manure (grass), and sawdust to the soil, you should sprinkle a light application of fertilizer over the top. Water the fertilizer in with 1 quart of household ammonia and 1 cup of liquid soap (with 20 gallons of water over 3,000 square feet) to replace the nitrogen that the added materials remove from the soil and to help speed up decomposition.

(These ammonia and soap treatments are one of my lawn's favorite treats: They're inexpensive and they help the lawn in all kinds of ways—see pages 61 and 125.)

Don't Even Consider Spading

If your lawn area is larger than 2,500 square feet, I suggest that you check your local want ads for someone with a power tiller. Get him to disc the area in every direction you can think of—four, to be exact: north to south, east to west, northwest to southeast, southwest to northeast. The more the organic materials are blended into the existing soil, the better base you will have to work with.

Existing Modification Is a Face-lift

Each spring you'll see dump trucks going up and down residential streets selling and broadcasting topsoil over old or existing lawns (this is also known as topdressing), with the promise of improving clay soil or root- and thatch-compacted lawns.

These people are giving bad advice, either because they don't know any better or because they're con men. This kind of treatment is both a waste and dangerous. First, don't expect the texture to improve just because you sprinkled material on top of the grass or soil; it will do nothing to improve the texture. On the contrary, if the material has a heavy peat moss content, it can crust over and *smother* the ex-

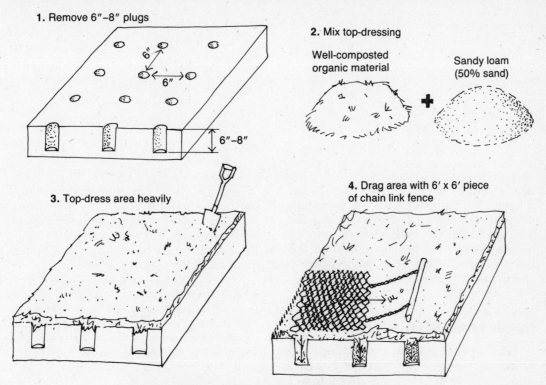

1. Remove 6"–8" plugs

6"

6"

6"–8"

2. Mix top-dressing

Well-composted organic material

Sandy loam (50% sand)

3. Top-dress area heavily

4. Drag area with 6' x 6' piece of chain link fence

Rejuvenate an old lawn by force-feeding the soil.

isting grass. Second, it will bring many, many different weed varieties into your lawn. Finally, it can either blow away or wash away.

To help rejuvenate old, compacted soil or poorly textured clay soil, you must remove plugs 6 to 8 inches deep and 6 inches apart. Next, mix a good amount of well-composted organic material with a sandy loam (50 percent sand) and heavily top-dress the turf area. Now, drag a 6-by-6-foot piece of chain link fence back and forth over the treated area to force the mixture into the plugs. This should be done once a year for at least 3 years. Don't worry, you'll see the difference during the first growing season and be amazed with the improvement by the third.

Sandy Soil Is Lots Easier

The problem with sandy soil is that wa-ter and nutrients run right through it and the grass gets left high and dry. A mixture of organic compost and clay loam top-dressed over a newly plugged area and brushed in with a 6-by-6-foot chain link fence section will add years of life to your lawn—and make it look younger and healthier.

Surface Tension Is Half the Problem

Surface tension can be caused by dry winds, hot or cold weather, static electricity, airborne pollution, and traffic compaction. It is also referred to by most turf experts as stress. It is often mistaken for poor soil structure. Fill your hose-end jar half with water and half with cheap, cheap, cheap liquid dish soap and apply it with 20 gallons of water over 5,000 square feet of lawn twice a month. Half of your problems should be eliminated. Both heavy and sandy soils will stay moist longer. On hilltops, where the grass can dry out quickly, I fill an Ortho whirley spreader full of dry laundry soap, set it to the number-one setting, apply it to the dry turf, and water it in. (The whirley spreader has four settings: 1 is the lowest, 4 the highest.)

Nature to the Rescue

Two super-duper natural materials—lime and gypsum—can help turn bad dirt into good dirt and are safe, inexpensive, and easy to apply. Lime is used to control soil pH, while gypsum helps break down heavy, dense clay particles. Both are added to the dirt before the final tilling. Here's what you can expect from these two hard workers:

Sweet Soil Means Greener Grass

When we hear people talk about sour soil and liming to "sweeten" soil, most of us probably wonder what it can have to do with our lawn's health.

No doubt we use the terms *sweet* and *sour* to describe our soil because we're frightened by the idea of soil chemistry. Many of us shy away from things that sound too technical and believe that you'd have to be a chemist to understand soil chemistry. This can cause us to ignore a very important part of lawn and garden care and as a result waste hundreds of dollars putting fertilizer on our lawns without getting the benefits.

Soil chemistry, as it applies to home gardening and lawn care, really isn't any harder to understand than the concept of a balanced, healthy, human diet. Liming, for example, can be compared to taking an antacid for a "sour" stomach.

"Sour" soil has an excess of hydrogen ions $(H+)$ and is acidic. We think of it as being sour because acids like vinegar are sour to the taste. When we treat soil to "neutralize" the acid, we call it "sweetening" the soil, since sweet is the opposite of sour.

Why Is Our Soil Bad?

Unlike a sour stomach, which can develop an ulcer, sour soil causes problems by interfering with the lawn's feeding. The acidity acts something like the goalie in a hockey game. In the soil, nutrients become positively charged particles (called ions) that are taken in by the plant's roots as food. These positive ions are also called *cations* (pronounced "kat-ions"). For some strange reason, hydrogen ions $(H+)$, like a hockey goalie, just won't let the puck (cations or nutrients) get past them to the goal (the plant's metabolism). They block out the nutrient cations. Even if the nutrients are abundant in the soil, the plant roots can't get to them.

Lime, which contains calcium carbonate, is often applied to the soil as a remedy for sour soil. The carbonate part combines with the $H+$ ions to form water and carbon dioxide (CO_2). The remaining calcium acts as a needed plant nutrient.

5.0	5.5	6.0	6.5	7.0	7.5	8.0	8.5	9.0
Range of Acidity				Range of Alkalinity				
Strong	Medium	Slight	Very Slight	Slight		Medium	Strong	

Nitrogen

Phosphorus

Potassium

Sulfur

Calcium

Magnesium

Iron

Manganese

Boron

Copper and Zinc

The absence of H+ ions is called a basic, or alkaline, state. The degree of sour (acid) and sweet (alkaline) is measured according to what's called *the pH scale*. This scale ranges from 1 to 14, with the number 7 indicating neutral. Numbers smaller than 7 indicate acidity, and numbers larger than 7 indicate alkalinity.

Availability of Elements to Plants at Different pH Levels

Soil pH has an important effect on the comparative availability of eleven important plant nutrient elements. In the accompanying table the width of each element's band shows how available it is at different pH levels.

What Turns Soil Sour?

Some lawns and gardens end up with high soil acidity as a result of the transposition of subsoil and topsoil, especially when new areas are developed for residences. With time, long-established lawns and gardens can also develop acidity. There are many causes for this build-up of hydrogen ions in the soil. The most common are the hydrogen content of rain, fertilizers, and the decomposition of plant matter.

The Cure

Liming is one of the oldest soil management practices. The benefits of applying lime have been known since before the time of Christ. Lime was apparently applied to soils in ancient Egypt. Both Benjamin Franklin and Thomas Jefferson wrote about applying lime to sweeten sour soils.

In the past it's been standard practice to apply ground limestone in the fall, at a rate of 50 pounds per 1,000 square feet for each point of pH change needed. Unfortunately, even though ground lime seems powdery, in terms of the soil's chemistry it is really like tiny rocks. It can take, at best, months and even years of freeze/thaw stress and a lot of rain to break the particles down to the point where any measurable amount moves from the surface to the root zone, where it can be involved in soil chemistry.

This old-fashioned way of sweetening soil doesn't work in the summer because by the time any sweetening can take place, the nutrients have leached into the subsoil where the plant roots can't reach them and the season for growing has long passed.

A New Form of Lime

A new product, called Nutra Nuggets, is made with lime ground so fine that more than three-fourths of it will fall through a 20 wire per inch mesh sieve. This superfine lime is then formed into pellets with a soluble binder. The process creates a dust-free product that can be spread with any garden spreader. It can also be used at any time of the year. It dissolves so quickly that as soon as it rains, the calcium carbonate will seep into the root zone, where it does its work.

The most important benefit of this new form of lime is that it takes only about one-quarter as much to raise the soil pH one point as did the coarser grades of lime.

Other pelletized lime products on the market look like this product, but they don't work the same way. Other manufacturers just pelletize the coarse limestone. Any pelletized product that won't pass at least 90 percent through a 100-mesh sieve will not work fast enough to be effective within the growing season. (This information should be printed on the product's bag.)

How Often Should the Soil Be Treated to Maintain a Neutral Condition?

The soil pH should be maintained on a constant basis, so that whenever fertilizer or nutrients are applied, your plants will be able to use them. If you apply this new form of lime once every spring—and add a corrective application any time the soil pH goes to the sour side—your soil will always be "sweet."

It's a good idea to have your soil tested for acidity by a laboratory that is equipped with accurate instruments. A county extension agent can usually do these tests for you. If he can't do them himself, he'll know where you can get the tests done.

In the absence of a soil test, you'll have to watch for the telltale symptoms of sour soil. If your grass or garden fails to respond to a fertilizer application with a noticeable greening, it is very likely that the nutrients are being blocked by acid (sour) soil.

Another Contribution from Ben Franklin

I keep a silhouette of Ben Franklin hanging over my desk. The inscription below it reads, "The Garden Godfather." He was, among many other things, a farmer, scientist, writer, humorist, poet, and scallawag—which is how he discovered the gardening use of land plaster.

Land plaster, which is now known as gypsum, is a natural white, sandy powder that is mined in the United States, Canada, and Mexico. It is made up of calcium and sulfur, for the most part, and is often referred to as the "Hadacol" of the garden—a sort of all-around tonic.

Gypsum should be spread onto untilled soil at a rate of 50 pounds per 1,500 square feet. It will help break down clay and neutralize any oil, salts, or other junk that could be in the builder's backfill. Gypsum can be purchased under many brand names (for example, Hyponex or Sof'n Soil) at most garden centers.

Oh! How did Ben discover its merits? He saw it used to keep the soil loose in a French vineyard while running away from a paternity charge.

If You Have Read This Far, You Are a Serious Contender

When we hear of people who have "green thumbs," we often credit them with some kind of mystical luck. I credit these people with intelligence. Their gardens are green because they took the time to learn about plants and soil—and then practiced what they'd learned by exercising consistent and organized lawn care.

I meet dozens upon dozens of people who make their living as landscapers who don't know half of what you have just read. What makes it even worse is that they often don't believe that this kind of care is necessary. They can cause more harm to lawns than all of the insects and diseases that plague our lawns.

The simple soil science lesson you have just been through will eliminate many, many hours of extra work and extra dollars that you would have wasted barking up the wrong tree looking for a solution to a soil problem that didn't have to exist.

3

Building or Rebuilding a Lawn
*Try It One More Time...
My Way!*

The most discouraging sight I can think of is looking out the front window of your brand-new home and seeing a patch of brown, barren earth that looks like Death Valley. The second most discouraging sight is seeing your checkbook balance so close to empty that you wonder whether rebuilding a lawn is really worth it—or whether you've made an addition error.

Perk up! Building or rebuilding your lawn doesn't have to be all that bad. In fact, just about all of us have been down that road before. Now that we've taken a close look at the basic building blocks of your lawn—grasses and soils—let's see how you can turn them into your own green, beautiful lawn.

When you build a new lawn, you have a choice between three different methods: seed, sod, or plugs. Seeding is the least expensive. Sodding is the most expensive (but is instant). Plugging is the in-between solution—and as a rule takes the longest. There are advantages and disadvantages to each method.

The advantages of seeding are that:

• The costs are lower
• There is a greater selection of turf grass species and cultivars
• A greater range of grasses are available for shade, heavy traffic, wet or dry locations, and low-maintenance lawns.

The disadvantages of seeding are that:

• Grasses establish themselves more slowly and require more care
• The period during the growing season when grasses can be established is limited
• There is an increased risk of poor establishment
• It is more difficult to establish a lawn on sites subject to erosion or heavy wear.

The advantages of sod are that:

• It rapidly establishes itself
• It can be laid at any time that the soil can be prepared

• It is easier to establish sod on high-use areas

• It gives more dependable results on banks and slopes where erosion can be a problem

The disadvantages of sod are that:

• The cost is higher

• A limited number of grass cultivars are available as sod

• There is a limited availability of sod with grasses adapted to shady locations, heavy traffic, or utility areas

No matter which method you choose, you must prepare your soil properly (see chapter 2).

Let's See How Much You Have Learned About Grass Seeding

Seeding can provide a satisfactory lawn for a wide range of site conditions, uses, and maintenance levels. To obtain good results and adapt to these variable conditions, carefully pay attention to the following factors:

1. Provide adequate site and soil preparation.
2. Select properly adapted turf grass species and cultivars according to site conditions, usage, and maintenance levels.
3. Follow proper steps for establishment.
4. Supply the required cultural care (water, mowing, fertilizing, and weed control) during and after establishment.

Seeding Methods

Moisture and temperature conditions are most favorable during the late summer. The preferred time to seed is between August 15 and September 15. Gentle fall rains are best for turf grass establishment with minimal weed competition. Turf grass seeded later in the fall may fail if the seedlings aren't able to grow enough to survive the winters. A *dormant* seeding—after early November—is also acceptable, since low temperatures will prevent germination until the following spring. An alternate time for seeding is early spring. Both spring and midsummer seedings are often unsuccessful because of high temperatures, lack of moisture, and competition from weeds, particularly annual grasses.

Proper seeding requires a uniform distribution of the seed at the recommended rate. It is best to seed when there's little wind activity because of the light, chaff-like nature of turf grass seeds. Apply one-half of the total amount of seed in one direction, and the remaining half at right angles. Use a cyclone or drop-type spreader for seeding. After seeding, rake the lawn lightly to mix the seed into the top 1/8–1/4 inch of soil. (An inverted metal or bamboo leaf rake dragged over the seedbed is excellent for this job.) Then roll the seedbed to ensure good seed-to-soil contact.

Apply a straw mulch to provide consistent moisture and cool temperatures during the establishment period and to reduce soil erosion and displacement of the seed. Oat straw is preferred on fall seedings because volunteer oat seedlings will be killed during the winter. Approximately 1 bale of straw should cover 500 square feet of seeded area. Spraying the straw with water after it is spread will help stabilize the mulch during windy conditions. On steep areas where erosion is a problem, burlap or twine netting can reduce the mount of seed and soil that wash away.

Watering is extremely important for effective turf grass establishment. The soil surface should always be kept moist, because young seedlings can die within a few hours if water is not available. A light sprinkling several times a day is best. Apply water lightly to avoid displacing the seeds.

When the grass seedlings are 1½ to 2 inches tall, remove approximately one-half of the straw. In a spring seeding, the remaining straw will decompose during the season. In a fall seeding, the remaining straw should be removed prior to snowfall, unless erosion is a potential problem. Redistribute windblown piles of straw to avoid smothering the grass. Burlap, cloth, or netting do not need to be removed.

Hydromulch Seeding. In hydromulch seeding, a mixture of seed, fertilizer, water, mulch, and a binder are applied from a spray tank onto a prepared seedbed. This hydromulch mixture provides an excellent medium for germination and rapid establishment. The water-holding capacity of the hydromulch reduces the need for irrigation during the establishment period. This cover also helps stabilize moderate slopes. The guarantee of satisfactory results that most seeding companies provide is an additional benefit for homeowners.

Postestablishment Care

Mow a newly seeded turf when the grass is 2½ to 3 inches tall. Mow to a height of 1½ to 2½ inches. The mower blade must be sharp so that the grass is cut cleanly and the plants not pulled out of the ground.

When the grass seedlings reach a height of about 1½ to 2 inches, applying a high-nitrogen turf fertilizer will help them get established. The first number on the fertilizer bag is a measurement of the nitrogen content, so a suitable fertilizer would be a 30-4-4 or a 23-4-6. Apply this fertilizer at one-half the rate recommended on the bag. Water immediately after application to prevent possible foliar burn.

Broadleaf weeds that germinate during the establishment period can seriously compete with the developing grasses. Herbicides can help control these weeds. However, to avoid injuring your lawn, make sure to apply the right herbicide at the right time.

Water will continue to be a primary concern for a new lawn. About 1 inch of water per week (counting natural rainfall plus your irrigation) is required to maintain a quality lawn. July and August are especially critical periods, and watering may be necessary.

Lawn Seeding on Frozen Soil

Almanacs sometimes advise seeding on the last snow of winter. This isn't a bad idea. Melting snow certainly settles lawn seed into a seedbed gently and uniformly. More practical advice, however, might be to distribute Adelphi, Fylking, Merion, or other standout varieties onto frozen ground that's clear of snow. Bluegrasses like these are small-seeded (from 1 to 2 million seeds to the pound), and the seeds stand a good chance of becoming embedded in the pits and cracks that result from the freezing-thawing cycle. In the weeks to come, the seed will probably work its way deeply enough into the soil so that seedlings will successfully strike root at the first onset of warm weather.

The idea of distributing seed while the ground is still frozen may not appeal to a warm-weather gardener, but it's certainly easier to seed at this time than later onto the mushy, thawing ground of spring. A spreader works very effectively on the solid footing of frozen soil, and there is not a lot of lush growth to get in the way. The seed sifts uniformly into the turf, unimpeded by damp foliage to which it might stick or wad. Moreover, freezing weather almost guarantees there won't be rain. If snow does follow, you are merely abiding by the almanac advice and thereby "mulching" a well-dispersed sowing.

Instant Green for You, Eh?

Sod Selection

Sod should be free of weeds and weedy grasses (such as bent grass, quack grass, and tall fescue) and should contain species and cultivars recommended for the location to be sodded. Most sod grown today has been selected for higher-quality lawns in sunny locations. There are usually blends of improved bluegrasses that respond well to watering and fertilization. Blends of several cultivars also provide better resistance to disease than does a single cultivar. A few growers provide sod adapted for shady or utility areas. If your needs for sod are unique, be sure to inquire about specially adapted sod.

Sod Installation

The grass plants in sod produce heat that cannot be dissipated when the sod is rolled or tacked for too long. This heat can kill the sod. To prevent this damage, sod should be laid within 24 hours of its harvest during warm weather, and always within 48 hours.

Sod can be laid at nearly any time of the year if the soil is dry enough to allow for soil preparation. Problems may exist with early winter sodding because the sod may dry out and die if the roots aren't established before the ground freezes. Don't sod during dry spells if watering won't be possible.

Avoid laying sod on powdery, dry soil. A soil that is moist, but not saturated, to a

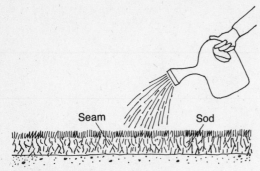

Before laying out sod, *and until the sod knits to the soil*, keep the soil bed moist to a depth of 6 inches. Seams and edges dry out more quickly and may require more frequent watering.

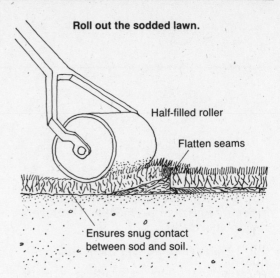

Roll out the sodded lawn.

Half-filled roller

Flatten seams

Ensures snug contact between sod and soil.

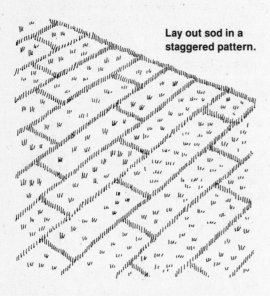

Lay out sod in a staggered pattern.

depth of 6 inches allows the new roots to establish rapidly. The end of the sod pieces should be staggered to prevent lines from forming across the turf. (These are caused by the slower establishment of the edges.) Make sure that the edges of the sod are in good contact with each other but *not* overlapping. Avoid stretching the sod, or gaps will develop between the pieces when the sod dries. Once the sod is laid, roll it to ensure good contact with the soil. The roots will dry out rapidly if

air pockets are left between the sod and the soil. If sod is laid on a slope, it may be necessary to peg the sod strips with wooden stakes to prevent slippage.

Thoroughly water the sod immediately after rolling. As a general rule, you should water every day to keep the sod moist until the roots have grown into the soil. Water the sod during midday to obtain the most rapid results. Be sure to apply enough water to wet the soil under the sod. Rooting normally requires 2 to 3 weeks. Once the sod is established, watering can be reduced gradually to once a week or less, depending on when the grass begins to wilt.

Mowing should begin when required by the growth of the grass. The recommended mowing height for bluegrass sod is 1½ to 2½ inches. Avoid removing more than one-third of the leaf surface at any one mowing.

After the sod is rooted, follow a fertilization program suggested for established lawns. Generally, at least four fertilizer applications per year are suggested for higher-quality lawns. Once the sod is established, good management practices will be necessary to maintain a high-quality turf.

Here's how to figure out how much sod you'll need.

Lot size:	5000 sq. ft.
House:	– 750 sq. ft.
Garage:	– 480 sq. ft.
Drive:	– 987 sq. ft.
Stoop:	– 48 sq. ft.
Walk:	– 30 sq. ft.
Area remaining to be sodded:	**2705 sq. ft.**

Area to be sodded

How Much Sod Do You Need?

This question is on all new sod layers' minds. Since most sod is sold by the square yard, simply measure your property length by width, subtract the house, walks, drives, and garage from that total, and divide what is left by 9. This will tell you exactly how many rolls of sod you will need. Here is an example:

Your lot size is:
$50' \times 100' = 5,000$ square feet
House: $30' \times 25' = -750$ square feet
Garage: $20' \times 24' = -480$ square feet
Drive: $23' \times 19' = -437$ square feet
$50' \times 11' = -550$ square feet
Stoop: $6' \times 8' = - 48$ square feet
Walk: $3' \times 10' = - 30$ square feet
This leaves you with 2,705 square feet to sod.

Divide 2,705 by 9 = 301 square-yard rolls to purchase

If You Become a Friend to Your Sod, Your Sod Will Be a Friend to You

If this little bit of wisdom seems rather simple to you, then let us consider its origin. When you finally decided that you could afford to sod your lawn, went to the trouble of preparing the soil, and purchased and rolled out your thick, green, luscious, healthy, instant lawn, you were accepting the results of many, many hours of hard work by the sod grower who prepared, drilled, watered, and fed that

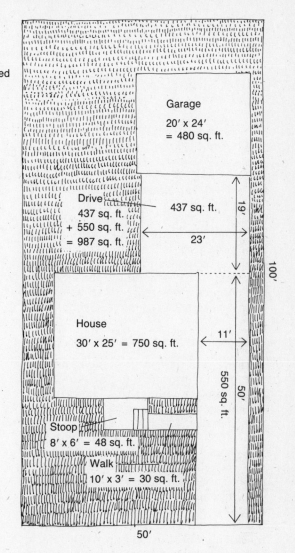

grass—for nearly two years! Now its future is in *your* hands. Feeding is the deciding factor as to whether your sod will continue to look as good as it did when you rolled it. From the time the new seed sprouts until it comes to your home as sod, it is fed every two weeks. You read that right: every two weeks! You must stop thinking of a lawn as a massive green blob and remember that you are caring for several million constantly hungry individual plants. In the sod field, they are fed a 1-1-1 ratio fertilizer (12-12-12, 10-10-10, or 8-8-8). Two weeks later they're fed a serving of 43, 44, 45, or 46% urea-nitrogen. This feeding cycle continues until it comes to your house. Don't feed it just in the spring and then wonder why it lost its color! Please follow the advice in the chapter on fertilizers so that your lawn never regrets its move to your home.

Give Your Old Lawn a Face-Lift

Every year thousands of lawns deteriorate due to improper maintenance, disease, or insect damage that leaves bare or thin areas. Steps can be taken to improve these lawns.

The cause of the deterioration or damage should be determined first, so that you can avoid the same problem in the future. If the area has good drainage and contours and the topsoil is of a desirable texture, you can renovate the lawn. Renovation is any practice—beyond routine maintenance—used to improve a deteriorated or damaged lawn. It can be as simple as seeding small bare spots or as complex as overseeding the entire lawn. Areas that need soil modification and/or recontouring should be reestablished rather than renovated.

The best time to renovate a lawn is late summer through early fall. Gentle rains and cool temperatures help seeds germinate and turf grass grow along with reducing competition from weeds. Early spring is another good time for renovation, although competition from weeds

and summer heat may reduce its effect. Before you start, make sure that supplemental watering will be available after renovating to protect the new seedlings from drying out.

Spot Seeding or Sodding

Bare areas larger than about 6 inches in diameter should be spot seeded or sodded. If good growing conditions prevail, smaller bare areas will tend to fill in naturally as the grass spreads laterally. Bare areas that require spot seeding or sodding should first be cleared of any weeds or dead grass to expose the soil. A stiff rake or small hoe can be used to loosen the soil thoroughly. Additional soil should be added if the spot is below the level of the lawn.

When spot-seeding, spread a seed blend or mixture similar to the existing lawn by hand. Cover the area uniformly with approximately 15 seeds per square inch. The seed should then be raked lightly into the top 1/4–1/2 inch of soil, and the soil firmed. Then apply straw or another mulch to the spots. Following mulching, irrigate the newly seeded spot thoroughly. Keep the new seedbed moist for a few weeks, or until the grass is well established. A light application (about 5 pounds per 1,000 square feet) of a complete fertilizer (such as 12-12-12) may help new seedlings grow.

With spot-sodding, cut a piece of sod that fills the area completely. The soil below should be loosened thoroughly, as in spot-seeding, but be sure to account for

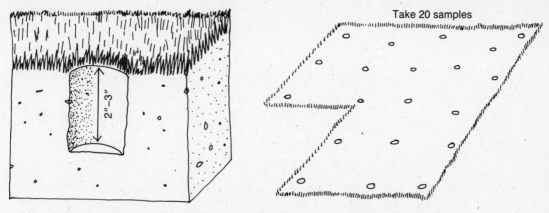

Collect soil samples from different spots to give an overall picture of your lawn.

Take 20 samples

the thickness of the sod when establishing the soil level. The sod should be tamped down and then watered thoroughly. Keep the sod moist until it is well rooted. A light application of a fertilizer (5 pounds per 1,000 square feet) high in phosphorus and potash will help it get established. You can spot-sod any time during the growing season, provided that enough water is available.

Further Renovation

Areas that have too many bare spots to make spot seeding or sodding practicable, or areas that have undesirable weedy grasses present, will require more extensive renovation. The following sequence should be followed to ensure a successful renovation (alternative options are suggested for some of the steps).

1. Soil Sampling. Collect soil samples to a depth of 2–3 inches from twenty locations throughout the area to be renovated. Use clean equipment when sampling. Mix these subsamples together. Air dry about one-half pint of the soil, package it securely, and send it to your local county Cooperative Extension Service or a reputable laboratory for testing. The test report will indicate the soil acidity level and the phosphorus and potassium content of your soil. Pay particular attention

to the phosphorus level, since an adequate supply is essential for establishing grass seedlings. Follow the soil-testing lab's recommendations for adding fertilizer and lime.

2. Perennial-Weed Control. Control perennial and broadleaf weeds before seeding. Complete your broadleaf weed control program several months before renovating. Control is most effective while the weeds are actively growing, which normally occurs during the spring and fall.

Weedy perennial grasses pose a more difficult problem and may themselves be the reason for renovating. A few grasses, such as tall fescue, spread very slowly and form unsightly clumps in the lawn. These clumps can be dug out with a shovel. Remove the grass and the soil below to a depth of 4 to 6 inches. Dig out about 4 inches around the outside of the clump to make sure you remove all the weedy grass.

Most perennial grasses spread aggressively by underground shoots, called rhizomes or by aboveground shoots, called stolons. Because of the way these grasses spread, digging them out is extremely difficult and may even aggravate the problem. You're better off applying a nonselective herbicide, which will kill both desirable and undesirable grasses in the area. Glyphosate (the active ingredient in Shoot-Out, Roundup, and Kleenup) is a particularly useful herbicide because you only have to wait 7 days after using it before reseeding. Follow the label directions carefully when using this—or any other—herbicide.

If these weedy grasses are confined to small areas, spot seeding or sodding can be used for reestablishment. Unfortunately, these grasses will usually be spread throughout your lawn, making spot treatment impracticable. When faced with this problem, killing off the entire lawn area where these grasses have established themselves is recommended. Skip two or three mowings before applying glyphosate to improve the plants' uptake of the herbicide.

3. Cultivation. After weed control and before seeding, use a lawn mower set at the lowest cutting height to remove most of the green grass or dead grass killed by the herbicide. This will provide better light for the seedlings and reduce the competition from the existing grass. Excessive clippings should be removed prior to seeding and can be stockpiled for later use as a mulch.

The seed must have good contact with the soil to germinate and grow properly. Some cultivation is necessary to ensure this contact. The easiest piece of cultivating equipment for the homeowner to obtain and operate is a dethatcher. This is also referred to as a power rake or vertical mower. The rotating tines remove some of the thatch layer and may be set to cut into the soil. Dethatch in several different directions to thoroughly expose the soil and obtain a good seedbed.

Coring is another form of cultivation that can help provide a good seedbed. This piece of equipment brings small cores of soil up to the surface. Core in several directions. After the cores have dried, break up the soil plugs by dragging a piece of fence or an inverted rake over the area. A dethatcher also can be used to break up these plugs. If much of the area has exposed topsoil with very little thatch, cultivation can be done *after* the application of fertilizer and seed. This will save time while still providing a good seedbed.

4. Fertilizer and Lime. It is best to follow recommendations based on a soil test for your soil's lime, phosphate, and potash needs. Nitrogen should be applied at a rate of 1 to 1½ pounds of actual nitrogen per 1,000 square feet. If you didn't get a soil test, a good general rule is to apply 10 to 12 pounds of a 1-1-1 ratio fertilizer (such as 12-12-12) per 1,000 square feet. (See page 135 for the method of calculating "actual" nitrogen). Rake lime and fertilizer into the seedbed, or mix it in by lightly going over the area with a dethatcher.

5. Seeding. Take half the seed and apply it in one direction, with the remaining seed applied at right angles to the first. This ensures good seed distribution. Use either a drop-type or a cyclone spreader. Seed with species and varieties of grass similar to the existing lawn. Areas that

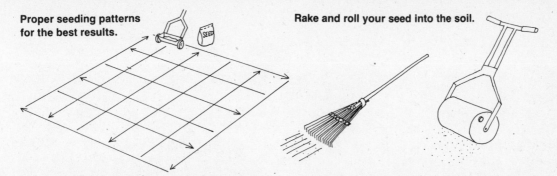

Proper seeding patterns for the best results.

Rake and roll your seed into the soil.

were killed with a nonselective herbicide prior to renovation should be seeded with species and/or cultivars recommended for use in your area. Follow the seeding rates listed on the package.

Mix the seed with the soil by dragging a leaf rake lightly over the area. Then roll the area to improve the seed contact with the soil. A thin mulch applied over the seeded area will help stabilize the seed and trap moisture. I make a mulch of Hyponex topsoil mixed with sphagnum moss. The combination of the two holds moisture over the seed longer and ensures a more even germination. Mulching materials include peat, straw, or dry clippings. Existing stubble will also provide a mulching effect.

6. Pro Tricks to Speed Up Renovation. A great number of homeowners hang on to an old, worn-out lawn because a new lawn takes a good deal of work and, as a rule, looks worse than the old lawn did until the new grass seed sprouts. The main problem is getting enough ambition to start. Well, I have a reputation for finding shortcuts and methods that make your yard and garden work faster, easier, and more fun, so let's try a couple of lawn renovation innovations:

Grass seed should always be stored in the refrigerator until it is needed. The lower temperatures keep the seed "asleep," so that it saves all of its energy for growing once you plant it in the ground.

Grass seed shells keep the baby seed inside safe, sound, and well-nourished until it is planted into soil. In order for the young seed to sprout through the shell, the casing must be softened up by the moisture and heat in the soil. This can take some time if the soil dries out because the weather is hot and dry, or if you don't sprinkle it enough. You can avoid this problem by pregerminating the seed.

Three days before you are going to sow the seed, place it in the legs of an old nylon panty hose or pillow case and submerge it in a clean garbage can filled with lukewarm water with ½ cup of Epsom salts added. Let it set for twenty-four hours. Remove the seed and pour off the old water, refill the container with lukewarm water (clean) and return the seed to soak another 24 hours (no Epsom salts this time). Your yard area should be almost ready for seeding. Spread the seed out on a dry, hard surface (driveway, patio, porch, etc.). Keep moving it around until it is dry enough to pour into your spreader. Pregermination will speed up sprouting by about 300 to 400 percent, as well as decrease the mortality rate of your seed.

7. Postrenovation Care. Once the seed is applied, water the area thoroughly. The surface should be kept moist during the germination period. Water daily at midday if your rainfall is inadequate. Once the grass is well established, watering can gradually be reduced.

Mow the area as you normally would. A sharp blade is important to keep the seedlings from being pulled from the soil.

8. Baby Lawn Food for Baby Grass

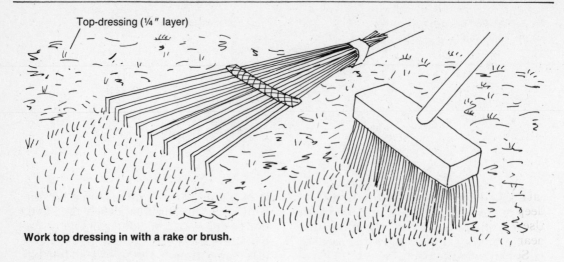

Top-dressing (¼″ layer)

Work top dressing in with a rake or brush.

Plants. New grass plants will get some help from the fertilizer that you added when you applied Neutra Nugget lime and lawn food. It takes a little while for your lawn to get those nutrients so I fill my hose-end sprayer jar half full of household ammonia, add water and ½ cup of liquid dish soap, and spray my newly sown seed. The soap keeps the Hyponex topdressing and seed damp. The ammonia is predigested nitrogen—a sort of baby food for your new seedlings.

A Little Dab'll Do Ya

Most of us have felt or noticed an unevenness in our lawn surface. Perhaps this roughness affects our accuracy in croquet or boccie. In any event, such humps and hollows form in the best of lawns. Frost heaving during winter months may cause these formations, and the activity of soil fauna, such as earthworms, can create additional roughness.

Perhaps the ultimate in turf grass surface smoothness is required on golf greens. In order to maintain these true putting surfaces, the greens are topdressed regularly. Home lawns seldom need regular topdressing. At times, however, a little dab of dressing is just what the lawn doctor ordered, as, for example, over tree roots that corrugate a surface.

Topdressing for lawns should consist of a soil that is as much like the soil in the root zone as possible. If anything, it should be a little more sandy. It should not be highly organic in nature, because lawn grasses build organic matter in the soil much more effectively than it can be added as topdressing. And, of course, it should be as free from weed seed as possible.

A layer of about ¼ inch brushed or raked into the lawn will help to smooth the surface. Such an application will also help prevent the formation of thatch, a layer of undecomposed organic matter that has a tendency to form at the soil surface between roots and foliage. Just a little dab of topdressing will do a lot of good.

Autumn Grooming Eases Winter Lawn Stress

Lawns don't need crackers or cheese or warm milk before being put to bed for the winter, but there are some grooming practices that will help your lawn have a less stressful and more restful winter.

First, check to see that all undesirable bedfellows, either weed or insect, have been controlled. This would involve use of an herbicide formulated to eliminate dandelions, plantains, perennial chickweed, and others. Grubs and other harmful insect pests will be getting ready to dig deeper in the soil for winter protection. Use an insecticide early, while they are near the surface, for best control.

Second, autumn fertilization may actually start with application in the late summer. This provides nutrients for building the reserves that will keep the lawn going through the winter months of dormancy and snow cover. During this period there are few green leaves active in photosynthesis (nature's food-making process), and lawn grasses must rely on food supplies stored in stems and roots. However, the roots can continue to absorb and assimilate some nutrients from autumn or early-winter applications of fertilizer.

Third, mow the lawn regularly throughout the autumn and check to see that the thatch is not unduly thick. If needed, use a power rake to thin this out. The last mowing or two should be just a little lower than the regular clipping height. Not much lower, but enough to ensure that the lawn is well groomed as it enters the dormant season. This helps prevent winter injuries caused by cold-weather fungi or smothering under slush and ice.

These three practices will help your lawn to sleep tight all winter and jump out to a fast start next spring.

Lazy, Shady Lawns

Trees, shrubs, and lawn greatly enhance the beauty and value of a home.

However, maintaining a lawn in the shade of trees and large shrubs can often be difficult. Trees compete with the grass for sunlight, water, and nutrients. The grass usually ends up on the short end of this competition. However, grasses may coexist with trees and shrubs, depending on the severity of the competition, if you follow certain management practices.

Establishment

As we have discussed, the first step in maintaining any lawn area begins with proper establishment. Site preparation and correct seeding or sodding methods are necessary for a uniform and healthy lawn. Selecting shade-tolerant grass varieties is particularly important for shady areas. The fine-leafed fescues, rough bluegrass (*Poa trivialis*), and a few varieties of improved Kentucky bluegrass perform acceptably in the shade. Rough bluegrass should only be used in very wet shaded areas where the fine-leafed fescues or the shade-tolerant improved Kentucky bluegrasses do not do well. Other grasses are prone to disease or lack vigor in shaded areas and should not be planted.

Tree Root and Branch Pruning

Certain steps can be taken to reduce competition from trees and shrubs. A sharp shovel or ax can be used to cut the surface roots of the tree that extend into the lawn, or a special root-pruning machine can be rented. Deeper roots will still supply nutrients and water to the tree. Root pruning should be done gradually so that the tree or shrub will not be severely damaged. Some shallow-rooted trees and shrubs, such as maples, beeches, and evergreens, will not tolerate extensive root pruning, so proceed with care.

Selective pruning or thinning of trees and shrubs will increase the light available and improve the air circulation to the lawn. Normally, only inside or low branches of the tree are removed. Maintain the shape and beauty of trees with selective pruning. In some cases, trees or shrubs can be removed or replaced with dwarf types. This will eliminate or significantly reduce the competition between the trees and shrubs and the grass.

General Care

Shaded lawns need different care than sunny areas. Grass grown in the shade is normally thinner than grass grown in the full sun. Foot and vehicle traffic easily damages grass in shaded areas and should be restricted whenever possible. Traffic also increases soil compaction, especially when the soil is wet.

The grass in shaded areas should be mowed 3–4 inches high, rather than 1½–2½ inches normally recommended for sunny areas. Do not remove more than one-third of the green leaf tissue at each mowing. In the fall, it is critical that tree leaves be removed promptly. Leaves left on the ground will eventually smother the grass.

Shaded areas tend to stay moist much longer than sunny areas and must be watered carefully. Water shaded areas deeply but infrequently. Allow the area to dry before the next application of water; avoid light, frequent applications. Apply enough water to supply the roots of shrubs and trees as well as the grass.

Shaded lawns need to be fertilized less than sunny areas because there is less growth. Light applications of fertilizer for the grass but deep root feeding of trees works the best. Heavy fertilization will give succulent turf growth that is prone to disease and traffic damage. A soil test will help to determine the proper rates for phosphate and potash application.

Shade-tolerant improved Kentucky bluegrass should have fertilizer applied at the full rate in late September, with a follow-up application at one-half to three-quarter rate in mid-November. (A full rate of fertilizer is the rate specified on the bag, which is close to 1 pound of actual nitrogen per 1,000 square feet.) Fine fescue will often thrive in shady areas with no fertilizer, especially if it is already dense and well established. Newer stands of fine fescue or thin areas may benefit from a three-quarters to full-rate application of fertilizer in September. Avoid any fertilizer application to shady areas in spring or summer.

I have found that keeping a quantity of Super K-Gro Shady Mix Seed in the refrigerator, and overseeding—spreading it with my whirley spreader—every 22 days, helps keep the grass green even under trees and other shady spots.

Alternatives to Grass

In some circumstances it may be best to avoid the use of grass in shaded areas. This is especially true in areas that receive a great deal of traffic, or in the especially deep shade of trees such as beech, maple, and evergreens.

In areas that receive heavy traffic, wood chips, crushed rock, or other mulches are alternatives. These mulches can be separated from the grass by edging or can be naturally contained using railroad ties or other permanent material if no clear edge exists. Shade-tolerant flowers can add color to the area.

Shade-tolerant ground covers can be used in areas that receive no traffic. They add diversity to the range of materials that can be used for landscaping shaded areas. Once established, these areas require little maintenance. The following table lists several shade-tolerant ground covers.

With proper selection and care of plant material, shaded areas can be beautiful.

SHADE-TOLERANT GROUND COVERS

	Growth Habit	Height (in inches)
Baltic Ivy *Hedera helix baltica*	Evergreen, creeping	8
Bugleweed *Ajuga reptans*	Herbaceous, creeping	6
Evergreen Candytuft *Iberis sempervirens*	Evergreen, spreading	8
Japanese Spurge *Pachysandra terminalis*	Evergreen, upright spreading	6
Many Fern Species (Native)	Herbaceous, spreading	12–24
Paxistima *Paxistima canbyi*	Evergreen, spreading	10
Periwinkle *Vinca minor, V. major*	Evergreen creeping	6
Purple Wintercreeper *Euonymus fortunei colorata*	Evergreen, spreading	24

Checklist for a Beautiful Lawn

The following rules are designed to make lawn care easy, enjoyable, and successful. Develop and maintain a beautiful, uniform, green lawn by using this information as it applies to your specific growth conditions.

• **Design for Use.** Lawns are to be used. This means they should be walked on and played on and still be pleasing to look at. Care should be taken in the design of lawns and gardens to provide adequate space for the uses intended, and to reflect your personality.

• **Encourage a Mixture of Grasses.** Use mixtures of grasses rather than pure seedlings of one variety. Mixtures of turf grass adjust better to a constantly changing environment. Mixtures also increase hardiness. *Mixtures of varieties* means a combination of several different types of Kentucky bluegrasses, and so on.

• **Don't Fight Shade.** Lawns need sunlight. Use ground covers where there is insufficient light to grow turf grasses. Attempts to grow lawn grasses in shady areas often fail because of the combined effects of low light intensity, root competition from woody plants, and poor air movement that increases disease within the turf. You can, however, overseed every 22 days, as I have suggested.

• **Have Lawn Soils Tested.** A soil test will indicate whether your lawn needs lime and will help you choose the right fertilizer for a specific soil. Brand-name lawn fertilizers are recommended for average conditions. The soil test will indicate how close your conditions are to the average. The small soil-test kits that you buy at your garden center work very well if you will just read and follow the directions.

• **Fertilize in the Early Fall.** Fertilize in the early fall every year. Where lawns are irrigated, fertilize in spring and fall, but consider fall fertilization a must. Turf grasses store reserves for the winter during the fall. Don't let your lawn go into winter dormacy in a starved condition. Feed with a liquid lawn food like Super K-Gro Rapid Green every 3 weeks throughout the summer.

• **Feed with Nitrogen and Potassium.** For established lawns, use more nitrogen than potassium and more potassium than phosphorus. A ratio of nitrogen to phosphorus to potassium of 3-1-2 is recommended. Phosphorus should only be used during construction of a new lawn or if a soil test indicates that it is needed.

• **Renovate Lawns in the Fall.** Lawns can become "pot bound..." (This means that the roots get so thick that none of them can get food.) Thin your turf grass (if needed) as part of a fall renovation program that should also include an application of fertilizer. Remember that turf grasses, like any plant, need room to grow. Add new, improved varieties of seed for a more beautiful, easy-to-maintain lawn. De-thatching in the fall will give you results you won't believe.

• **Kill Nongrassy Weeds in the Fall.** Use herbicides to control lawn weeds (all except the grassy weeds) during cool fall weather. Ornamental plants that are easily damaged by drifting herbicides are more hardy and less likely to be injured by treatments made after the first frost in the fall. Lawn weeds are easily controlled at this time by proper use of the right herbicide spray. Always spray the weeds with soap and water first; then spray with weed killer.

• **For Grassy Weeds, Use Preemergent Herbicides.** Grassy weeds are best controlled by use of a pre-emergent herbicide in midspring. Post-emergent herbicides should be considered for those weeds that cannot be controlled by a pre-emergent chemical. Do not spray postemergent herbicides when the temperature is over 75 degrees F.

• **Mow Frequently.** Mow as frequently as necessary to remove ½ inch of clippings when the height of cut is set from 1½ to 2 inches. Mow all lawns that consist of mixtures of turf grasses at this height. Keep your mower blades razor-sharp. Remember, it pays to have more than one blade so that you always have a sharp one on hand.

● **Water Well or Don't Irrigate at All.** Lawns should be watered adequately or they should be left unwatered, so that adjustments to draught and dormancy will be made in a natural way. More harm than good can result from watering with sprinklers set to apply less than 1 inch of water per setting. Use sprinklers that minimize water runoff. Remember, if you spray the lawn at least once every 2 weeks with the soap solution, you will save water and save your grass.

● **Limit Pesticide and Herbicide Use.** Use fungicides and insecticides as "special purpose" treatments to control specific disease and insect problems. Use pesticides only on lawns that are well cared for, that is, mowed, fertilized, and watered. Use herbicides only when the turf is not able to crowd out weeds on its own.

● **Control Thatch and Constantly Spike.** Be sure you spray the lawn area in early spring with a mixture of half beer and half ammonia to help control thatch. Celebrate the Fourth of July with your lawn by spraying it with 1 quart of beer mixed with 15 gallons of water. Wear your lawn spike sandals (see page 68) at least every third time you mow to keep the soil healthy.

Green Is Clean

There's an old saying that lawns are most beautiful when they are so uniform that they are hardly noticed. In effect, we should pass over the lawn in our anticipation of observing the beauty of the overall landscape. Any weeds or blemishes that attract attention to the lawn tend to spoil the overall picture and decrease the impact of the moment. Litter on or about such lawns is seldom seen, for *green* is *clean*.

The quality of lawns provides a measure for determining pride in neighborhoods and the degree of individual caring within a community. According to Dr. Eliot Roberts of the Lawn Institute, evidence across the country supports the green-is-clean concept. Where people have been unable to develop, or have lost their interest in, lawns and gardens, or where adequate space in unavailable, litter and trash collect and soon replace green grass. On the other hand, residences that boast the ultimate in high quality turf are clean and well taken care of. Real estate values are high. Green is clean—and an important part of our quality of life.

Campaigns to pick up and remove litter are not likely to succeed unless people care. It takes the cultivation of living ground cover to make a habitat suitable for humankind. Without lawns and gardens, we are likely to lose ground, literally, to the pressures of a "throw away" society.

4

Fertilizing

Give It a Shot of Bo Peep and A Beer Chaser

I can drive down a street during the lawn-growing season and tell you who has sincere pride in their lawn, who is doing just enough to keep their lawn from being a fire hazard during the dry season, and who just doesn't give a hoot.

I've subtitled a chapter a little further along in this book "Green Lawns Don't Just Happen—They're Caused!" There I recapped all of the steps you'll have to follow to ensure a better-than-average lawn on your side of the fence.

But the one step that can cause the most green—both in your grass and in your neighbor (who'll be green with envy because he didn't put as much effort into his lawn), is to fertilize your grass in the right way, at the right time, and with the right materials.

Why Bother to Fertilize Your Lawn?

Proper fertilization helps a lawn in many ways. The grass turns a richer, healthier color. Its growth is stimulated, making the turf thicker and better wearing. Balanced fertilization improves the grass's health and thwarts disease. Fertil-

ized grass competes more vigorously with weeds; many weeds are simply squeezed out, while others (such as crabgrass) are shaded into submission.

More esoteric benefits will occur on a physiological level. Fertilized grass is hardier and responds to stresses better. New tissue steadily replaces senescent growth for a healthier and more attractive appearance.

Sparse foliage that covers the ground poorly is characteristic of underfertilized turf. Ecologists tell us that poor fertility generally encourages biomass below ground rather than above. In an effort to compensate for the low level of nutrient intake, grass plants allocate their resources to root growth rather than to growing green foliage. In severe cases, plants will languish, and even die, since they need ample green leaf for making food by photosynthesis.

Adopt a commonsense approach to lawn feeding—avoid overdosages and imbalances; both can cause real problems.

Soluble fertilizer salts can wilt grass due to "dehydration"—direct contact can burn grass foliage. A deluge of nitrogen unaccompanied by adequate amounts of other nutrients can cause lushness, but the grass will lose some of its ability to resist disease and wear. Although nitrogen is the main nutrient required by grass, it is best parceled out steadily and sparingly rather than in gushes.

In fertilizers, "gradual-release" is a highly valued feature.

Fertilizers can be thought of as transients: They are just passing through. That's why they're designed to "release" slowly. If they released all their nutrients at once, they wouldn't be as effective before they leached into the subsoil.

Keep Your Lawn on a Diet

No, I'm not fooling. The professional turf manager probably watches his grasses' diet more closely than he does his own. Our health is controlled by our diet: If we want to look good, feel good, and perform physically without cramps, injuries, or illness, we have to eat foods with the minimum daily requirements of vitamins and minerals as well as control the number of calories we consume. We must follow a similar program for our lawns if they are to stay in peak appearance and perform properly (grow).

Get Your Lawn a Regular Lab Test

I have my soil tested twice a year, on April 1 and September 1, just to make sure that my soil is not too hot (alkaline) or lacking in a necessary element.

If you want your soil tested, take a spoonful of soil from several different spots in the yard, digging 3 inches down under your turf. Mix the samples together, let them dry, and place them (locked tight) in a plastic bag. (Do not take soil samples from areas that have had fertilizer or lime applied within the past 4 weeks.)

Lable the sample with your name and address and send it, along with $15.00, to: McCue & Associates, Consultants, 4458 Seventeenth Street, San Francisco, California 94114.

You will get a good qualitative interpretation of the content of your soil and its needs. Your county extension service may also provide a soil testing service.

Building Stronger Grass Sixteen Ways

Grass needs sixteen essential elements if it is to continue to grow all season. These sixteen elements are divided into three groups: primary, secondary, and minor nutrients. If you don't make sure that all sixteen elements are available to your lawn, then your grass's appearance will suffer. It will also become more prone to disease, weeds, and insect problems.

The Sixteen Essential Elements

I. Primary Nutrients	II. Secondary Nutrients	III. Minor Nutrients
Nitrogen	Calcium	Iron
Phosphorus	Magnesium	Manganese
Potassium	Sulfur	Copper
		Boron
		Zinc
		Chlorine
		Molybdenum

I could, should, and would tell you about each of these sixteen elements, but you would get bored, and I promised that I would keep this fun and easy.

The primary elements, especially nitrogen, are absolutely necessary if you want green grass and not the all-too-common yellow to yellow-green variety.

Your grass uses up nitrogen faster than kids can eat a box of cookies. Use a dry lawn fertilizer that combines several forms of nitrogen in its formula. Different forms of nitrogen work faster or slower than others, so a fertilizer that includes several kinds will make nitrogen available to your grass over a longer period of time.

Nitrogen compounds can be divided into two groups, each with its own characteristic behavior:

Water-Soluble Group

- Are quickly available to the grass—results are seen very soon
- Quickly leach out (wash away)
- Can burn the grass if not watered in
- Are less expensive

- Are applied more often, but at lower rates
- Tend to lower the soil pH
- Work well in both cool weather and warm

Slow-Release Group

- Are slowly available to the grass (the type of soil, temperature, air, and water control how quickly the nutrients become available)
- Are more dependable as a source of nitrogen
- Are slow to leach out
- Seldom burn lawns
- Are more expensive
- Are applied more heavily
- Do not work well in cool weather

All Appetites Aren't the Same

The seventeen most common kinds of lawn grasses divide into four groups of different eating preferences: ¼ pound, ½ pound, ¾ pound, and 1 pound of nitrogen per growing month per 1,000 square feet. This won't mean a hill of beans to most of you in the beginning, but you will eventually find that you can control the color, growing speed, and density of your lawn by what and how you feed it.

The "Nitrogen Requirements" chart is a basic guide to the preferences of the most popular lawn grasses.

Phosphorus, The Paranoid Element

If you don't keep your soil's acidity in

check, phosphorus (P) won't come out from under the bed—it gets locked up chemically in the soil. This can be really bad news, because phosphorus helps your grass develop a good root system.

Potassium, the Caviar of Lawn Food

Potassium (K) has been described as the caviar of lawn food, because grass plants take in much more than they need. (This is called luxury consumption.) Potassium acts like the plant equivalent of vitamin C in humans: It helps grass fight off the stress from cold and heat.

Characteristics of Fertilizers Used on Lawns

The table on page 56 shows how some of the more popular fertilizers deliver nitrogen, phosphorus and potassium (N, P, and K).

The Second Team Makes the First Team Look Good

Secondary elements are really the keys that unlock the primary nutrients (N-P-K) or keep them from getting locked up in the soil.

Calcium does lots of good things, but what it does best is neutralize salt damage and help the grass grow to be tougher.

Sulfur both releases the nitrogen in the soil and helps control the soil's pH. You can feed your lawn both calcium and sulfur by applying agricultural gypsum in the fall (in all zones) at a rate of 50 pounds per 1,000 square feet. Gypsum contains large quantities of both these elements.

NITROGEN REQUIREMENTS

	Lbs. of N/Mo.	Grass Season	Best Zones
Bahia Grass	1/4	O	3, 5, 7, 8
Bermuda Grass		O	3–8, best in 9, 10 and West Coast
Common	3/4		
Improved	1		
Buffalo Grass	1/4	O	3, 6, 8
Centipede Grass	1/4	O	3, 6, 8
Chewings Fescue	1/4	*	3, 9
Colonial Bent	3/4	*	3, 9
Creeping Bent	3/4	*	3, 9
Dichondra	3/4	O	2, 5
Hard Fescue	1/4	*	4, 8
Italian Rye	1/2	*	3, 9
Kentucky Bluegrass	1/2	*	3, 6, 9
Perennial Ryegrass		*	3, 9
Classical	1/2	O	2, 9
Improved	1/2	O	2, 9
Red Fescue	1/4	*	4, 8
Rough Bluegrass	3/4	*	4, 8
St. Augustine Grass	3/4	O	3, 5, 7, 8
Velvet Bent Grass	3/4	*	3, 9
Zoysia Grass	3/4	O	3, 6, 8

* Cool-Season Grass
O Warm-Season Grass

Characteristics of Fertilizers Used on Lawns

Type	N	P₂O₅	K₂O	Soil-Acidifying Effect	Water Solubility	Potential for Burn
		Nutrient Content (in percent)				
Ammonium Nitrate	Synthetic inorganic	33	0	0	Moderate	High	Very high
Ammonium Sulfate	Synthetic inorganic	21	0	0	Great	High	High
Urea	Synthetic organic	45	0	0	Moderate	High	High
Monoammonium Phosphate	Synthetic inorganic	11	48	0	Slight	Moderate	Low
Diammonium Phosphate	Synthetic inorganic	20	50	0	Moderate	Moderate	Moderate
IBDU (Isobutylidine Diurea)	Synthetic organic	31	0	0	Undetermined	Very low	Low
Sulfur-Coated Urea (SCU)	Synthetic organic	32	0	0	Undetermined	Very low	Low
Ureaformaldehyde	Synthetic organic	38	0	0	Undetermined	Very low	Low
Milorganite	Natural organic	6	4	4	Undetermined	Very low	Low
Methylene Urea	Synthetic organic	38	0	0	Undetermined	Very low	Low
Superphosphate	Inorganic	0	20	0	Low	Low	Low
Treble Super Phosphate	Inorganic	0	45	0	Low	Low	Low
Muriate of Potash (KCl)	Inorganic	0	0	60	Low	Moderate	Moderate
Sulfate of Potash (K₂SO₄)	Inorganic	0	0	50	Low	Moderate	Low
Potassium Nitrate	Inorganic	13	0	44	None	Moderate	Very high

How much of each nutrient is available from the fertilizer can be determined by looking at the three-number formula on the bag. The first number stands for the amount of nitrogen (N), the second number for the amount of phosphorus (P), and the third number for the amount of potassium (K). If the formula is 30-4-4, for example, the fertilizer contains 30 percent nitrogen, 4 percent phosphorus, and 4 percent potassium.

If you have a pet dog or if you use rock salt as an ice or snow-melting agent, you and your lawn need gypsum.

Magnesium keeps the grass from getting sore feet. It's a root builder, skin thickener, and color deepener. Magnesium is the main element in Epsom salts. I apply a mixture of 70 percent Epsom salts and 30 percent diatomaceous earth (the "dust" used in swimming-pool filters) from a broadcast spreader in mid-May. I use the Epsom salts as a carrier for the diatomaceous earth, which controls the snails and slugs that hide in the damp tall grass.

The Minor League Never Gets as Much Attention

With the exception of iron, the minor nutrients are usually taken for granted. According to horticulturist J. D. Butler of Colorado State University, lawns grown on alkaline soils are often deficient in iron, and yellow-grass foliage is often noted under these conditions.

The presence of iron in the soil deepens the green of most grasses. Since the amount of green chlorophyll in grass leaves is directly related to the amount of iron in the grass, iron is critical to the culture of uniformly green turf.

Applications of nitrogen fertilizer will also make lawns a darker green color, but they increase the growth rate of the grass. As a result, the lawn will need more frequent mowing. Under most soil conditions iron improves lawn color without stimulating growth. This is especially desirable during warm weather. If you are feeding your lawn on a frequent basis and the grass still has a yellow cast to it, add ferrous sulfate at a rate of 1½ pounds per 20,000 square feet. (I use a whirley-type spreader.)

Acid mine tailings and iron salts, such as ferrous sulfate and ferrous ammonium sulfate, will produce a longer-lasting effect on color than the chelates, such as Ferriplex 128, Pay-Plex, and Sequesterene 138 and 330.

Since only small amounts of iron are required for lawn greening, application rates should closely follow those recommended on the package of the product used.

The rest of the minor elements are provided out of the mild and acceptable buildup of ¼ to ⅛ inch of thatch. Here are a few facts about the other minor elements:

Manganese helps the plant take in carbon dioxide and transform the carbohydrates within the plant.

Plants use hardly any *zinc*, but it acts as sort of a sex hormone—helping the reproductive process.

Copper promotes growth and activates some important enzyme systems.

Boron helps the plants digest calcium and phosphorus.

Molybdenum keeps your grass plants from being runts.

Open Your Mouth and Say Ah-h-h-h

If you are even halfway serious about having a better-than-average lawn, you should always keep your eyes open for trouble. If you know what to look for, it won't take you even one season to recognize the elemental deficiencies in your lawn (see accompanying table):

Deficiency	Symptoms
Nitrogen	Older leaves will turn yellow green, and there will be very little new growth
Potassium	Leaf tips and edges will look burned
Phosphorus	Foliage will go from dark green to a reddish cast
Calcium	New leaves will be small and foliage will be reddish brown
Magnesium	Foliage will be yellow green with reddish margins
Sulfur	Mature foliage turns yellow
Iron	New foliage turns yellow
Manganese	New foliage turns yellow
Copper	Seldom if ever a problem on turf
Zinc	Leaves look shriveled up, thin, and small
Boron	Yellow foliage and stunted growth
Molybdenum	Mature foliage is gray-green.

If you are feeding your lawn with a well-balanced lawn food on a regular basis, odds are you won't be bothered with any of these symptoms.

Brand-Name Preferences Should Depend on Price and Performance

When you're choosing a fertilizer, remember that the highest-priced fertilizer is not always the best and that the lowest-priced lawn food is not the worst. Before you go to buy fertilizer, take a good look at the fertilizer ingredients listed in the "Fertilizer Characteristics" chart (see page 56). Now look at a few different brands of lawn food and check to see if they have a combination of high, moderate, and low (slow-release) forms of nitrogen. Check the coverage and then check the price.

There is nothing wrong with buying broken bags for a good price and mixing them together (as long as you pay attention to the nitrogen sources) to feed your lawn. No, I don't care if you use three or four or five different brands together.

Feeding Time

Earlier I stated that your grass eats every 2 weeks until it comes to your house. And then guess what? It's lucky if it gets fed twice a year!

I feed my lawns every 2 weeks, and I spend less money and probably less time on it than my neighbors who, out of shame, feed their lawns once a month. No, I don't expect you to feed your grass every 2 weeks (although it would be better off if you did), but once a month is not too much to ask, is it?

Getting Off to a Good Start

Grasses are just like people. Some folks wake up with an appetite that could compete with a bear just out of hibernation, while others prefer to be up and about for an hour or so and then have a light breakfast. Still others want nothing more than a cup of coffee.

That's how it is with some grass types. I have found that sulfur-coated urea (SCU) fertilizers are the greatest things to come down the pike for "waking up" a lawn.

Try feeding your lawn with an SCU as soon after the first of the year as possible (with an Ortho whirley spreader on a *number-3 setting*)—even between snows in the North. Then just forget you ever fed it.

Apply a regular well-balanced lawn food brand at half the recommended spreader setting at the normally accepted time. Water it in with your hose-end jar filled with household ammonia and 1 cup of liquid dish soap (per 10 gallons of water over 2,500 square feet). Your grass will chase you into the garage for a second helping. This simple source of nitrogen (household ammonia) can be eaten and digested by the grass immediately. The other types of nitrogen used will gradually feed your lawn as moisture and temperature release them from their carriers.

Once again, I'm going to advise you to wear your lawn spike sandals or golf shoes (see page 68), not only when you mow, but everytime you feed the lawn, even if you are using liquid fertilizer.

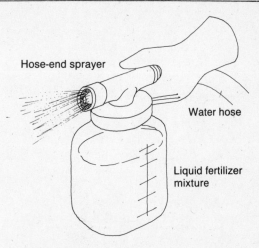

Hose-end sprayer

Water hose

Liquid fertilizer mixture

Spoon-fed Grass Always Wins the Prize

After the second feeding (the first was the SCU, which you were supposed to forget), wait until you have mowed the lawn twice before feeding it again. Then fill up the whirley spreader with your selected lawn food, set it on *number 2*, and let 'er rip. Two mowings later, repeat the application. And so on and so on until September 30; then feed it at half the recommended rate again.

Lawns Like to Drink Their Lunch

The popular liquid fertilizer applicators began to appear on the green scene about fifteen years ago. At first, fuel oil distributors got into the liquid-fertilizer business to keep their equipment and men working all season. Since most of their employees had little knowledge of turf needs, spraying techniques, or chemicals, this venture turned out to be a rather costly one in terms of damaged equipment and plants. Next came the professional landscaper with specially designed equipment and chemical formulas.

The bottom line is that liquid-fertilizer application is an excellent method. No, it's not magic—nor is it the best.

As a matter of fact, a combination of liquid and dry applications works the best. Whether you hire a professional or apply it yourself, apply dry fertilizer at half rate in the spring and fall and use liq-

uid fertilizer for the rest of the season. You can help the commercial operators by watering the lawn the days before and after the application. These days, most grass damage caused by fertilizers is the result of missing this follow-up irrigation.

Do-It-Yourself Liquid Application Can Save You Money

Since the custom applicator has become so successful and taken a significant share of the lawn food market, many major fertilizer brands now offer their own excellent premixed liquid applications. The prices for these are reasonable. Simply attach the prefilled sprayer to your hose and do the same job that the custom applicator does—for about 25 percent of the cost.

K-Mart probably has the biggest sellers, called Rapid Green Lawn Food and Liquid Weed and Feed. K-Mart's Super K-Gro Lawn Fertilizer is also the largest-selling national brand of dry fertilizer on the market today. I use them both. When I am using the liquid, I forgo the in-between dry applications.

Spread the Word

While you are at it, spread your fertilizer with a broadcast spreader—they come

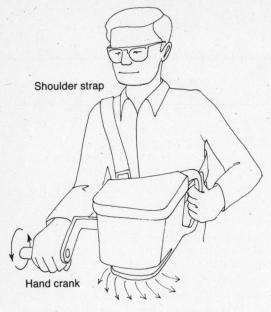

Shoulder strap

Hand crank

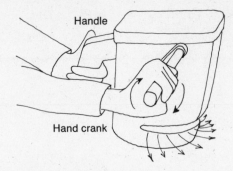

Handle

Hand crank

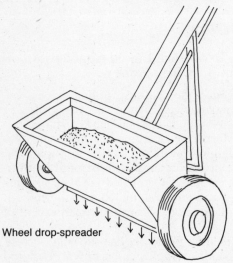

Wheel drop-spreader

Three popular ways to spread fertilizer.

in wheeled or chest- or hand-held models. I personally prefer the chest- and hand-held versions because I don't have to worry about wheel and turnaround marks. No, they are not heavy. My pride and joy is a hand-held whirley-type spreader from Denmark that comes with a small hopper attachment. I purchased it

through the Brookstone catalog* for under twenty-five dollars and I use it at the drop of a hat. Ortho makes one that is just as handy but does not have the portable hopper.

The old drop spreader is on its last leg. I have not used one in eighteen years and cannot think of any reason to invest in one now.

Please, please, please, wash out your spreader after every job. Rinse it well. I use a warm soap solution to clean mine.

Organic Gardening Lawns

Do the principles of organic gardening work for lawn care? Lawns are a natural for the treatment, according to Dr. Eliot Roberts of the Lawn Institute. First of all, lawn care does not place emphasis on yield, but on quality. High clipping yields will only cause the gardener mowing grief. Therefore, chemical fertilizers that push growth are unnecessary. Slow-release, natural sources of nutrients are good choices for lawns.

Natural materials that contain heavy metals, such as cadmium, should be used cautiously where there's a chance that the lawn area may someday be converted into a vegetable garden. The same caution holds for the use of wood ashes. Otherwise, the ash can sweeten the soil and is a good source of potassium.

*Brookstone Company
5 Vose Farm Road
Peterborough, New Hampshire 03458

The "Something Specials"

Every gardener or superintendent I ever studied under had his own little tricks when it came to making grass grow or slow. Over the years I have developed a couple of my own: beer, household ammonia, liquid cow manure, and soap. You can also throw in my golf shoes and turf spikes (see page 68). Now you know why I am referred to as a lawn nut—but it's the results that count, right?

● **Beer.** I start the season by filling my hose-end jar half full of ammonia and half full of beer and spraying my lawn with 15 to 20 gallons of water over 2,500 square feet. The ammonia provides a quick shot of nitrogen, while the beer starts the thatch decomposing. I repeat the treatment, but with beer only, on the Fourth of July.

● **Ammonia** (household). It's like baby food for my young lawns and chicken soup for the older ones. Ammonia is a cheap, quick shot of nitrogen.

● **Liquid cow manure** (now odorless). When I worked in England, we saved cow pies in the spring and mixed them into a slurry thin enough to pour through two thicknesses of burlap, with which we then drenched the turf. Now I use a material (still made from cow pies) called Bov-a-Mura from P.B.I. Gordon Corporation (Acme Chemicals).*

Liquid manure does sixteen things,

and all of them are good. Its two biggest assets are that it tears the hell out of thatch, but it also turns the grass greener than green. I mix half Rapid Green (from K-Mart) and half cow juice. Wow! What great results!

● **Soap.** I don't know why folks make such a fuss over a practice that originated hundreds of years ago. Soap kills bugs, disease, protects the wax coat on foliage, cleans pollution off of the same leaves, softens up the soil, and makes chemicals stick. I use the cheapest liquid dish soap for spraying. I broadcast powdered laundry soap from my spreader in the spring after cleanup or mix it with my first fertilizer treatment. There are also expensive professional turf and plant soaps.

To Feed or Not to Feed—There Is No Question!

If you want a lawn to be proud of, you must follow a good, sound feeding program designed to get the best performance out of the grass variety you have selected. Remember what I said earlier: Your grass was fed every 2 weeks for 2 years at the sod field. Don't make it sorry that it came to live at your house.

*PBI Gordon (Acme Chemicals)
1217 W. 12th St.
P.O. Box 4090
Kansas City, Missouri 64101

5

Mowing
Have You Priced a Lawn Mower Lately?

Would you be surprised if I told you that improper mowing prepares lawns for weeds, insects, and disease damage and destroys more lawns than the insects and diseases do on their own? It's true!

Very few home gardeners give lawn mowing any more attention or respect than taking out the trash, and that's a deadly shame (for the lawn). For turf care professionals, mowing grass properly is as important as feeding, watering, fertilizing, and insect and disease care.

If you really want the greenest grass on the block to be on your side of the fence, you must change your attitude toward mowing. My neighbors would most likely describe me as a "lawn nut": The first lawn mower you hear in the spring is mine, as is the last one heard before the snow flies. I love to cut my grass. When I am finished mowing, trimming, and edging my lawn, it is a sight to be proud of. I also know that the lawn is comfortable and working as hard as I am to stay picture-perfect.

Grass must be mowed regularly for both good looks and healthy growth. When grass is cut on a regular basis, at

the proper time (of day), at the proper height (for the variety), and with the proper type of lawn mower—one that is well maintained and has a sharp, sharp, blade—both its looks and its quality will be truly spectacular.

What You Buy Is What You Get

Most people answer the question I asked at the beginning of this chapter with a shocked, "I can't believe it."

Lawn success begins with your mower. Get comfortable—I am going to give you a lesson on lawn mowers that will knock your socks off.

First off, did you know that very few lawn mower companies actually manufacture their own mowers? Most *assemble* parts manufactured by others, attach their brand name, and then package and sell them. (In many cases, service for these machines is practically non-existent.)

A good mower should adjust easily to different mowing heights. It should have enough power not to stall in tall grass. Sufficient power ensures that the blade

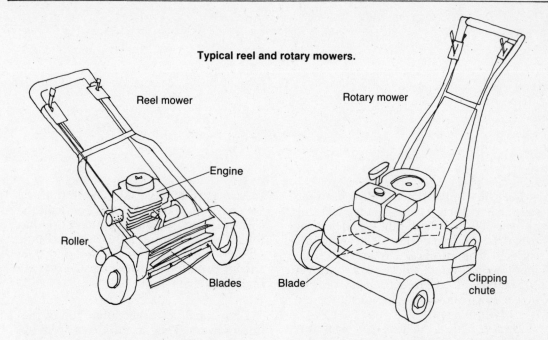

Typical reel and rotary mowers.

Reel mower

Rotary mower

Engine

Roller

Blades

Blade

Clipping chute

can properly lift and cut the grass as well as provide adequate pull for the mower itself. If the power for the cutting blade is independent of the forward propulsion, you can ease into patches of tougher grass at a slower pace, putting less of a burden on the mower's power source.

Reel mowers give the best-looking finish to a lawn, but they're too expensive for most homeowners and require more maintenance than rotaries.

Rotary mowers are more versatile for higher and rougher cutting, while reel mowers do a neater job on low-cut turf. Most reel mowers can't approach obstructions as closely as rotaries can, since their wheels are outside of the cutting cylinder.

Rotary mowers are more popular because of their lower price. As a rule there aren't many moving parts on a rotary mower, outside of the engine itself.

It used to be that if your mower had an engine made by a name-brand motor manufacturer, you could count on getting high quality and performance. Today, this is no longer the case. Producers of

small engines have had to manufacture "special versions" of their engines to stay competitive and to satisfy the large mower assemblers they sell their engines to.

A rotary-mower engine spins the mowing blade at 3,000 rpm, or over 200 mph. As a rule, you will find engines with power ratings between 2.5 and 3.0 horsepower on the lower-priced rotary mowers. When these engines are asked to propel a machine forward as well as cut heavy grass, they can bend their crankshafts. Replacing a crankshaft can cost you from one-half to two-thirds the original cost of the mower. For my money, the engine capability of your mower should be at least 3.5 horsepower.

Rotary-Mower Features

Design. For one reason or another, homeowners seem to think that they need a high-fashion mower with sleek lines and a classy engine shroud. The professional prefers an uncluttered, round deck that fits tight to the outside edge of the blade. The round design permits him to mow close up to objects.

Deck. The only thing standing between me and a tempered piece of steel whirling at over 200 mph is the mower deck. My friend, I want that deck *and* the toes of my shoes to be made of steel. A national commission on product safety says that over 100,000 people are injured every year by power lawn mowers—safe design is extremely important!

Trailing Shield. Most of you probably think that the trailing shield was added to your mower to aggravate you when you have to pull the mower backward. It's really there to stop objects from being thrown by the whirling blade from under the deck. I want my trailing shield to be made of steel, *not* rubber or plastic.

Discharge Port. If I am following a mower equipped with a rear bagger, I want the cover that fits over that port to be made out of steel—*not* plastic or rubber.

Engine Shroud. The fancy cover over the engine should also be made of steel—*not* fiberglass or plastic.

Wheels. Make mine wide, soft, and round so that they do not leave grooves in my lawn. If your mower doesn't have wide, soft tires, see if you can convert to them on your own.

Riding Mowers

If you are going to purchase a mower to cut the grass *and* haul you around, make sure that it's big and strong enough to do both jobs.

For your lawn's sake, make sure that the tires are big and fat enough that the weight of the mower doesn't compact the soil. For your own safety, make sure that the throttle automatically shuts the blade off if you fall out of the seat and that steel shields protect you wherever the moving blade could shoot out debris.

I have just described a few top-of-the-line mowers. They usually cost from six hundred dollars on up, but if properly maintained, they can last from eight to ten years. The current assortment of cheaply made, often unsafe mowers usually don't last more than two to three years.

"In Dew Time" Is *Not* the Proper Time to Mow

If I had spelled it "due," I could have gotten away with it. If you can fit it into your schedule, and you really want a picture-perfect lawn, plan to mow near 6:00 P.M. The late start will give the grass blades plenty of time to recover before they're exposed to the hot sun and dry wind the next day. Mow with a razor-sharp blade (remember that only the outer 3 inches of the blade actually cut) and water your lawn as early as possible the following morning (watering at sunup is best).

Never, never, never mow wet grass! You will ruin all of your hard work by tearing out entire grass plants.

Make sure to cut your lawn at the proper height. For example, bluegrass can be:

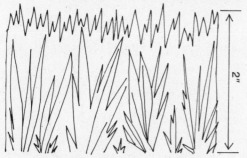

Cut when grass reaches 2″ in height.

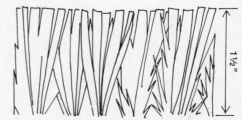

Cut grass to 1½″height.

How High Is High? How Low is Low?

There are as many different answers to this question as there are varieties of grass and personal preferences. Cutting the grass too high leaves it looking shaggy, fat, and uncared for. Too-tall grass can also lead to an excessive thatch build-up—encouraging insect and disease damage. Cutting it too short, on the other hand, damages the crown of the grass plants, which leaves them almost incapable of manufacturing their food or resisting weed invasions.

How Often to Mow

You should mow your lawn frequently enough that only a small portion of the vital green leaf is lost at any one clipping. Mow, if you can, each time the grass gains one-third again its customary clipping height.

In general, lawns that are mostly bent grass are clipped at heights ranging from ½ to 1 inch tall; lawns that are mostly fine-leaved fescues, bluegrasses, and perennial ryegrasses are clipped at heights ranging from 1 to 2 inches tall. Only workaday species such as tall fescue are clipped much above 2 inches tall.

A Guide to Mow By

Here is a list of the suggested heights for the different types of lawns:

Type	Height (in inches)
Bahia grass	2–4
Bermuda grass	
Hybrids	¼–1
Common	½–1½
Blue Grama	2–2½
Buffalo grass	¾–2
Carpet grass	1–2
Centipede grass	1–2
Colonial bentgrass	½–1
Creeping bentgrass	¼–½
Crested wheatgrass	1½–2½
Fine Fescue	1½–2½
Kentucky bluegrass	1½–2½
Perennial ryegrass	1½–2½
St. Augustine grass	1½–3
Tall fescue	1½–3
Zoysia grass	½–2

None of these heights is carved in stone, but keep in mind what can happen if you mow too high or too low.

HOW YOU MOW DOES MAKE A DIFFERENCE

Most of you probably don't give much thought to the pattern you use when you mow your lawns. This can be a big mistake in terms of the looks of the lawn, the comfort of the person mowing, and the health of the lawn. Mowing patterns should be kept clean and straight if you want an attractive-looking lawn. It is important that you regularly vary the directions you cut your lawn so that the grass does not begin to grow with permanent ridges, develop permanent ruts, or become compacted from constant traffic.

YOU JUST CAN'T WAIT TO MOW YOUR NEW LAWN

Every spring and fall, as new lawns are started or overseeding (with cool- season grasses) begins in the south, I am asked (many, many, times) when to start mowing. Here is one answer straight from the professional's professionals:

Research at Pennsylvania State University has shown that the best way to produce a good-looking, uniform lawn with a mixture of Kentucky bluegrass and perennial ryegrass seed depends heavily on proper mowing.

These two seeds are a popular mixture because they give both quick turf cover, contributed by the ryegrasses, and high turf quality, from the bluegrasses. It's difficult to produce a lawn that contains a balanced mixture of these different grasses, though, because the ryegrass seedling grows so much more vigorously than the bluegrass seedling.

The Penn State research shows that early mowing practices influence these competitive relationships. Essentially, starting to mow the lawn 2 weeks after planting—and about 9 days after the first emergence of the ryegrass—can help the bluegrass develop. (At this point, there is usually about a 50 percent turfgrass ground cover.)

For example, mowing the new grass at a 1½ inch height, starting 2 weeks after planting, produced a fifty-fifty mixture of bluegrass and ryegrass after 2 months, even though the seed mixture contained 95 percent bluegrass and only 5 percent ryegrass.

Mowing at a ½ inch height, starting 2 weeks after planting, also produced a fifty-fifty mixture of the grasses after 2 months—even though the amount of bluegrass seed in the mixture had been lowered to only 50 percent.

Early close mowing seems to favor the bluegrass at the expense of the ryegrass. This makes it possible to develop a high quality turf from a seed mixture that contains less bluegrass and more ryegrass. Increasing the percentage of the ryegrass in the mix means that the lawn cover will develop more rapidly—and leads to a happier lawn owner.

Grass Roots—Out of Sight, But Not Out Of Mind

Lawn grass roots may be out of sight, but they shouldn't be forgotten. All of our ornamental plants obtain their essential water and mineral nutrients through their roots. How much they receive depends on the size of the root system and the volume of soil in contact with the roots. The more roots there are and the deeper they grow into the soil, the better.

All grasses establish a balance between growing foliage and growing roots. Grasses that are not clipped, or are perhaps cut infrequently, have the most extensive root systems, but the resulting cover looks more like pasture than lawn.

When lawn grasses are mowed frequently (for example, once a week), lowering the height of the cut will lower the amount of root growth. Good mowing practice calls for the removal of leaf tips when the grass is about one-third higher than the standard cutting height. For example, a lawn cut with a mower set at 1½ inches should be mowed soon after growth has reached 2 inches. Clippings of this length (about ½ inch) will filter down through the lawn, decompose, and enrich the soil below.

Setting the mower at the proper clipping height is important, not only because it causes the grass plants to grow more leaves but because these leaf surfaces provide the energy the grass needs for root growth.

Make Lawn Mowing a Money Maker

Fuel costs are high enough that anything that helps make mowing more efficient is worthwhile. Planting modern low-growing cultivars rather than lanky unselected grasses is an obvious way to economize. How often the grass needs mowing and how much horsepower it takes to trim the grass both decrease.

Several other tricks of the trade can save time and gasoline, too. A lawn mower set to mow a bit taller than our standard heights won't take as much effort. More power is required to cut the stiff lower portions of grass clumps than the soft upper blades. There will be less clogging detritus present in the canopy of the turf, as well. As an added bonus, the grass grows better because more of the green leaf is spared.

Contrary to popular belief, a high-cut lawn needs mowing somewhat less frequently than a low-cut lawn. A lawn clipped tall does not show irregularities quite as quickly as one mowed short. (Lawns look neat if they have a smooth surface—not because they are a particular height.)

Naturally, a well-built mower in good running condition is more efficient (and more pleasant to use) than one that is balky and out of adjustment. So, keep your mower properly "tuned up." A reel mower uses less power to mow a given swath of grass than a rotary does, although, of course, rotaries have advantages of their own, especially for high-mown grass. You can save some fuel if your reel mower has fewer rather than many blades. A five-bladed reel is sufficient for ordinary mowing, although more blades are better for the especially low-mown bent grasses, Bermudas, and zoysias.

Stop-and-Grow Isn't for You

Have you ever asked yourself why they can't invent a fertilizer additive that keeps the grass green but stops it from growing? That's a question I hear a lot. The answer is that they *have* invented it.

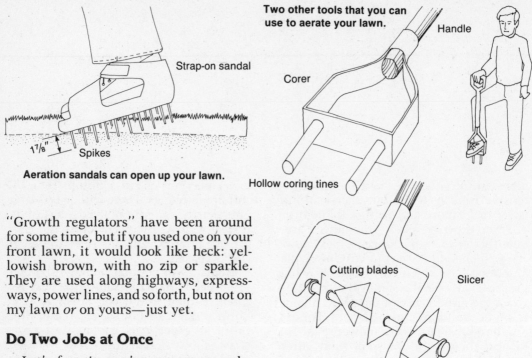

Aeration sandals can open up your lawn.

Strap-on sandal

1⁷/₈"   Spikes

Two other tools that you can use to aerate your lawn.

Handle

Corer

Hollow coring tines

Cutting blades

Slicer

"Growth regulators" have been around for some time, but if you used one on your front lawn, it would look like heck: yellowish brown, with no zip or sparkle. They are used along highways, expressways, power lines, and so forth, but not on my lawn *or* on yours—just yet.

Do Two Jobs at Once

Let's face it, you've got to mow the lawn anyway, which means walking behind your mower, one foot in front of the other, in 18- to 20-inch-wide paths up and back—so why not *aerate* your lawn at the same time? Look in a garden catalog for a pair of *aeration sandals*. These heavy-duty plastic soles strap onto my regular shoes. The 1 7/8-inch steel spikes that stick out through the bottom will penetrate through the thatch, sod pad, and root mass of any lawn. (I used to wear my golf shoes but they didn't quite dig in deep enough.) I wear these spiked shoes about every third time I mow the lawn to help food, water, air, and soap get to where they'll do the most good. The spikes will also give your grass plants room to breathe—as you stomp on their heads! You won't believe the difference a couple of trips around the lawn will make.

You Have Heard of Plugged In? Well, A Good Lawn Is Plugged Out!

If you worked half as hard as your lawn

does manufacturing oxygen, you would get so tuckered out that a nice massage would feel great. Well, that's what your lawn needs, too. Body treatments for lawns are called coring and slitting.

Coring. Coring is the removal of thumb-size plugs of soil and turf to relieve soil compaction. The holes let more water, fertilizer, air, and chemicals into the root zone. Coring can be done at any time of the growing year without damage. Cores should be removed, crushed, and used in other places, for topdressing or building up low spots. Coring can be done by hand (actually, by foot!) with a two-core foot tool from the garden shop— or you can rent a power "plugger."

Slit Slicer. Lawns are usually "slit" in the fall or early spring before seeding, to help give the seeds a foothold. The blades are triangular shaped, and simply cut a slit in the turf about every 10 inches with

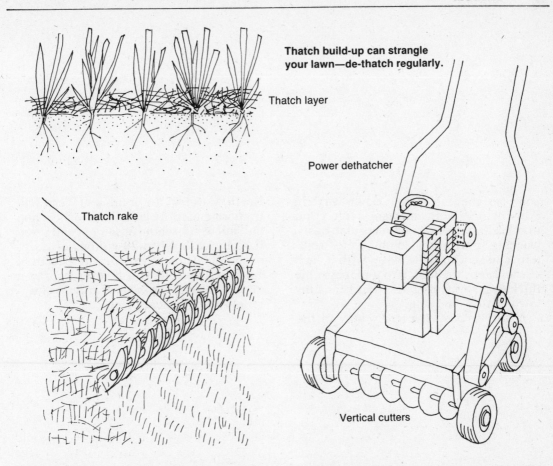

Thatch build-up can strangle your lawn—de-thatch regularly.

Thatch layer

Power dethatcher

Thatch rake

Vertical cutters

a foot between rows of slits. You can rent a slitting attachment for your tiller. Lawns should be slit (or pin) sliced from both north to south and east to west for best results. This is an excellent method of aeration and should not be overlooked.

Aeration is the one single chore that can make the difference between a good lawn and a great lawn. Do it!

Raise the Roof on a Bad Lawn

Don't ever let anyone talk you into not picking up your lawn clippings. Lawn clippings left on the lawn cause a heavy buildup of decayed material called thatch. Thatch is where many lawn problems begin. Insects breed, disease grows, and grass seed dries out quickly in the

thatch. Water, food, weed controls, and fertilizer can't get where they're needed. Thatch must be kept to a minimum of 1/8–1/4 inch high at the most.

Mechanical dethatching is best done in the first week of September. You can use a "lawn groom" rake (designed for small areas) or a gas-driven power rake (usually rented) to remove thatch. Yardman now makes a homeowner's version of a dethatching machine. You can also purchase special dethatching blades that attach to many mowers. Any of these methods will do the trick.

This Method Will Not Give Your Lawn a Drinking Habit

There are biological products available designed to break down thatch. Some of them work and some don't. I find that feeding my lawn on a regular basis, washing it with a soap-and-water solution, and sharing a few beers with it each season keeps the thatch to a manageable thickness, saves my back, and keeps my lawn healthy and safe.

In the early spring (early May in the North, March in the South and West) I fill my hose-end spray jar half full of beer and half full of household ammonia and spray it along with 15 to 20 gallons of water over 2,500 square feet. On the Fourth of July, as I've told you before, I spray a quart of beer along with 20 gallons of water over 2,500 square feet.

6

Watering
Don't Count on Rain

As you read through this book, you should be developing a lot of respect for that patch of green surrounding your homestead. It's so much more than just a glob of green. Now that you know that 20,000 square feet of lawn can produce the very air you and your family live off of, you should begin to show a little more interest when it comes time to taking care of the "damn lawn" (as I hear all too often).

If you check the table at the end of this chapter, you'll see exactly how many rainy days and how many inches of rain you'll typically get in your neck of the woods. In some cases, it can seem like a lot of water, but not when you figure that on a sunny, windy, hot, dry day, a 20,000-square-foot lawn (that's ½ acre) will give more than 5,000 gallons of water back into the atmosphere!

And if you don't think watering your lawn can run up your water bill, then you've got another thought coming!

First Comes Water

Grass can live on water alone. Your lawn wouldn't be very attractive, but it can survive without fertilizer. The grass plant itself is made up of 80 to 90 percent water (if you let it dry out to below 60 percent, you can kiss it good-bye).

It takes between 50 and 60 gallons of water to grow a pound of grass clippings. Just how much water your grass plants need depends on the variety, weather, depth of roots, quality of care (that's you, Bub!), amount of foot traffic, kind of soil, and last but not least, what kind of appearance you'll settle for. All of these factors determine the size of your water bill and how green your valley will turn.

Most lawns don't require a lot of water, but those located in areas where rainfall is limited will not survive without some irrigation. Lawns in the cooler more humid regions of the country may need only about an inch of water a week—some twelve inches or so over the summer. Evenly distributed rainfall will usually supply this much water and more.

Lawns are most likely to wilt during the warm summer months. The temptation to water is greatest when summer showers are irregular and the water supplied by rain ends up short of the inch per week that the lawn needs. Then it helps to know a little about how grasses use water, in order to conserve moisture.

Water conservation is everyone's business. Wasting water is not only costly but can lead to community restrictions on water use. Unfortunately, lawn watering is often viewed as a culprit during water shortages, and lawn irrigation can be prohibited.

Lawns lose water in two different ways. First, they lose it by direct evaporation from the soil surface. The best way to prevent this is to develop a dense turf cover over the soil, which will help retain moisture in the roots.

Lawns also lose water by transpiration. Moisture absorbed through the roots is used by the conductive system of the grass plants and then transpired as a vapor through leaf pores. Transpiration is necessary for healthy growth and tissue cooling. Chemical sprays that reduce transpiration—by coating the foliage or by stimulating the pores to close—have been tried, but without much success.

A Little Dab Will Do You

For many years this slogan was used to advertise hair cream. When I watch some of you folks water your lawns, it looks to me like you think it applies to you. You'll have to stop thinking that way if you want a great or even a good lawn.

I've told you about the high price our lawns must pay in moisture just to produce our oxygen, so let's give them all the water they need.

How Much to Water

You can tell that your grass needs water when the blades begin to look dry and gray green to blue green in color or when it doesn't spring back when you walk on it or drive machinery over it. You can also use a knife, trowel, or hollow pipe to remove a core sample down to 6 inches. If the soil is dry from 4 to 6 inches deep, it's time to water.

How much water to apply depends on the type rather than the variety of grass.

If your soil is sandy, watering every 3 days should be often enough. Apply as close to 1½ inches of water per 1000 square feet of lawn (that equals 920 gallons or 125 cubic feet of water). On clay soil, watering every other day will return attractive results.

To find out how much water you are applying, place three tin cans of the same size on the turf. The first should be 1 foot from the sprinkler; the second, 2 feet away; and the third, 4 feet away.

After an hour of watering, pour all of the water from the three cans into one of the cans and measure the depth. Divide that amount by three—the answer will tell you how much water you're applying per hour.

Match Lawn Watering to Soil Thirst

Newly seeded lawns certainly require watering, if it fails to rain, in order to trigger sprouting and promote seedling growth. The surface of a cultivated seedbed is generally loose enough to ac-

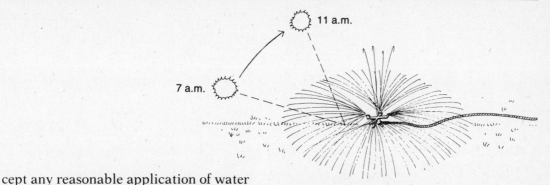

Always water before 2 p.m.
The best time to water? Between 7 a.m. and 11 a.m.
Never water at night.

cept any reasonable application of water without sealing itself, especially if it has been mulched. Once the planting has been soaked, only light sprinkling should be necessary to keep it from drying out. Initially, these should be fairly frequent, but they can be tapered off as the grass roots more deeply.

Watering established lawns can present problems. Some clay soils are quite recalcitrant, with water soaking in as slowly as ¼ inch per hour (perhaps half or less the normal application rate of a sprinkler). Fortunately, once grasses are flourishing, their roots improve the soil structure and increase the rate at which water can soak in. But make sure that you aren't watering faster than the ground can absorb, which will cause wasteful runoff. Check that your irrigation apparatus applies water at a rate suited to your soil and lawn conditions.

Water only so long as the moisture soaks into unsaturated soil. Make sure that enough water is applied, at the proper rate, to soak the grass's root zone thoroughly. It may take 2 or 3 inches of water to moisten the top 10 inches of clay soils (the water will probably have to be applied slowly). In a sandy soil this may take only a few minutes, as a half inch or so of water can penetrate the root zone completely and is as much moisture as the soil can hold.

There Is a Right Time to Water

I don't give two hoots and a jaybird what you have heard from anyone else about the proper time to water a lawn. You paid for my advice by buying this book—and I am telling you to water before 2:00 P.M. in the afternoon. The best time is between 7:00 A.M. and 11:00 A.M. Don't ever let me catch you watering your lawn at night or I will give you the gee-by-golly's like you've never heard them before. Damp grass is a welcome wagon for bugs and disease.

I know what your argument is: If I'm right, why do golf courses water at night? The reason is pretty simple: You can't very well water when you have dozens of fee-paying members on the course. Golf course superintendents end up sacrificing a major part of their budgets to the cost of fungicides.

Your Lawn Deserves Quality Water

In most cases your lawn water comes right from the tap, but that's not always best for your lawn. Some water systems use too much chlorine. Use an ordinary pool-test kit from time to time to test city tap water. Take a water sample out of the system ahead of a softener. Some folks make the mistake of trying to use soft water on their lawn, don't! Rivers, ponds, lakes, and wells are great sources of water but should be tested from time to time, as well.

Lawns Are Like Sponges

A good lawn shouldn't look much like a sponge, but when it comes to soaking up water, there is a similarity. According to the Lawn Institute, your lawn soil is a natural reservoir for holding and purifying water as it seeps down through the topsoil and into underground aquifers. Keep all the rainfall you can on your land by maintaining a lawn with thick, healthy, green grass and a good, deep root system that soaks up every drop—like a sponge.

Regular mowing will help to keep the turf dense and minimalize the foliage's exposure to water loss. See the chapter on mowing for optimum lengths, but cutting your lawn 1½ inches high works well for most grass types.

For the most efficient watering, try to avoid runoff when sprinkling your lawn. This often requires setting the sprinkler differently for sloping lawns than for level areas. Thatch—the layer of undecomposed organic matter between the roots and the foliage—often sheds water. If the thatch is thick and dense, get rid of it with a power rake.

Lawn grasses usually enter dormancy in response to cold weather, but the process can also be caused by hot, dry summer spells. Dormancy develops gradually as the turf makes adjustments that prepare it for survival during adverse conditions. Dormant grasses stop growing, and the foliage may turn brown. In locations where irrigation must be limited, it is of-ten better to allow the lawn to turn dormant than to "tease" it along with minimal irrigation. More damage can be done to the grass by improper watering than by dormancy. Of course, a brown lawn is not as attractive as a green one; however, if it is uniformly brown, and unpocked by weeds, it can be tolerable.

The newer lawn grasses, which generally provide a denser, deeper-rooting turf, are proving their value by reducing moisture requirements and preventing the waste of irrigation water. If you are thinking of renovating an old lawn this autumn, you might want to introduce some of these new grass cultivars to help your lawn conserve water.

How Much Is Not Enough?

According to horticulturist J. D. Butler of Colorado State University, lawn care is best defined in terms of the turf quality that can be expected for the amount of irrigation water applied.

Applying less water than a lawn grass can use is called *deficit irrigation*. How long can your lawn live with deficit irrigation? As it turns out, you don't have to reapply 100 percent of the water used (metabolized) by the plant/soil system in order to produce fine turf. In recent tests, Kentucky bluegrass lawns decreased only 10 percent in quality when provided with only 73 percent of the water they used.

When less than 70 percent of water used by the grass was reapplied, the quality of the lawn grasses was lower when turf was mowed to one inch in height than when it was mowed at 2 inches. When less nitrogen fertilizer was used, the lawn used less water, but the lawn quality also suffered.

It's important to consider the temperature of the grass when planning your watering. You can expect higher temperatures whenever your irrigation rate falls below the water use requirements of the grasses in your lawn. The temperature of the turf grass canopy will increase about 4 degrees for each 10 percent decrease in irrigation.

Buildings, trees, and privacy fences all restrict air movement. They slow the mixing between the air directly above your lawn and higher air currents, which can also raise the lawn temperature. These higher temperatures can not only inhibit your enjoyment of your lawn and outdoor activities but can increase your home airconditioning bills.

If You Have a Choice, Make It Wise

Surprisingly, Kentucky bluegrass and perennial ryegrasses are fairly tolerant of summer drought. Of course, any turf needs to be watered when wilting threatens in order to look its best. Fine fescues such as Banner, Ensylva, Highlight, Koket, and Ruby are well known for their ability to persist on dry soils in the shade. These fescues often dominate under trees where grass and trees compete for moisture. Fine fescues are generally not at

their best on wet ground in hot weather, but they do beautifully in cool climates.

If you are of a mind to change, build, or strengthen your lawn, I've listed how well some of the more popular grasses will adapt to drought:

E = Excellent
G = Good
F = Fair
M = Medium
P = Poor

Bahia grass	E
Bermuda grass	E
Buffalo grass	E
Centipede grass	P
Chewing fescue	G
Colonial bent grass	P
Creeping bent grass	P
Dichondra	M
Hard fescue	G
Italian rye	F
Kentucky bluegrass	M
Perennial ryegrass	F
Red fescue	G
Rough bluegrass	P
St. Augustine grass	F
Velvet bent grass	P
Zoysia grass	E

Let this guide you in selection, care, and caution.

Can I Buy You a Drink?

This could be an awfully expensive question, depending on which lawn grass sidles up to the bar (water, that is) with

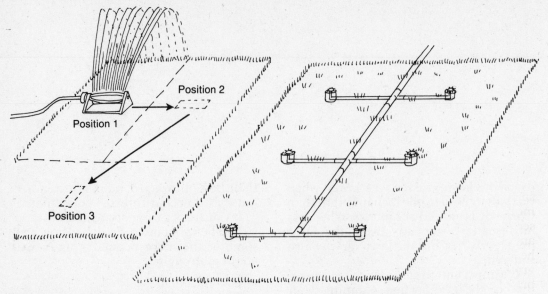

Your watering system can either be above-ground or a below-the-ground sprinkler system.

you. Here are the drinking habits of some of the popular grasses:

L = Low
M = Medium
H = High
W = Wet

Bahiagrass	L
Bermudagrass	L
Buffalo grass	L
Centipede grass	M
Chewing fescue	L
Colonial bent grass	P
Creeping bent grass	M
Dichondra	M
Hard fescue	L
Italian rye	M
Kentucky bluegrass	M
Perennial ryegrass	M
Red fescue	L
Rough bluegrass	W
St. Augustine grass	H
Velvet bent grass	M
Zoysia grass	L

Quality Really Counts

Use a high-quality sprinkler—not just a toy that the kids can run through, but a strong, sturdy, tough, high-volume lawn sprinkler.

I guess you could classify me as old-fashioned in my thinking when it comes to quality. I am a brass, lead, iron, steel, and concrete man. I avoid plastics, fiberglass, and exotic metals. I know they are supposed to be easier to replace! That's the trouble: most of them are so flimsy that they had to be made easy to replace.

Don't get me wrong, I am all for progress—but not at the expense of quality. Quality can be more expensive, but I would rather pay half again more for something and have it last for ten years than pay less and have it last only six months. My favorite pair of grass shears is over fourteen years old. I oil them, clean them, and sharpen them often. I have probably been given twenty-five to thirty new pairs of all kinds of shears over the years. They are lighter, fancier, cost more, and wear out, bend, or don't hold an edge at all.

I feel the same way about my lawn sprinklers. Give me brass moving parts, metal bases, and lots of noise. I want to see and hear my sprinkler work. I prefer an impact-type sprinkler with a brass head. Yes, for both in-ground and above-ground watering systems. Both Nelson-brand sprinklers and irrigation equipment and Rain Bird sprinklers are my kind of quality—and friends to my lawn.

Sprinkler Systems Are Great

When I say in-the-ground systems are great, I mean it! However, not everybody can afford them. Folks have told me that it costs $3,000 to $5,000 to have a system installed. That's a lot of money, but you can now install your own sprinkler system and end up with a super job—and it won't cost you an arm and a leg. Doing the work yourself on a 10,000-square-foot (¼ acre) lawn should cost you about $700 to $800. A system that will irrigate a 20,000-square-foot (1/2 acre) lawn will set you back $1,000 to $2,000. And it won't take you the rest of your life to install—it should take about one full week (after work) and the weekend. Here is the schedule my friends from Nelson propose:

1 to 2 days to lay out your pipe
4 to 6 hours to put one zone above-ground and test it
4 to 6 hours to install it below ground

If you are really serious about installing an underground sprinkler system, send your name and address to:

L.R. Nelson Corporation
7719 North Pioneer Lane
Peoria, Illinois 61615

They'll send you a fifteen-page book entitled, "Learn How to Install Your Nelson In-Ground Sprinkler System Without Losing Your Mind, Temper, or the Shirt Off Your Back." I have installed several different types of sprinkler systems, and if I can do it, so can you.

How Much and How Often?

The following chart will give you an idea of just how much rain, in inches, you can usually expect in your neck of the woods and the number of rainy days it will take for you to get it.

	Average Rain in Growing Season (in inches)	Rain Days in Growing Season
Alabama		
Birmingham	33	75
Mobile	58	90
Montgomery	38	77
Alaska		
Anchorage	8	49
Fairbanks	4	51
Juneau	15	92
Arizona		
Phoenix	7	24
Tucson	11	38

	Average Rain in Growing Season (in inches)	Rain Days in Growing Season
Arkansas		
Fort Smith	29	60
Little Rock	31	66
Texarkana	28	64
California		
Bakersfield	6	
Eureka	40	71
Fresno	10	22
Los Angeles	14	33
Marysville	21	
Palm Springs	31	
Pasadena	19	
Red Bluff	22	
Riverside	10	
Sacramento	17	
San Diego	9	42
San Francisco	21	66
San Jose	14	
Santa Barbara	17	
Santa Rosa	30	
Colorado		
Denver	15	42
Pueblo	12	
Connecticut		
Bridgeport	18	49
Hartford	21	59
New Haven	21	54
Delaware		
Wilmington	23	56
Florida		
Jacksonville	48	103
Miami	60	127
Tampa	51	105
Georgia		
Atlanta	29	72
Augusta	34	74
Savannah	41	89
Hawaii		
Hilo	119	282
Honolulu	25	101

	Average Rain in Growing Season (in inches)	Rain Days in Growing Season
Idaho		
Boise	11	23
Pocatello	23	
Illinois		
Chicago	21	61
Peoria	21	55
Springfield	21	59
Indiana		
Evansville	24	73
Fort Wayne	20	59
Indianapolis	22	60
Iowa		
Des Moines	20	55
Sioux City	18	52
Kansas		
Topeka	26	59
Wichita	24	56
Kentucky		
Lexington	24	66
Louisville	25	68
Louisiana		
New Orleans	47	93
Shreveport	29	67
Maine		
Bangor	17	47
Caribou	15	54
Greenville	14	43
Portland	16	54
Maryland		
Baltimore	26	68
Massachusetts		
Boston	23	73
Pittsfield	19	49
Worcester	18	50
Michigan		
Detroit	18	58
Grand Rapids	16	52
Marquette	16	60

	Average Rain in Growing Season (in inches)	Rain Days in Growing Season		Average Rain in Growing Season (in inches)	Rain Days in Growing Season
Minnesota			North Dakota		
Duluth	15	47	Bismark	10	42
Minneapolis	17	55	Ohio		
Saint Paul	17	55	Cincinnati	21	65
Mississippi			Cleveland	20	68
Biloxi	58	90	Columbus	21	64
Jackson	27	80	Oklahoma		
Missouri			Oklahoma City	25	56
Kansas City	28	61	Tulsa	27	56
Saint Louis	23	60	Oregon		
Springfield	26	59	Bend	12	
Montana			Eugene	43	
Great Falls	15	38	Portland	34	
Nebraska			Pennsylvania		
North Platte	14	45	Altoona	22	62
Omaha	23	58	Harrisburg	21	68
Nevada			Philadelphia	26	70
Las Vegas	4	19	Scranton	19	63
Reno	7		Williamsport	19	61
New Hampshire			Rhode Island		
Berlin	12	41	Providence	21	62
Concord	14	48	South Carolina		
New Jersey			Charleston	44	94
Atlantic City	27	65	Columbia	34	74
Newark	24	69	South Dakota		
Trenton	25	67	Huron	12	44
New Mexico			Rapid City	11	44
Albuquerque	8		Sioux Falls	16	45
Santa Fe	13		Tennessee		
New York			Knoxville	25	73
Albany	17	58	Nashville	24	68
Binghampton	18	56	Texas		
Buffalo	17	60	Corpus Christi	27	73
New York	24	69	Dallas	23	51
Syracuse	17	60	El Paso	6	33
Watertown	16	50	Houston	38	80
North Carolina			Lubbock	15	40
Ashville	26	69	Utah		
Raleigh	30	71	Ogden	16	
Wilmington	40	79	Salt Lake City	15	

	Average Rain in Growing Season (in inches)	Rain Days in Growing Season		Average Rain in Growing Season (in inches)	Rain Days in Growing Season
Vermont			**Wisconsin**		
Burlington	16	58	Green Bay	16	55
Saint Johnsbury	14	46	La Crosse	19	54
			Milwaukee	18	61
Virginia			**Wyoming**		
Norfolk	34	79	Cheyenne	15	50
Roanoke	25	66			
Richmond	29	68	**Puerto Rico**		
			San Juan	70	219
Washington					
Centralia	46		**Virgin Islands**		
Seattle	36		Saint Croix	50	180
Yakima	8		Saint John	50	180
			Saint Thomas	50	180
Washington, D.C.					
Capitol	26	68			
West Virginia					
Charleston	22	71			
Parkersburg	21	66			

7

Weed Control
Even Weeds Are Welcome When All You've Got Is Dirt

As the old saying goes, "There's no such thing as a weed—it's just a plant that we haven't found a use for." Another old saying is that a weed is just a plant that is out of place. Even a rose is a weed when it's growing in the middle of a wheat field.

It's impossible to have a weed-free lawn. As long as the wind blows, birds fly, man walks, and animals run, the seeds of weeds will be planted in your lawn. But don't get discouraged! Just because a few weeds pop up in your green scene from time to time, don't think that you have failed. Weeds are a constant challenge and a reminder that we need to keep our lawns well fed and well groomed. When more than an occasional weed drops by and stays for a while, it's just a gentle reminder that you may be mowing your lawn too low, feeding it too little, or have too much thatch. If weeds become a problem, check your general lawn care habits first.

My national recognition and current career success are due directly to Dinah Shore. Being a regular member of her long-running and highly successful daytime show (*Dinah's Place*) exposed me to millions of home gardeners each week.

Dinah's sister, Bessy, insisted that I write *Plants Are Like People*, the first of my many books, answering the show's viewer mail so that she and her staff wouldn't be permanently crippled with writer's cramp. "Write the book, Junior," were her words. I did.

The most important character (I can't say person, even though I do think plants are like people) in establishing my credibility with you folks was a Dandelion. That's right! When a reporter photographed a dandelion growing in the middle of my front lawn, it was international news. Front-page news in papers around the world! EVEN AMERICA'S MASTER GARDENER GETS WEEDS IN HIS LAWN, the headlines blared!

That, my friends, is when you and I became real green-thumb partners. I had been telling you all along that I learned everything I know the hard way—from the ground up. I live in a neighborhood just like yours, mow my own lawn, carry out the garbage, help Ilene with the heavy chores around the house, and travel several thousand miles a week, just like many of you.

But the greenest grass on the block is

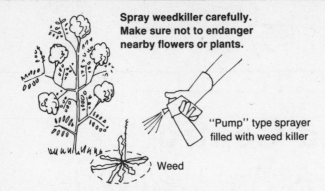

Spray weedkiller carefully. Make sure not to endanger nearby flowers or plants.

"Pump" type sprayer filled with weed killer

Weed

still on my side of the fence—even with an occasional weed, brown patch, or even a stray bug or two camping on my lawn.

First Steps

I keep two old window-spray bottles on my gardening shelf. The first one is filled with 10 to 15 drops of liquid soap mixed with water. I spray this soap-and-water solution on plants, weeds, and bugs before I apply a chemical treatment. It makes the treatment work faster.

The second spray bottle has a big WEED KILLER ONLY label on it. When I see uninvited weeds in my lawn, I mix just enough (and no more) spray to kill them. Two or three days after spraying they are dead.

No Thrill-Killing or Mass Punishment

If a larger area is invaded by weeds, you should apply a weedkiller with a hose-end sprayer (which is reserved for that use only). K-Mart sells a combination liquid fertilizer and broadleaf weed killer solution—called Rapid Green—in a special hose-end sprayer. It really does a complete job (it feeds and kills).

Whenever you use a herbicide, be extremely careful to apply it only to the lawn and the weeds you want to remove. Don't spray when its windy or when rain is predicted within 24 hours, and do not water the area for 24 hours after application.

Be sure that the apparatus you'll use to apply it is in good working order. Of course follow the directions for the product of your choice carefully.

In any case, keep in mind that it is not fair or healthy to spray anything on the regular lawn grasses that they don't need—as well as being a waste of time and money.

Stop Weeds in the Fall

Weeds make their biggest advances in your lawn during the summer months. Your lawn grasses are less aggressive at that point and provide less competition for both grassy and broadleaf weeds.

Properly timing your herbicide treatments is extremely important. They'll be most effective while the weeds are still growing well—which in most cases is during early spring and early fall.

Shoot-Out at High Noon

The best time of day is to go after the weeds is when the sun is bright and the temperature is in the 70s, which is usually between noon and 2:00 P.M. However, this may also be the time when the wind is rather strong.

My friend, spraying when it's windy out is a no-no! The drift of even a little bit of weed killer can destroy flowers, vegetables, evergreens, bushes, and darn near everything dear to a gardener's heart. So be sure to check the wind. If I am spot-

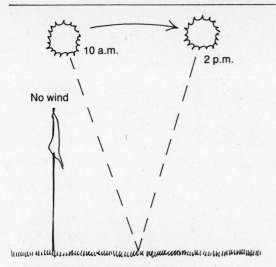

Spray between 10 a.m. and 2 p.m.
***Never* spray in a strong wind!**

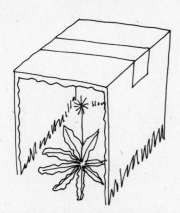

**Use a cardboard box as a
wind shield for spot spraying.**

treating a small area, I'll cut the side out
of a cardboard box and use it as a
windshield.

Stop Weeds Dead

Depending on which weeds you're
faced with, you'll end up using either
unblended chemicals or chemical mixtures. Some weeds are sensitive to a
particular ingredient, while others may
be more resistant. Some will succumb

only to a synergistic combination of
chemicals.

In order to be certain that you've selected the most effective herbicide for
your problem, you might want to take a
sample of your weeds to a garden supply
center for identification. The descriptive
literature that comes with most products
will help you make this identification.

Dry Versus Liquid Weed Killers

For my money, and for most of my professional friends, liquid weed killer wins
hands down. Dry weed-and-feeds are effective but the weed-killing chemical
must break loose from the carrier material the manufacturer used to fill up the
bag, and soil temperature, air temperature, and moisture must all be right for
the chemical to do its job.

Liquid weed killers, on the other hand,
are as a rule taken into the root or foliage
system right away—and knock the weeds
out in short order.

The soap-and-water treatment I described above will speed up the action of
both dry and liquid weed killers. Fill up
your hose-end jar with water, leaving
room for 1 cup of liquid soap to each 10
gallons of water. (To mix the solution in
smaller quantities, mix 10 drops of liquid
soap to 1 quart of water, or 1 shot glass
full to 1 gallon.) Spray the solution on the
weed area, wait a half hour, and then
broadcast or spray your weed killer. The
soap removes the surface tension from
the soil, dusty pollution from the leaf,

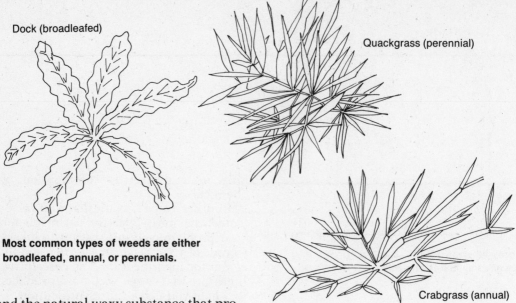

Dock (broadleafed)

Quackgrass (perennial)

Crabgrass (annual)

Most common types of weeds are either broadleafed, annual, or perennials.

and the natural waxy substance that protects the plant's skin, all of which can prevent the weed killer from doing its job.

Don't Even Let Them Get a Foothold

There are basically three different kinds of weeds: the annual, perennial, and broadleaf varieties.

Those that can be stopped before the seed germinates (sprouts) are referred to as annual weeds, since this year's plant produces a seed for next year's growth before it dies.

Here are the most common ones that you'll encounter:

Bluegrass (annual)
Browntop Panicum
Bur clover
Bur marigold
Buttercup
Carpetweed
Chickweed
Crabgrass
Florida pusley
Foxtail
Goose grass
Johnson grass (from seed)
Lamb's Quarters

Love grass
Nodding Spurge
Purslane
Sandbur
Spotted spurge
Spurge
Spurry
Veronica (creeping speedwell)
Wild geranium
Witchgrass

This group of weeds can be prevented from maturing by spraying or broadcasting a type of weed control referred to as a preemergence herbicide. Good timing is the secret to success. I strongly advise you to apply your "preemerge" as close to 2 weeks ahead of the weed's expected germination date as you can.

Look for one of these common herbicides from your favorite brand of garden products:

Benefin
Bensulide
DCPA
Ethofumesate
Oxadiazon

Pronamide
Siduron
Metribuzin

Make darn sure that you read and understand every word on the label before you even purchase any of these products and that you know they can be used on your type of grass.

Here is a rough idea of when some of these annual weeds germinate. (For more precise dates, don't be afraid to call your county extension agent and ask.)

Annual Bluegrass	August 15 to October 1
Crabgrass (*Poa Annua*)	March 15 to May 15
Goose grass	June 1 to August 1
Spurge	May 15 to August 15

To answer your question before you even ask it: If you use a preemerge, don't sow grass seed until after August 15.

Crabgrass, for example, loves hot weather. It completes its annual growth cycle by late summer, just as the cool-season grasses and perennial ryegrasses get their second wind for cool-weather growth.

Crabgrass-infested lawns are characteristically thin and weak by summer's end. They are also loaded with crabgrass seed that will lie dormant in the soil until lilac-blossom time the following spring.

It's easy to prevent crabgrass from coming back. Small areas can be raked out easily by hand. Larger areas will require a power rake, which you can usually get through landscape outlets or rental agencies. Where crabgrass is abundant, the power rake will remove both weeds and weak grasses, readying the gound for overseeding.

You can then plant new permanent grass in place of the crabgrass without fear of it competing with the new grass. Given reasonable care, it will overwhelm your crabgrass the following spring.

And Then There Are the Be-Backs...

Just when you think you've got the weed problem whipped, or at least understood, here's yet another unwelcome group of weed grasses. These are perennial visitors, which means that they live more than 2 years. Some reproduce by seeds and some reproduce from stolons, rhizomes, and bulblets (white clover, nut sedge, and quackgrass are excellent examples). For your perusal, I have listed the perennial grasses:

Bent grass
Bermuda grass
Carpetweed
Chickweed
Chicory
Cranesbill
Creeping beggarweed
Creeping buttercup
Curly dock
Dallis grass
Dandelion
Dichondra
Dock

English daisy
Field beggarweed
Ground ivy
Hawkweed
Heal-all
Hop clover
Johnson grass
Kikuyu grass
Knot grass
Nimble will
Nut grass
Orchard grass
Oxeye daisy
Quack grass
Rushes
Smut grass
Tall fescue
Torpedo grass
Velvet grass
White clover
Wild carrot
Wild onion
Yellow sorrel

I've Got Good News and Bad News

As the old joke goes, which do you want first? Well, let's get the bad news out of the way! It is *almost impossible* to control perennial weed grasses without hurting the regular grasses as well. A common practice for the turf professional is to spot-kill perennial weeds in the early fall. The best chemical killer is *Glyphosate*, available under the brand names of Super K-Gro Shoot Out and Roundup, as well as other brands. I use an old window sprayer that I can destroy when I am done.

Now for the good news! You can re-plant grasses seven days later without harm or injury to the new seed or grass. The big problem is that most of us don't want great big dead spots all over our lawn—because our neighbors will talk about us. Well, if it makes you feel any better, just think what gets said when the big dead spot is in the middle of *my* yard!

Here is what I suggest you do. Try treating a couple of relatively hidden spots this fall. When you see how quickly they recover, you won't be afraid to expand the treatments.

If You Got's to Have Weeds, Let Them Be Broadleafs

Most popular weed killers are formulated to destroy broadleaf weeds. On top of that, broadleaf weeds are the easiest kind to kill. In case you have never met the more famous broadleaf weeds, let me introduce you:

Birdseye pearlwort	Mallow
Black medic	Mugwort
Broadleaf plantain	Pennycress
Buckhorn plantain	Pennywort
Common purslane	Pigweed
Common yarrow	Prostrate spurge
Ground ivy	Prostrate vervain
Hawkweed	Red sorrel
Heal-all	Shepherd's purse
Henbit	Speedwells
Knapweed	Spotted spurge
Knotweed	Spurweed
Lamb's-quarters	Thistle
Lespedeza	Wild garlic

Wild mustard   Wild violet
Wild onion   Yellow rocket
Wild parsley   Yellow wood sorrel
Wild strawberry

As I stated earlier, this group of weeds is easily destroyed by the many broadleaf weed killers on the garden shop shelves with combinations of several different chemicals. Dicamba, 2,4-D, and Mecoprop (also known as MCPP) are the more popular ingredients, and are found in Super K-Gro Broadleaf Weed Killer.

Here is a list of which chemicals work best for specific broadleaf weed problems:

Control of Broadleaf Weeds by Popular Products	Dicamba** (Banvel)	Mecoprop (MCPP)	2,4-D***	2,4-D MCPP***	2,4-D MCPP Dicamba (Banvel)***
Aster			X	X	X
Bedstraw					X
Black Medic	X		X	X	X
*Bundweed				X	X
Burdock			X	X	X
Buttercup					X
*Canada Thistle			X		
Carpetweed	X		X		X
Chickweed	X	X		X	X
Chicory	X		X		X
Clover	X	X		X	X
Dandelion		X	X	X	X
Dichondra		X			X
*Dock	X		X	X	X
English Daisy	X			X	X
*Ground Ivy		X	X	X	X
Hawkweed	X				
*Heal-all			X		X

	Dicamba** (Banvel)	Mecoprop (MCPP)	2,4-D***	2,4-D MCPP***	2,4-D MCPP Dicamba (Banvel)***
Henbit	X				X
Knotweed	X	X		X	X
Kochia			X		
Lamb's-quarters		X	X	X	X
Lawn Burweed	X				
Lespedeza					X
Mallow			X	X	X
Morning Glory			X		
Mustard			X		
*Pennywort			X		
Peppergrass					*
Pepperweed	*				
Pigweed		X	X	X	X
Plantain			X	X	X
Purslane	X	X	X	X	X
Ragweed			X	X	X
*Red sorrel	X		X	X	
Shepherd's Purse			X		X
Speedwell	X			X	X
*Spurge	X		X		X
Spurry	X				
Spurweed	X		X	X	X
Stitchwort				X	
Weed Carrot			X		X
Weed Garlic			X	X	X
Weed Lettuce			X		X
*Weed Onion			X	X	X
Wood Sorrel				X	X
Yarrow				X	X
Yellow Rocket			X		

*Requires two applications of 2,4-D 7 days apart
** Do not use under trees
***Do not use on St. Augustine grass or carpetgrass

One Sprayer Just for Weeds

I have seen some pretty sad sights during my career: 200 rosebushes dead, a vegetable garden wiped out overnight, a flower bed damaged so badly that it would be three years before anything could grow there again, and dozens upon dozens of other horror stories.

Every one of them was caused by using a sprayer that had previously been used to spray weed killer. Sure, they had been cleaned out, but not well enough. If you don't pay attention to anything else I tell you, pay attention to this bit of advice. Save your money until you can afford a separate hose-end sprayer, or a tank sprayer (compression 1 gallon), and save your old window-cleaner spray bottles and clearly mark them to be used for weed killer only.

Before using any weed killer on your lawn, make sure that it is safe to use on your lawn grass varieties. Here's a list of how safe certain chemicals are to use on specific grass types:

Weed Killer Safety on Popular Lawn Grasses	Dicamba (Banvel)	Mecoprop (MCPP)	2,4-D	2,4-D MCPP	2,4-D Dicamba (Banvel)	2, 4-D MCPP Dicamba (Banvel)
Annual Bluegrass	1	1	2			
Bahia Grass	1	1	1	1		1
Bermuda Grass	1	1	1	1		1
Buffalo Grass	1		2			
Centipede Grass		1	1			
Creeping Bentgrass	2	1	3			
Kentucky Bluegrass	1	1	1	1		1
Perennial Ryegrass		1	1	1		1
Red Fescue	2	1	1	1		1
St. Augustine Grass						
Tall Fescue		1	1	1		1
Zoysia Grass	2	1	1	1		2

1 = Safe if used as directed on label
2 = Some injury may occur to grass
3 = Some injury may occur to grass at high temperatures

Digging Weeds Multiplies, Not Subtracts

If you have put a lot of time, effort, pride, and money into your yard, the last thing you want to see is a fuzzy yellow head, blue trumpet, or skinny plantain stem sticking up in the middle of the lawn. So, typically, you go grab a dandelion digger and gouge the offending weed's roots out.

The question is, did you? Did you gouge out the roots? The answer is probably not. When you are tempted to dig up the weeds that occasionally pop up to mar your green scene, try to remember that in most cases cutting its root will lead to two weeds from the same spot.

No Scorched-Earth Policies

Every once in a while I see a homeowner burning the dry grass off his lawn in the spring or late fall. It takes everything I've got to hold myself back from telling him how dumb and unsafe that method is. Fire is a gardener's worst enemy. As a rule, when you burn a turf area containing good high-quality-type grass varieties, you'll scorch the root area, pop the seed cover, and leave nothing to grow back but the hardier wild grasses and deep-rooted broadleaf weeds. Even new seed will have trouble germinating for at least a year. Yes, it's true that in the seed-growing areas of the country, they burn off dry grass to destroy disease and maverick seeds, but they then till and repre-

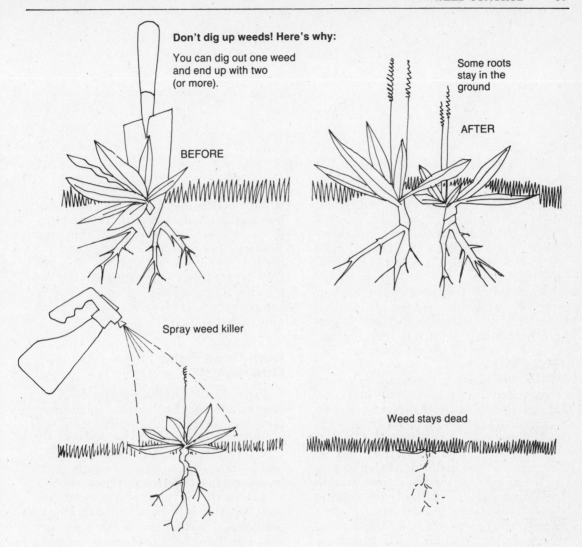

Don't dig up weeds! Here's why:

You can dig out one weed and end up with two (or more).

BEFORE

Some roots stay in the ground

AFTER

Spray weed killer

Weed stays dead

pare a brand-new seedbed, with all of the foods the new seed will need. Don't you try it!

Preposterous

Unthinking people sometimes suggest letting a lawn "go natural," saving the whole bother of mowing and other care. Neighborhood restrictions seldom permit this, but even if such swards were allowed to exist, they would, in short order, turn weedy, brambly, and become a thicket of honeysuckle and poison ivy. So, you've got nothing against brambles and poison ivy? Well, how about the trash and blowing papers that are likely to get caught up in the mess? And what would your insurance company think about the fire hazard?

Two Things Can't Occupy the Same Place at the Same Time

The old saying that two things can't occupy the same place at the same time has special significance for lawns. Which will it be, lawn grasses or weeds? Keeping weeds out of your lawn is often just a matter of growing lawn grasses vigorous enough to stop the weeds from establishing themselves.

From time to time we all slip up in caring for our lawns—sometimes until a weed infestation has reached critical proportions. At that point, it is probably necessary to remove the weeds selectively with a herbicide.

Once the weeds are gone, though, your weed control measures are only half completed. Special lawn treatments are often necessary to correct the cause of the original infestation.

These can include applying lime to sweeten the soil and/or fertilizer to provide nutrients for vigorous grass growth and/or changes in watering or mowing that favor lawn grasses rather than weeds. You may need to provide for more adequate light and air movement or relieve soil compaction though aerating so that the grass roots penetrate more deeply.

Once good growing conditions have been restored to the lawn, you should sow a seed blend of the new cultivars or any mixture recommended for your area. Renovate bare spots and bolster thin grass or areas of lower-quality growth. New cultivars will upgrade your grass population and should bring new life and vitality to your lawn.

To avoid wasting your time and money, sow only high-quality seed. For most of the country, seed mixtures are compounded from topflight cultivars of bluegrass, fescue, and perennial ryegrass. Seeding in late August or early September is ideal because the grasses will have little competition from the weeds during the months ahead. Liming and fertilizing before seeding will help get the new grass off to a fast start.

Lawn Grass Fights for Its Own Rights!

Lawn grasses produce many different compounds as they grow. Some may serve as protective agents that help the grass resist insects and disease, or prevent the encroachment of weeds. Allelopathic effects are known to be important in interactions between plant species within both cultivated and natural systems. Grass rhizomes and blades, for example, may sound the death knell for weeds as they age or die from winterkill. They contain compounds that seem to inhibit the growth of other plants—for our purposes, hopefully, weeds!—directly upon decomposition.

Investigations on how allelochemicals can be used in lawn care are under way at the University of Rhode Island. Breeding lawn grasses to increase their production of the chemicals that inhibit weeds and deriving natural herbicides from the phytotoxic chemicals that some plants synthesize are two areas that show promise. Someday our lawns may do their own weedkilling for us!

If you don't know what the weeds in your lawn are, it'll be tough to get rid of them. Here are descriptions of thirty-two of the most common and undesirable lawn weeds that you'll encounter:

Bedstraw (*Galium aparine*)–A cool-season annual that prefers dense shade. Leaves develop in whorls along spindly, square stems with burrlike surfaces. Flowers are small with four white petals.

Black Medic also known as **"Yellow Trefoil"** (*Medicago lupulina*)–Summer annual legume with extensive stems (which do not root at the nodes). Leaves consist of three leaflets, similar to clover leaves. Flowers are bright yellow and seedpods almost black. Yellow trefoil is similar but has light-brown seeds and paler, round flower heads.

Broadleaf Plantain (*Plantago major*)– Ground-hugging perennial. Large shiny, oval-shaped leaves with rosette growth habit. Seeds produced on rattaillike spikes. Aggravates hay fever.

Buckhorn Plantain, also known as **Narrowleaf Plantain** (*Plantago lanceolata*)–Perennial with broad, grasslike elliptical leaves with prominent veins. Seeds are confined to the tip of a high-rising fox tail. Commonly found in undisturbed soil.

Common Chickweed (*Stellaria media Cyrillo*)–Spreading annual that flourishes in spring and fall. Many branches, with opposed and oval-shaped leaves. Roots at the nodes. Small white star-shaped flowers in clusters. Vigorous in cool weather and shady areas.

Common Purslane (*Portulaca oleracea*)–Fleshy warm-season annual that grows prostrate and roots wherever the stem touches the ground. Leaves are succulent with reddish hue; flowers, yellow; seeds, small and black.

Common Yellow Wood Sorrel or **Oxalis** (*Oxalis stricta*)–Warm-season annual or perennial. Branching stems and leaves have cloverlike appearance. Small yellow funnel-form flowers. Seedpod is cylindrical.

Curly Dock (*Rumex crispus*)–Hardy perennial noted for its large rosette and long leaves with crinkled edges. Prefers wet, low areas, with heavy soil and little shade. Has a carrotlike root, and greenish flowers. The seed stalk grows 2 to 3 feet tall.

Dandelion (*Taraxacum officinale*)– Most common perennial-weed pest in lawns. Yellow flowers appear in spring, continue to bloom all season in warm areas, then ripen into white "puff balls" full of seeds. New shoots come from the old taproot as well as from seeds.

Giant Ragweed (*Ambrosia trifida*)– Hardy annual. Opposite leaves, very deeply lobed. Upright stem and flowers are on a long spike. A major contributor to hay fever.

Ground Ivy also known as **Creeping Charlie** (*Glechoma hederacea*)–Hard-to-control and prolific perennial that spreads by seed as well as creeping stems. Identified by its round, scalloped leaves that are opposite each other on square stems that root at the nodes. Blooms early, with bluish, funnellike flowers.

Heal-all (*Prunella vulgaris*)–Perennial with large, long-stemmed opposite leaves sparsely placed on gangly stems. Purple or pinkish flowers in fingerlike clusters with bracts fringed with tiny white hairs. Related to the mint family.

Henbit (*Lamium amplexicaule*)–Winter annual with rounded, scalloped leaves about the size of a nickel on squarish, creeping stems that root on contact with soil. Lavender to blue flowers seen in early spring.

Lambs-quarters (*Chenopodium album*)–A major garden problem, this annual has a short, branch taproot and grooved stems frequently striped with red or light green. Also called white pigweed. Mature leaves have toothy edges and are white-coated underneath.

Mallow (*Malva neglecti*)–Grows as an annual or biennial throughout the United States. Leaves are large, rounded with serrated edges, and flowers are whitish blue. Found with a long, white fleshy taproot in new and problem areas.

Morning Glory (*Ipomoea pan purea*)–Difficult-to-kill perennial. Has white trumpet-shaped flowers and arrowhead-shaped leaves. Profuse vining may take over shrubs if not controlled.

Mouse-ear Chickweed (*Cerastium vulgatum*)–Creeping perennial with hairy, low-growing stems that root at the nodes. Leaves are clammy, fuzzy, dark green, and persist throughout the summer. The small white flowers have five petals.

Pennywort (*Hydrocotyle sibthorpioides*)–Low perennial creeper. Shiny green leaves are as rounded as ground ivy but smaller. An aggressive weed that does well in moist, shaded areas and crowds grass out.

Prostrate Knotweed, also known as **Knotgrass** or **Matgrass** (*Polygonum aviculare*)–Wiry stemmed and very leafy annual that germinates very early in the spring. In a dense mat, its bluish green leaves resemble grass. The joints where leaves attach to stem are swollen or "knotty." Flowers are greenish and inconspicuous.

Prostrate Pigweed (*Amaranthus graecizans*)–Annual with low, creeping growth habit, fleshy stems and small taproot. Small pear-shaped leaves and small, inconspicuous flowers in clusters.

Ragweed (*Ambrosia artemisiifolia*)–Erect annual with bracted stems possibly 1-3 feet tall. Leaves are smooth and deeply lobed, with a fernlike appearance. Greenish flowers, located at branch tips and leaf bases fill the air with pollen.

Redroot Pigweed (*Amaranthus retroflexus*)–Annual with distinctive red or pink taproot. Erect and branching growth habit. Leaves are rough and lance-shaped. Small green, inconspicuous flowers in late summer.

Speedwell (*Veronica filiformis*)–Both winter or early-spring weedy species exist. Plants have a prostrate growth habit, with small and numerous leaves. Blue flowers with white centers and heart-shaped seedpods are characteristics.

Red Sorrel, also known as **Sheep Sorrel** (*Rumex acetosella*)–Low-growing, rosette-shaped cool-season plant with lobed, spear-shaped leaves. Perennial. Lacey, flowering stalks (some red, others yellow). Three-sided reddish-brown seeds.

Scarlet Pimpernel (*Anagallis aruensis*)–Annual or perennial. Small oval leaves are opposite and lacking stalks. Stems are low and grow in a creeping form. Flowers are born in twos and have a reddish-to-purple color.

Shepherds-purse (*Capsella bursa-pastoris*)–Winter annual whose deeply lobed leaves and rosette growth pattern cause it sometimes to be confused with dandelion. Its flowers are white; seedpods are triangular and contain tiny reddish brown seeds.

Spurge (*Euphorbia supina*, Raf.)–Annual, warm season, low-growing plant. Hard-to-kill. Small oblong leaves, positioned opposite each other, with or without reddish brown spots. Sap and stems tend to be purplish. Fruits three-lobed, three-seeded.

White Clover (*Trifolium repens*)– Small perennial clover that spreads by underground and aboveground stems, as well as by seed. Sometimes planted in lawns, the seeds live twenty years or more. Pealike flowers, white to pinkish.

Wild Carrot (*Daucus carota*)–Biennial. Stems grow erect, with lace-like foliage and small white flowers in clusters. Has a white, fleshy taproot. Also called Queen Anne's lace or bird's nest.

Wild Garlic (*Allium vineale*) or **Wild Onion** (*Allium canadense*)–Probably the earliest of weeds to emerge, these perennials are easily recognized by their tubular leaves and distinctive odors. Wild garlic produces underground bulblets and has hollow stems; wild onion does not.

Wild Lettuce or **Prickly Lettuce** (*Lactuca serriola*)–Annual or biennial. Leaves and stems ooze milky sap when mowed. Long, pale green leaves have deep serrations. Small yellow flower heads emerge from stalks in summer.

Yarrow (*Achillea millefolium*)–Upright perennial. Leaves are soft and fernlike. White flowers form a flat flower cluster. Fine, gray-green hairs cover stems and leaves. Entire plant has a pungent odor.

8

Insect Control
How Much Grass Can a Little Bug Eat?

The answer to the question in the title of this chapter is: A little bug can't eat very much. The amount of grass that's injured by insects depends more on the size of the bug gang. Each insect only eats a little food, but the more bugs there are, the greater the damage will be to your lawn.

The number of insects in your lawn depends greatly on the weather. If the spring and summer are relatively wet, you'll generally end up with fewer grass-damaging insects. Most insects reproduce and mature better at higher temperatures and during drier weather.

In most parts of our country, insects spend the winter in a resting state. They stop eating in the fall as the weather cools down. When the warm weather returns in the spring, they are hungry enough to eat everything in sight—and from the looks of some of your lawns, they have.

In the Deep South, bugs just keep on trucking all year long. They won't give you or your lawn a moment's peace. Don't worry, though. If you spot the damage early, identify the culprits, and then apply the proper chemical control, you can, as a rule, keep them in check.

Out of Sight Does Not Mean Out of Mind

When it comes to the *root-feeding insects* that plague our lawns, the old saying that what you can't see can't hurt you is far from the truth. There are basically only *four* root feeders—with a catch: one family includes twelve different bug cousins.

Grubs. These are the larvae of a whole roster of beetles, including:

Asiatic garden beetle
Black turfgrass ataenias
Bluegrass billbug
European chafer
Hunting billbug
Japanese beetle
June bug
Northern mask chafer
Oriental beetle
Phoenix billbug
Southern mask chafer

In the early-summer months, grubs—after eating half the grass roots in your lawn—become adult beetles. They leave the soil and fly around looking for a mate,

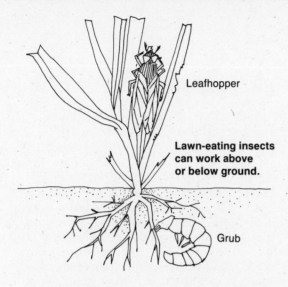

Leafhopper

Lawn-eating insects can work above or below ground.

Grub

driving you nuts in the process by bumping into your screens at night. After mating, the female lays her eggs. This generally happens in June. In July and August, the eggs hatch—and you and your lawn are in misery all over again. The grubs will then sleep all winter, resting up to start over again in the spring.

Billbugs. These are a double threat. The grub form eats the roots, while the adults attack the blades and stem. The phoenix billbug prefers Bermudagrass, the hunting billbug goes for zoysia. The bluegrass billbug's name is a dead giveaway of its dietary preference.

Mole Crickets. I have to bite my tongue whenever I face a turf problem where the mole cricket is the culprit; these critters can give even a preaching man reason to curse. Mole crickets eat *everything*: grass roots, stems, blades, stolons, rhizomes, other bugs, and earthworms. They will even eat your sweater if you leave it out overnight.

Mole crickets prefer Bahia grass. They dig down 5 to 6 inches into the soil and come out to eat at night.

Several insecticides do a good job of controlling mole crickets. Your local garden center can tell you which are avail-able in your area. Bo Dundee always told me to spread diatomaceous earth (used in swimming-pool filters), mixed with a cheap laundry soap, over the turf area. He said that it gave them the runs and blinded them. He never had mole crickets on *his* golf course.

Nematodes. These are microscopic worms which survive in the soil or grass debris as eggs, cysts, or larvae, and feed on the roots of grass plants.

Wireworms. These are skinny, smooth, shiny, hard-shelled worm-type larvae, which eat grass roots in wet areas. They turn into click beetles (their noise will drive you nuts when you try to sleep).

Ground Pearls. These very little ball-shaped critters clamp onto the roots of warm-season grasses and are sometimes mistaken for nematodes. They like centipedegrass. Ground pearls are tough to fight because they dig way down deep, where most chemicals can't reach. Try soaking the area with a quart of household ammonia plus 2 cups of liquid soap in 15 to 20 gallons of water (through a hose-end sprayer) before you apply your chemicals. I think you will be amazed at the results.

Butterflies. All butterflies ain't beautiful. These are just one of many stem and leaf feeders. On an early, pleasant summer evening, you'll see what appears to be a dainty Y-winged butterly flitting from grass blade to grass blade. Some people think they are *so* cute. I don't, and if you value your lawn, neither will you.

Sod Webworms. These are the babies of

lawn moths. They lay their eggs directly on the grass; they then hatch into worms (tan, green, or gray). These worms eat the dickens out of your lawn, but most soil insecticides will control them well. To make their life really miserable, wash your lawn with soap and water every two weeks. One cup of liquid dish soap per 10 gallons of water will drive them nuts.

Chinch Bugs. There are two types of chinch bugs. The hairy chinchbug lives in the North. The southern chinch bug causes his trouble down South. Chinch bugs bunch up in bright, warm, sunny areas. Thatch is their favorite hiding place. If you apply 50 pounds of gypsum per 2,500 square feet of lawn, wash the turf every 2 weeks with a soap solution, and keep the thatch under control, you may not need to invest in insect control.

Cutworms. They work alone and eat the grass stem off at the soil. They work the midnight shift. Soap (as above) works well as prevention.

Armyworms. These guys bivouac in large groups and feed on grass blades at night. Soap and water will help prevent them from invading your lawn.

Mites. I always get hysterical calls from people whose bedroom wall is covered with millions and millions of tiny red, green, or yellow crawling bugs. These are mites. *Never* grow grass right up to your house if you don't want mites. Wash the turf and spray it with a miticide.

Scale. These tiny, waxy-coated insects not only suck the life out of many of our garden plants, but hold a real destruction derby on our lawns. The ground pearl is a kind of scale that attaches itself to the roots, while the Bermuda grass scale does a number aboveground on the grass it is named after. The other aboveground scale insect is the Rhodes grass scale. It's favorite meals are Bermuda grass or St. Augustine grass.

Aphids. Anyone who has ever grown a rose knows what these tiny little sap-sucking pests look like. The aphid that enjoys your lawn is called a greenbug. It is a wingless creature that multiplies faster than a computer. If you find one greenbug in your lawn, you probably have hundreds, and you had better deal with them quickly. A soap-and-water wash with tobacco juice added will give them a belly-ache and diarrhea. Follow this with a local insecticide spray a half hour later. Always apply turf insecticides in the late evening, just before the bugs come out for dinner.

Grasshoppers. These hippety, hoppity creatures are more a nuisance than a threat to the grass itself. (Unless, of course, there are enough on your lawn at one time for them to be mistaken for extras in a movie plague scene.)

Leafhoppers. These guys interfere more with your nap on the lawn than anything else. If they do show up en masse, they'll usually stick around for a day or two and then move on. If you are getting a little bored with my soap-and-tobacco-juice bug-aggravation spray, then here is one more nail in the box: It works on leafhoppers, too.

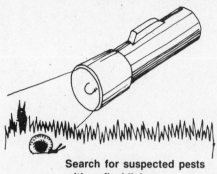

Search for suspected pests with a flashlight.

Bluegrass Weevil. This bug's name makes it sound like the principal performer in a banjo concert, but you won't applaud its appearance on your green scene. Its professional name is the hyperodes weevil. At golf courses on the East Coast and in the Northeast he is a major contender for "Most Unwanted Member"—because he eats their new spring grasses. He is not yet a big threat to home lawns, but could turn out to be a major-league bug batter.

Fruit Fly. This tiny, shiny, black fly has an expensive taste for bent grass, Kentucky bluegrass, and annual bluegrass. She flies around, laying her eggs, which look like small cream-colored nuggets— and which bore their way into grass stems at ground level. To see if you have fruit flies in your lawn, lay a small white card on the grass for a few minutes and then check the results.

Ants. I have added these dum-dums only because they can make your lawn look like a mess and because they have been accused of carrying lawn diseases from one turf area to another.

The dreaded *Fire Ant* of the Southwest, which has now been found in lawns in the Midwest, is another story. These can kill, maim, or scar adults who accidentally wander into their territory. Be careful!

My advice to anyone who calls, writes, or stops by to ask how to treat a fire-ant colony is to call a professional pest-control operator. They are experienced in this sort of thing—and the cost is well worth the results. *Carpenter Ants* and *Ter-*

mites also fall into this category.

Bees and Wasps. There will be no doubt in your mind what you've found if you run your lawn mower into a nest of either of these. They don't hurt the grass; just you, the kids, and the pets. Apply soap and water first, and then a combination of methoxychlor and Sevin late at night.

Don't Be Afraid to Look for Trouble

Whenever I go onto my lawn, whether it's to work on the grass itself or to cross over it to work on other plants, I am on the lookout for off-color grass or unexplained dead spots. Early in the evening, I look for hopping, skipping, jumping, flying, and crawling insects on the turf. If I have any reason to believe an uninvited guest has moved into the lawn, I take a flashlight along to inspect the grass.

No, I am not suggesting that you become paranoid. If you can stay one jump ahead of trouble, you'll save time, money, effort, grass, and discouragement. Be alert!

An Ounce of Prevention Can Be Dangerous and Costly

Until about 1973 we had a pretty good arsenal of insecticides (called chlorinated hydrocarbons) for soil and grass insects. Where these chemicals were applied, you could expect protection from insects for

Hose-end sprayer

Spray affected areas with soap solution first. If that doesn't work, use controlled amounts of insecticide.

anywhere from 3 to 5 years. Today, the major chemical group used for insecticides is the organic phosphates and they are comparatively lazy. You're lucky if you get 2 weeks' worth of protection.

With this in mind, make sure that you apply your insecticide at precisely the right time. As soon as you see insect trouble, identify it—and start treating it right away.

There is no reason to apply "preventive" insecticides, since they probably won't stay available in the soil until they're needed. This "overkill" style of home gardening can also add to the unwarranted bad reputation of vital insecticide chemicals. Insecticides and pesticides do not pollute. Man pollutes through misuse and abuse. DDT, chlordane heptachlor, and a whole list of other effective insect and disease control chemicals have unfairly taken the rap for man's thoughtlessness and thanklessness.

Be a Natural Faddist

If you think this makes me sound like a walking contradiction, you are right. My Grandma Putt, who taught me the greatest part of what I know, always believed in starting small—with both human and garden cures—and only building up to the heavy artillery if those don't work. I agree!

I am a great believer in using simple treatments like soap (liquid detergent) for insect prevention, for removing sur-face tension and static barriers, and for discouraging lawn diseases. The old wives' tale about throwing laundry, dish, and bath water on roses, flowers, and gardens is now considered a scientific breakthrough in the type and price of insect controls.

I always add chewing-tobacco juice to the soap solution. One cup of each per 10 gallons of water sprayed over 1,500 square feet helps control the insect pests in my lawn area. (To make tobacco juice, tie 3 fingers of chewing tobacco in an old nylon stocking and then soak it in a pint of hot water overnight.)

Spike the Bums

Insects that live and eat deep in the soil are often the toughest to get at. If you want to check to see if you have grubs in your soil, you dig a hole and look. Why not dig a lot of holes? (No, not with a shovel.) Buy a pair of aerator sandals (see page 68). If you have an insect problem, wearing the sandals will make it possible for insecticide chemicals to get deep into your lawn through the hundreds of holes the sandals have punched in the soil— stopping the bugs dead in their tracks.

The Names Change But the Principles Remain the Same

Well, things do change, but they still

always seem to stay the same. The same insects we're fighting now will be here many generations after we are gone, and home gardeners trying to keep an attractive lawn will use their era's most popular chemicals to control them.

Today's turf professional has a much larger assortment of chemical tools than the homeowner does, but the new, longer-lasting organic phosphates may soon be available to you. Isofenphos (trade name Olflanol), from Mobay Chemical*, is a good example. Its effects last several months—instead of days. In the meantime, you can use diazinon, Dursban, Sevin, and Kelthane with excellent results—if you follow the directions carefully and try a few of the additional steps I've recommended.

New lawn grasses that resist insects and diseases virtually eliminate the need for chemical insecticides and fungicides. The increased vigor of these grasses also helps crowd out weeds and reduces the need for chemical herbicides.

Look for the select-named grass varieties on the label of lawn seed blends and mixtures. For more information on the grasses best suited for improving your old lawn, send a stamped, self-addressed, number-10-size envelope to the Lawn Institute.**

*Mobay Chemical
 P.O. Box 4913
 Kansas City, Missouri 64120

**P.O. Box 108
 Pleasant Hill, Tennessee 38578.

9

Disease Control
Pythium Is Not A Bad Word

Actually, *pythium* is an extremely bad word in grass-growing circles. Pythium is one of several dozen lawn diseases that can destroy an entire lawn within 24 hours. Lawn diseases do not limit their devastation to poorly-cared-for lawns. Some of the most serious gardeners, those who try to follow all of the rules, sooner or later come face to face with one of these grass killers. I have on more than one occasion. The thing to remember at all times is that you must never intentionally create a comfort zone for fungus diseases. Two conditions that are necessary for fungi to breed that you have no control over a day temperatures around 90°F, and humid evenings where the temperature stays near 75°. If you stay alert, though, and you can take the necessary cultural steps for a good defense.

Defensive Disease Controls

You may have heard me say that there are no magic motions or potions for having a great and green lawn—just plenty of common sense. Here are some facts from the turf experts (that's someone called in at the last minute to share in the blame) on how to defend against lawn disease—a Baker's dozen to be exact:

1. Fungi and nematodes cause all of the serious infectious diseases in lawns in the Midwest. The fungi usually produce microscopic spores that are spread by wind, water, mowers or other equipment, and infected grass clippings.

2. Fungus spores need proper moisture and favorable temperatures to cause trouble. Lawn diseases are most common and damaging during wet, humid, seasons or as the result of frequent light waterings during dry periods.

3. Water properly. The more often grass is wet and the longer it remains wet, the greater are the chances of disease problems occurring. During dry periods, enough water should be applied at one time to provide adequate moisture for a week. This means that the soil should be wet 6 to 8 inches deep. It may help to water at short intervals on clay soils or where the thatch layer is thick in order to ensure penetration instead of runoff.

4. Remove excess thatch in early spring or early fall, when ½ inch has accumulat-

ed. Use a vertical mower, power rake, or similar equipment.

Thatch is a tightly intermingled layer of living and dead stems, leaves, and roots of grasses that develops between the layer of green vegetation and the soil surface. Too much thatch keeps water from penetrating the soil, makes some disease problems worse, and apparently prevents the grass from putting down a deep root system. Thatch is often an ailment of "good lawns."

Grasses differ in their inclination to develop thatch, but common Kentucky bluegrass is less likely to have a serious thatch problem than is bent grass, modern Kentucky bluegrasses, or red fescues.

5. Do not mow upright grasses, such as Kentucky bluegrass and fescues, too closely. Clipping to 2 inches tall or higher is recommended, somewhat higher in summer. Creeping grasses, such as bent grass, Bermuda grass, and zoysia, may be mowed to ½ inch tall or less.

6. Mow your grass frequently, so that no more than one-third of the leaf surface is removed at any one time. Mow the lawn throughout the fall until the grass stops growing.

7. Lawn areas where air movement is restricted can be problem spots. Thinning or removing the surrounding shrubs and trees allows sunlight to penetrate and increases the air flow. This speeds the drying of the grass and aids in disease control. Space landscape plants properly to allow adequate air movement and to avoid excessive shade.

8. Grass diseases may build up and spread rapidly in pure stands of a susceptible variety because every plant is susceptible. The severity of diseases is lower in lawns containing a comparable blend of two or more locally-adapted disease-resistant grass varieties or a mixture of grass species. It's necessary to pay increased attention to the destructive diseases when you're growing a single variety. Adjust your lawn care operations and perform control measures regularly.

9. Provide good surface and subsurface drainage when establishing a new turf grass area. Fill in low spots where water may stand.

10. Fertilize according to local recommendations and the results of a soil test. These recommendations will vary with the grasses grown. Do not overfertilize to promote fast, lush growth, especially in hot, humid weather or early spring. Overfertilizing may promote disease development.

11. Aerate hard, compacted areas, using a hand corer or a power machine. Coring is a form of cultivation that uses hollow tines or spoons to remove soil cores and leave holes or cavities in the soil.

12. Follow the suggested insect-and weed-control programs for your area and the grasses you are growing.

13. Do not plant grasses that are not adapted to your area. Be careful of seed mixtures that may contain some "weed" grasses; plant only at the recommended rates. You can get additional information

by contacting your local county extension office or the turf grass specialist at your local state land-grant university.

Never Laugh at an Old-Timer's Advice

Those of you who know me through my books, TV, and radio know that I have a reputation for using plenty of old wives' tales to tame the garden tigers. These old wives' tales are now often referred to as scientific breakthroughs. I learned many of these tried-and-true methods from my Grandma Putt, the lady I went to live with when I was expelled from kindergarten (I truly was). As I then grew up gardening wise, I had the opportunity to study under some of the best gardeners in the world. Old Zachary Beudreau used to make a solution out of a bar of old-fashioned Fels Naptha soap, cut up and dissolved in a jar of hot water. When the temperature went up, he would dip into this jellylike solution, dump it into a sprayer, and spray the greens and approaches on the golf course. We never had sick golf greens. Bo Dundee, another grass guy, always applied milorganite (from the Milwaukee Sewage Company*) on the turf area just before snow flew to help prevent early-spring turf diseases. Sid True Heart (his real name) made me wear a special pair of wooden-sole shoes

*Milwaukee Sewage Company
 Milwaukee Natural Sewerage District
 735 N. Water Street
 Milwaukee, Wisconsin 53202

with 2 inch spikes through them. When I had nothing else to do, I had to walk around the greens and wet the dry spots. We washed the dew off lawns early each morning to prevent diseases from growing in the damp turf. Mowers and equipment were washed and rinsed before storage. Newly purchased, used equipment was sterilized with steam. Lawn diseases can and in many cases are spread from lawn to lawn by landscapers and liquid applicators—so beware!

Here Are the Descriptions of the Enemy

The following diseases are the more common ones that the average homeowner will come in contact with. I want to warn you right now that the fungicides that cure, contain, or prevent lawn diseases are extremely expensive, and strongly suggest that you shop for the least expensive of the recommended chemicals.

PYTHIUM BLIGHT

Pythium blight (cottony blight) is an important disease in regions of the United States where daytime temperatures are routinely in the ninety's, night temperatures stay above 75 degrees F, and where high humidity is common. Under these conditions, pythium blight can devastate large areas of turf within 24 hours.

Symptoms: Pythium blight consists of spots initially ranging in size from ½ to 6 inches. These spots first appear as dark, greasy, or slimy water-soaked areas on the turf. When the spots dry, the leaves shrivel and turn light brown or straw-colored. In the early morning, when the humidity is high, a fluffy white mold growth may be seen on these lesions. If the turf is mowed while the fungus is still active, the disease will spread in streaks. Remember that phythium blight appears during humid, warm weather and in poorly drained areas.

Cultural Control: Pythium blight management begins with improving soil drainage, which eliminates the problem in most cases. Other cultural practices that reduce the severity of pythium blight include lowering the amount of nitrogen applied to the lawn just before and during warm weather and improving air circulation.

Chemical Control: Chloroneb (Tersan SP) and ethanzole (Koban) are effective fungicides for pythium blight when an outbreak occurs. Here is a list of fungicides effective in the management of pythium blight:

Recommended Fungicides

Common Name	Trade Name	Manufacturer
Chloroneb	Tersan SP	Du Pont
	Koban	Mallinckrodt
Metalaxyl	Subdue	Ciba-Geigy
Propamocarb hydrochloride	Banol	Upjohn

DOLLAR SPOT

Dollar spot is one of the primary diseases of creeping bentgrass, annual bluegrass, creeping red fescues, and Kentucky bluegrass. More money is spent on dollar spot than on any other turf grass disease. The disease is easily recognized by the appearance of small bleached-out spots in turf, ranging in size from a quarter to a silver dollar. A good fungicide in combination with cultural practices that inhibit disease progression is the best way to attack the disease.

Symptoms: Dollar spot is characterized by circular straw-colored, bleached-out areas ranging in size from a quarter to a silver dollar. These areas appear as sunken spots, especially when the turf is mowed to ½ inch or less in height. Individual spots may merge and blight larger, undefined areas of turf. White, fluffy mycelium (fungus strands) are often seen in these spots while the grass is still moist in the early morning.

On individual grass blades, dollar spot symptoms appear as bleached-out or yellowing-blanching lesions extending the width of the blade. On bentgrass and Kentucky bluegrass, reddish brown bands occur on the ends of the lesions. The reddish brown banding does not appear on annual bluegrass.

Causal Agent and Disease Cycle: Dollar spot is caused by *Sclerotinia homeocarpa*. This fungus spends winters as dormant mycelium in infected plant parts in the thatch and soil. The dollar spot fungus resumes growth when the temperature reaches 60 degrees F, and peak activity for infection occurs between 70 and 90 degrees F. At least two strains of the fungus exist. One strain is favored by cool weather (below 75 degrees), while the other strain is favored by high humidity, warm days (78 degrees), and cool nights. The fungus produces a toxin that produces the disease symptoms. The fungus does not normally produce spores, so the disease is spread by the movement of infected plant material by water, wind, or carried on mowers, maintenance equipment, hoses, and shoes.

Cultural Control: No cultivars of creeping bentgrass or annual bluegrass are resistant to dollar spot. Most Kentucky bluegrass cultivars are resistant. Two susceptible cultivars that should be avoided are Nugget and Sydsport.

During periods of severe infection, the nitrogen levels should be kept high to help reduce dollar spot and to make the fungicide treatment more effective. Keep nitrogen levels high with light, frequent applications of ½ pound per 1,000 feet per month in June, July, and August to manage dollar spot and to promote the growth of grass plants during warm weather.

Chemical Control: The following list contains effective fungicides for dollar spot management. Remember, use all fungicides in accordance with label directions. Do *not* misuse or misapply fungicides.

Recommended Fungicides

Common Name	Trade Name	Manufacturer
Benomyl	Tersan 1991 DSB fungicide	Du Pont
Cadmium chloride	Caddy	W. A. Cleary
	Cad-Trete	W. A. Cleary
Cadmium succinate	Cadiminate	Mallinckrodt
Chlorothalonil	Daconil 2787	Diamond Shamrock
	Spectrum Fungicide	
Cycloheximide	Acti-dione TGF	Upjohn
Cycloheximide + thiram	Acti-dione + thiram	Upjohn
Dyrene	Dyrene	Mobay
	Dymec 50	P.B.I. Gordon
	Ortho Dyrene Lawn Disease Control	Chevron
Iprodione	Chipco 26019	Rhone-Poulenc
Thiophanate-ethyl	Clearly 3336	W. A. Cleary
Thiophanate-methyl	Fungo 50	Mallinckrodt
	Topmec 70 W Fungicide	P.B.I. Gordon
Thiphanate + thiram	Bromosan	W. A. Cleary
Thiopanate + anilazine	Spectro Turf Fungicide	W. A. Cleary

Fusarium Blight

Fusarium blight can cause severe losses on Kentucky bluegrass lawns and golf course fairways. The disease occurs most commonly on Kentucky bluegrass, although it has been reported on other turf grass species. *Fusarium roseum f. sp. cerealis* and *Fusarium tricinctum f. sp. poae* are thought to cause this disease, but controversy still exists about the exact cause.

Factors such as nematodes, other soil fungi that is, fairy ring-like fungi, and/or normal aging of the turf are thought to be involved in the fusarium blight disease.

Fusarium blight is usually seen from late June through August and is most severe when Kentucky bluegrass is suffering stress from drought. The optimum conditions for fusarium blight occur when daytime temperatures are between 80 and 90 degrees F. Kentucky bluegrass lawns 3 or more years old are most often affected.

Symptoms: The ring first appears as dark-blue-to-purple patches of wilted turf 6 to 24 inches in diameter. As the disease progresses, the turf turns a light straw color. Fusarium blight usually occurs in a circular pattern with healthy-appearing grass in the middle surrounded by a ring of dead turf. This symptom is referred to as a frog-eye pattern. Infected turf grass plants have rotted roots that are brown to reddish in color. The pinkish growth of *Fusarium roseum* and *Fusarium tricinctum* may be seen on the roots and crowns of the turf grass near the surface of the soil during times of high soil moisture.

Cultural Control: Proper care of turf grass can minimize the damage caused by fusarium blight. Fusarium-resistant seed or sod should be used when new turf areas are established. Kentucky bluegrass cultivars such Adelphi, Parade, Glade, Baron, Majestic, Touchdown, Fylking, and Kenblue are the most resistant. Since drought stress favors fusarium blight, infected lawns should receive light, daily irrigation during summer months. Keeping thatch at a minimum also helps prevent drought stress and reduces disease severity. Kentucky bluegrass plants going into summer dormancy are more susceptible to fusarium blight. Apply ½ pound of nitrogen per 1,000 square feet in June, July, and August to prevent summer dormancy, and 1 pound per 1,000 square feet in September and November. The November application should be made after the grass has stopped growing. Phosphorus and potassium should be added based on soil tests. Turf mowed shorter than 2 to 3 inches in height may be more susceptible to fusarium blight.

Chemical Control: Research has shown that the chemicals benomyl, thiophanate-ethyl, thiophanage-methyl, and triadimefon are the most effective fungicides for Fusarium blight control. Apply benomyl, thiophanate-ethyl, and thiophanate-methyl at the first sign of symptoms (wilting patches in the turf). Triadimefon is only effective when applied as a preventive. It should be applied around July 1 on lawns with a past history of the disease. Benomyl, thiophanate-ethyl, and thiophanate-methyl are only effective when they are drenched into the root zones. To achieve this, the lawn or fairway should be thoroughly irrigated (½ to 1 inch) the day before application, then irrigate immediately after application—before the fungicide dries on the foliage. It is not necessary to drench in triadimefon.

Recommended Fungicides

Common Name	Trade Name	Manufacturer
Benomyl	Tersan 1991	Du Pont
Thiophanate-ethyl	Cleary 3336	W.A. Cleary
Thiophanate-methyl	Fungo 50	Mallinckrodt
	Topmec 70 W	P.B.I. Gordon
Triadimefon	Bayleton	Mobay

Current Scuttlebutt on Lawn Blight

Fusarium blight of bluegrass may not involve *Fusarium* fungi at all. At least so goes one recent theory, especially as advanced by Dr. Smiley at Cornell. Fusarium is always present in lawns, part of the general population of microorganisms. Dr. Smiley has both good and bad news. The good news is that while *Fusarium* may incite disease at times, it also helps preserve the normal ecological balance. It can help the lawn by repressing "even worse" fungi and by helping to consume thatch.

The bad news is that fusarium blight is still very much of a puzzle. The disease starts in warm weather and is most likely to occur where the grass has been subjected to unusual stress. Could this result from too much water—or too little—too much fertilization—or too little? Could a pesticide treatment predispose the lawn toward blight?

The severity of a fusarium-blight outbreak can usually be reduced by watering the affected area and by using moderation in all phases of lawn care. An ideal control would be the sowing of bluegrass cultivars resistant to the disease. A recent tally from the Rutgers University proving grounds shows Adelphi, Enmundi, Majestic and Sydsport to have sustained no fusarium blight damage at all under normal growing conditions.

FUSARIUM PATCH (PINK SNOW MOLD)

Fusarium patch is a problem in areas with a cool, wet, spring or fall, or where there is a snow cover in the winter months. Annual bluegrass, creeping bentgrass, and perennial ryegrass are highly susceptible and easily destroyed by fusarium patch. Kentucky bluegrass and red fescue are moderately susceptible to the disease.

Symptoms: Without snow cover, pink snow mold occurs as reddish-brown spots in the turf. The spots may range from less than 1 inch to 8 inches in diameter, although larger ones may be found. When a snow cover is present, the circular spots are usually 2 or 3 inches to 1 or 2 feet in diameter and are tan, whitish-gray, reddish-brown. Shortly after the snow has melted, pink mycelium (fungal strands) can be seen at the advancing edge of the spot.

Occurrence: Pink snow mold is caused by *Fusarium nivale*. This organism survives in the turf thatch and will actively grow on turf residue. Infection takes place at temperatures below 60 degrees F because slowly-growing turf is more vulnerable to attack by the fungus, and there is less competition from other microorganisms at this temperature. *Fusarium nivale* and other snow molds are pathogens that have found ecological niches where they can survive without competition from other microorganisms.

Cultural Control: Fall nitrogen fertilization causes lush turf growth going into the winter. It also makes the turf more susceptible to fusarium patch and management with fungicides more difficult. The last date of application for nitrogen should be early enough to give the turf a chance to "harden off" before the first snow or frost. A good average date for the last nitrogen application for cool-weather grasses is August 15 through September 15. This is not to be confused with the dormant nitrogen application that is applied after the turf has stopped growing in November or December. Also, if the turf is lush and there is a winter without snow cover, large areas of turf may be lost to desiccation (drying out).

There is no creeping bentgrass or annual bluegrass cultivar that is resistant to fusarium patch, and all require preventative fungicide treatment.

Chemical Control: Several fungicides can be used to manage fusarium patch where there is no lasting snow cover. However, if there is a snow cover for three months or longer, either the mercury or systemic fungicides must be applied before permanent snowfall. They are the only fungicides capable of protecting the turf from fusarium patch during this time, as repeated applications cannot be made. Fusarium patch will occur in the spring during cool, wet periods and fungicide treatments should be applied at the first evidence of the disease.

Recommended Fungicides

Common Name	Trade Name	Manufacturer
Benomyl	Tersan 1991	Du Pont
Cadmium chloride	Caddy	W. A. Cleary
	Ca-trete	W. A. Cleary
Mancozeb	Fore	Rohm and Haas
	Formec 80	P.B.I. Gordon
Thiophanate-ethyl	Cleary's 3336	W. A. Cleary
Thiophanate-methyl	Fungo 50	Mallinckrodt
	Topmec 70W	P.B.I. Gordon

FAIRY RING

Fairy rings are caused by soil-inhabiting fungi that survive on dead organic matter. They can occur in any type of turf where conditions are suitable for fungal growth. Although the occurrence of fairy ring on a homeowner's lawn is generally of little concern, it can be a serious problem on golf course greens.

Symptoms: A circular fairy ring develops because the fungi starts from a central point and grows equally in all directions. The fungi break down the organic matter as they grow, releasing nitrogen (ammonia) that eventually is changed by other microorganisms to nitrate nitrogen. The nitrate nitrogen stimulates turf grass growth within the ring (known as the zone of stimulation or activity zone). The turf may appear dark green at first, but will eventually die if stressed by heat or drought. Sometimes the turf may simply turn yellow or be stunted. If the turf is adequately watered, it will usually recover from the yellowing, but the stunting may remain. The yellowing, stunting, and turf death within the ring has been attributed to a number of causes. Mushrooms are often found in the fairy ring circle.

Occurrence: Fairy rings are commonly seen in areas that were previously forested or where stumps or logs were used as fill. Many of the fungi that cause fairy ring are wood-decaying fungi, which survive in soils high in organic matter (for example, peat or muck). High nitrogen levels can also stimulate these fungi and cause the development of a fairy ring.

Control: Controlling or removing a fairy ring is difficult and expensive. If fairy rings are on a putting green, they should be removed. Fairy rings on golf course fairways can generally be ignored, unless there is a large concentration in a critical landing zone or on an approach to a green. Fairy rings in sod fields should be fumigated to prevent the movement of fungi with the sod. In athletic fields, commercial areas, or home lawns, they can be ignored unless a large area is covered or they are an irritant.

Cultural Control: Fertilization with nitrogen, to increase the growth of the surrounding grass, will help mask the dark-green grass in the zone of stimulation. However, it should be remembered that some fungi are stimulated by nitrogen and an application could cause more fairy rings to be produced. I have had excellent luck by punching holes 3 to 4 inches deep, 6 inches apart all over the infected area, mixing a solution of 1 cup of liquid soap per gallon of water, and pouring some over the area. Next, feed the area with a water-soluble lawn food like Super K-Gro at half the recommended rate, with a cup of household ammonia added for each gallon. I repeat the soap wash weekly for 3 weeks. Keep the infected area well fed and watered.

Another method is to drown the fairy ring by supersaturating the area for 48 hours or more. This is a temporary remedy; the fairy ring will normally recur later that season or the next year.

Some turfmen dig them out. Go a foot beyond the ring, square it off, remove the sod, and then remove the soil within the square to a depth of 1 foot. Fill the hole with uninfested soil and reseed or resod.

Chemical Control: Fairy ring cannot be controlled by fungicides. Fumigating or digging them out is the only real way to eliminate them. Drilling holes and pouring fungicides down them is not effective in controlling fairy ring and may even aggravate the problem. Fumigants should only be applied by licensed turf professionals.

HELMINTHOSPORIUM MELTING-OUT AND LEAFSPOT OF LAWN GRASSES

Helminthosporium melting-out (*H.vagans*) is most destructive during the cool, wet weather of spring and fall. *Helminthosporium* leaf spot (*H. sorokinianum*) is most destructive during the warmer summer months. Therefore, if conditions are favorable, lawns can be damaged by one or the other of these pathogens anytime between April and November. Leaf spot is mainly a problem on creeping bentgrass and fine-leaf fescues, while melting out is a problem on Kentucky bluegrass.

Symptoms: Both *Helminthosporium* diseases first appear as small, purple-to-black specks on the leaf blades, which quickly enlarge and become irregularly elongated. The tissue in the center of the spot may die and turn beige or straw-colored, while the margin varies in color from reddish brown to near black. If the spot extends across the leaf, the blades will wither and die. When cool, moist conditions persist, the leaf sheath and crown of the grass plant can become infected with *H. vagans*, causing the entire grass plant to die. The terms fading out, melting out, and *Helminthosporium* blight are often used to describe this stage of the disease. Because dead or badly diseased plants often lose the characteristic symptoms described, the injury is often blamed on drying out or insect damage.

Occurrence: H. vagans and *H. sorokinianum* survive the winter as spores and mycelium (fungal strands) in and on diseased grass tissue and in the thatch. In spring, when temperatures reach 55 to 60 degrees F and high moisture conditions (heavy dew or rain) prevail, *H. vagans* grows and produces spores. These spores are spread by wind, water, and mowing equipment, and under favorable conditions, large areas of turf appear to die (melting out) almost overnight. *H. sorokinianum* causes the same problem when the temperatures are between 80 and 90 degrees F.

Cultural Control: For established lawns, several cultural practices can be used to reduce *Helminthosporium* melting out or leaf spot:

● Mow the grass at a 1¾- to 2-inch height. Do not mow the grass too short, since this weakens the plant.

● Do not fertilize susceptible lawns with nitrogen in the spring, since lush growth favors infection and disease development. Fertilize moderately with nitrogen during the summer months.

● Keep the grass blades dry by avoiding evening or night watering.

When establishing new lawns in areas where *Helminthosporium* melting out is a problem, use resistant cultivars. Parade, Touchdown, Majestic, Adelphi, Cheri, Victa-Brunswick, and Baron are recommended.

Chemical Control: Several fungicides are available that provide excellent control of *Helminthosporium* melting out and leaf spot. Melting out is best controlled by applying protective fungicides during the spring and fall, when temperatures are optimum for disease development, but before the disease becomes severe.

Recommended Fungicides

Common Name	Trade Name	Manufacturer
Chlorothalonil	Daconil 2787	Diamond
	Proturf 101V	Shamrock
Cycloheximide + PCNB	Acti-dionRZ	Upjohn
Cycloheximide + thiram	Acti-dione-Thiram	Upjohn
Anilazine	Dyrene	Mobay
	Dymec 50 Proturf	P.B.I. Gordon
	Ortho Dyrene Lawn Disease Control	Chevron
Iprodione	Chipco 26019	Rhone-Poulenc
Mancozeb	Fore	Rohm and Haas
	Formec	P.B.I. Gordon

TYPHULA BLIGHT (GRAY SNOW MOLD)

Typhula blight is an important disease in regions where snow cover remains on the ground for 3 months or more without melting. It may be found in combination with another disease called fusarium patch (pink snow mold) (see pages 106–7), but unlike fusarium patch, some type of cover is necessary for typhula blight. This cover is usually provided by snow; but leaves, straw, mulch, and desiccation covers can cause the same effect.

Symptoms: The typhula blight fungus grows and infects grass at temperatures between 30 and 50 degrees F. As the snow melts, circular pinkish-to-grayish spots appear in the turf. The spots range from 3 inches to 2 feet in diameter, but most are between 6 and 12 inches across. As the snow melts, the grayish white mycelia (fungal strands) can be seen, especially at the outer margins of the spots. Typhula blight is worse during winters when snow falls on unfrozen turf that has not been hardened by frost. When snow falls on frozen ground, the disease usually develops only in the spring, when the snow begins to melt.

Occurrence: Typhula blight is most commonly caused by *Typhula incarnata*. The *Typhula* fungus survives that summer as sclerotia (the dormant stage). In early spring, as the snow melts, the sclerotia may be as large as 3/16 inch across and visible to the naked eye. Later, they dry up and are no longer detectable. The sclerotia are resistant to warm temperatures and fungicides that are part of summer disease-control programs. During cool, wet fall weather, the sclerotia swell, germinate, and produce spores, which are carried by wind and water to new sites.

Cultural Control: Typhula blight is more severe if the turf is lush going into the winter. Depending on the area, the last nitrogen application on actively growing turf should be made sometime between mid-August and mid-September. This should not be confused with dormant nitrogen feeding, which is nitrogen application after the top growth has stopped. Dormant feedings promote an early green-up in the spring and favor the quick recovery of turf damaged by snow mold. Whenever possible, fungicides should be applied to turf receiving dormant nitrogen feedings.

Resistant Varieties: All creeping-bentgrass cultivars are susceptible to typhula blight and require some type of fungicide treatment. The fine-leaf fescues and Kentucky bluegrasses are, in general, more resistant to typhula blight than are annual bluegrasses, creeping bentgrass, and perennial ryegrass.

Chemical Control: Chemical control of typhula blight is necessary on all annual bluegrass and creeping-bentgrass putting greens. PCNB is phytotoxic to some bent grass. Chloroneb is not effective against fusarium patch, so in areas where both typhula blight and fusarium patch occur, or where fusarium patch is the main problem, other fungicides must be used in combination with chloroneb.

Recommended Fungicides

Common Name	Trade Name	Manufacturer
Cadmium chloride	Caddy	W. A. Cleary
	Cad-trete	W. A. Cleary
Cadmium succinate	Cadimate	Mallinckrodt
Chloroneb	Tersan SP	Du Pont
Cycloheximide + PCNB	Anti-dione RZ	Upjohn

RHIZOCTONIA BROWN PATCH

Rhizoctonia brown patch, caused by *Rhizoctonia solani* Kuhn, attacks all turf grass species in the Midwest. It is most severe on perennial ryegrasses and creeping bentgrass in the southern coastal areas and can be a problem on Kentucky bluegrass lawns. The brown-patch fungus lives in the soil and competes well with other saprophytic microorganisms (organisms that live on decayed organic matter). *R. solani* is found in most soils and can survive for years without a suitable host.

Symptoms: Brown patch occurs as circular brown patches ranging from a few inches to several feet in diameter. Infected leaves first appear water soaked and dark, but eventually dry and turn dark brown. Brown-to-black sclerotia (survival structures) are sometimes found beneath the leaf sheath or on the stolons. When the disease develops under conditions of high humidity, a "smoke ring" often develops along the outer edges of the diseased area. Under conditions of low humidity, the smoke ring is usually absent. Brown patch has a "slimy" appearance when it occurs on perennial ryegrass.

Disease Cycle: R. solani survives the winter months in plant debris as mycelia and sclerotia. The fungus begins to grow as temperatures rise into the 60s. When day temperatures reach the middle 70s, it enters the leaf tissue through wounds (mowing) and stomates (leaf pores).

Symptoms usually do not appear at this stage because the plant is actively growing, and this keeps *R. solani* from causing serious damage. High humidity, daytime temperatures in the mid-80s, and nighttime air temperatures above 70 degrees F put the grass plant under stress, and can result in the appearance of symptoms. Under proper weather conditions, infected plants that previously showed no symptoms will exhibit them almost immediately.

Cultural Control: High nitrogen levels increase the severity of *Rhizoctonia* brown patches. Therefore, fertilize with no more than ½ pound actual nitrogen per 1,000 square feet per month as hot, humid weather approaches. Phosphorus and potassium should be maintained at normal levels, and the pH should be neutral. Removing dew early in the morning will help reduce the severity of the disease.

Chemical Control: Several fungicides are available that will control brown patch. Brown-patch infection begins to take place long before symptoms are evident, so the best use of these fungicides is preventive. Fungicides should be applied when average daytime temperatures begin reaching the 80s.

Recommended Fungicides

Common Name	Trade Name	Manufacturer
Chlorothalonil	Daconil 2787	Diamond Shamrock
	Proturf 101V	
Cycloheximide + PCNB	Acti-dione RZ	Upjohn
Cycloheximide + thiram	Acti-dione-thiram	Upjohn
Anilazine	Dyrene	Mobay
	Dymec 50	P.B.I.-Gordon
	Fungicide III	
	Ortho Dyrene Lawn Disease Control	Chevron
Iprodione	Chipco 26019	Rhone-Poulenc
Mancozeb	Fore	Rohm & Haas
	Formec	P.B.I.-Gordon
	Turfcide	Olin
Thiophanate + thiram	Bromosan	W. A. Cleary
Thiram	Spotrete	W. A. Cleary
	Tersan 75	Du Pont
	Thiramid	Mallinckrodt

HAS DECLINE OF ANNUAL BLUEGRASS (ANTHRACNOSE)

The loss or decline of annual bluegrass *(Poa annua)* has traditionally been attributed to direct high-temperature kill or to the natural dying of a winter annual. However, fungicide treatments have recently been used to prevent annual bluegrass from dying during summer heat stress. This suggests that annual bluegrass does not die from these stress factors, but rather as a result of other causes that can be mitigated by fungicides. Anthracnose, caused by *Collectotrichum graminicola*, has been shown to be the primary cause of annual-bluegrass decline during warm summer weather. *Helminthosporium sorokinianum*, the disease organism involved in leaf spot, and senescence also play a part in annual bluegrass decline. The proposed name for this disease complex is HAS Decline (*Helminthosporium*-Anthracnose-Senescence). Annual bluegrass will grow successfully during the summer stress period if this disease complex is managed by the use of fungicides. It is no longer necessary to try to eliminate annual-bluegrass decline through expensive, time-consuming, and unsuccessful overseeding programs.

Symptoms: The initial characteristic symptom of HAS Decline is a yellow-bronze coloring of the turf. This color indicates senescence and distinguishes it from wilt, which is dark-blue-to-purple in color. Later the turf darkens and irregular brown to purplish-black lesions appear on the leaf blades.

In cool weather, the turf will remain yellow, with little thinning or dying. But when temperatures range in the 80s and humidity is high, the yellowish-bronze turf will darken within 48 hours unless fungicides are applied. HAS Decline may initially appear as irregular spots 1 to 2 feet in diameter, but within 24 hours large areas, even an entire fairway, can thin out and die. At this point the black fruiting structures (acervuli) of the anthracnose fungus are visible in the yellow and/or newly stricken tissue. The black spines (setae) protruding from the fruiting structure distinguish the fruiting bodies of anthracnose from the fruiting bodies produced by saprophytic fungi. The acervuli can be seen with the aid of a hand lens or dissecting scope.

Occurrence: HAS Decline occurs when daytime temperatures are in the 80s for a week or more and is more severe when nighttime temperatures stay above 70 degrees F for 3 or more nights in a row. HAS Decline is most severe when annual bluegrass is under stress, as in compacted areas, heavy traffic, poor soil drainage, or improper nitrogen fertility.

Cultural Control: HAS Decline can be prevented in years of moderate temperature by proper nitrogen fertility. A nitrogen program of ½ pound of actual nitrogen per 1,000 square feet applied in June, July, and August, will help repress the disease. This nitrogen fertility program should be supplemented by applying 1 pound of actual nitrogen per 1,000 square feet in early September and after vertical plant growth has stopped.

Chemical Control: Systematic fungicides (benomyl, triadimefon, thiophanate-methylor, and thiophanate-ethyl) applied as a drench at 2 ounces per 1,000 square feet will allow newly infected areas to recover in about 10 days. One-ounce rates and nondrench applications also work, but recovery takes longer. However, a one-ounce rate is sufficient when applied as a preventive before the disease occurs. This application should be made around mid-July. Contact fungicides, such as chlorothalonil and mancozeb, can also be applied on a preventive basis every 7 to 10 days starting in mid-July.

Recommended Fungicides

Common Name	Trade Name	Manufacturer
Benomyl	Tersan 1991	Du Pont
Chlorothalonil	Daconil 2787	Diamond Shamrock
Maneb + zinc sulfate	Tersan LSR	Du Pont
Mancozeb	Fore	Rohm and Haas
	Formec 80	P.B.I. Gordon
Thiophanate-ethyl	Cleary 3336	W. A. Cleary
Thiophanate-methyl	Fungo 50	Mallinckrodt
	Topmec 70W	P.B.I. Gordon
Triadimefon	Bayleton	Mobay
Thiophanate-methyl + mancozeb	Duosan	Mallinckrodt

RUST SMUT

Rust smut is caused by the fungus *Ustilago striiformis*. Pale-green plants develop long gray streaks that rupture to release masses of black spores. Infected leaves later twist, shred, and die. Patches of smutted plants die during summer droughts. Smut is encouraged by excess thatch, frequent irrigation, and the growing of susceptible cultivars. I have found that a solution of 1 cup liquid soap and one cup mouth wash in a 20 gallon lawn sprayer works wonders.

RUST

Rust diseases are caused by about a dozen species of the fungus *Puccinia*. Yellow, orange, or reddish-brown dusty pustules form in leaves and sheaths of grass that are growing very slowly. Heavily rusted grass appears yellow, thin, weak, and is more susceptible to drought, weed invasion, winterkill, and other damage.

POWDERY MILDEW

Powdery mildew is caused by the fungus *Erysiphe graminis*. Superficial white-to-grayish patches of mold develop on leaves and sheaths. The turf appears dull white (as if dusted with flour), thin, and weak. The leaves may later turn yellow, wither, and die. Mildew is most serious on Kentucky bluegrass growing in moderate-to-dense shade.

RED THREAD AND PINK PATCH

Red thread and pink patch are caused by several fungi that infect turf grasses during prolonged cool-to-warm weather in very humid areas. Round-to-irregular light-tan-to-pinkish patches develop that are 2 to 12 inches across. The spots may merge to form large, irregular, bleached-tan or yellowish areas with a reddish brown cast. Bright coral-pink to blood-red "threads," up to ¼ inch or longer, commonly protrude from the leaf tips and sheaths. The threads are gelatinous at first but later dry and become brittle. This disease is promoted by slow-growing, nitrogen- and calcium-deficient turf grass, excessive thatch, lack of water, and weakening by other stresses.

SLIME MOLDS

Slime molds, caused by several soil-borne fungi, suddenly appear on grass, other low-lying vegetation, or objects during wet weather or following deep watering. The slimy masses, up to about a foot across, are watery white, gray, cream, or black. They soon dry to form bluish, bluish gray, grayish white, black, creamy-yellow, orange, or purple-brown spore masses that are easily wiped off, leaving the blades beneath a healthy green or somewhat yellow. Slime molds are favored by dense, lush, well-watered grass and excessive thatch.

WHAT YOU SEE AIN'T ALWAYS WHAT YOU GOT!

More often than not, people who have put their blood, sweat, and tears into a near-perfect lawn panic at the least blemish and run for the fungicide. Don't! Stop and take a real close look. It could simply be dog damage, a gasoline spill, or one of the many other nondisease problems. Here are a few of the common ones to check for:

Insect Injury—Numerous insects, including grubs, webworms, chinch bugs, ants, leafhoppers, and others may damage turf. Insect injury may closely resemble one or more lawn diseases. If you suspect a lawn insect problem, contact your county extension office or the extension entomologist at your land-grant university.

Chemical Burn—Agricultural chemicals (e.g., fertilizers, pesticides, or hydrated spray lime) may injure grass if improperly applied. Burned areas may occur in spots or streaks, or the entire lawn may be "scorched." Prevent lawn injury by following the directions printed on the package label. Apply fertilizers evenly in recommended amounts, when the grass is dry. Then water immediately. The use of calibrated lawn spreader is highly recommended. Ground agricultural limestone is safer to use on lawns than hydrated lime.

Chlorosis (Yellowing)—Areas or all of the turf may become yellowed and stunted. Chlorosis (yellowing) is usually caused by a nitrogen or iron deficiency or the temporary waterlogging of the soil. Most lawn fertilizers contain nitrogen. If a recommended fertility program is carried out, this element is probably being applied in sufficient amounts. If the lawn continues to remain yellow after nitrogen application followed by rain or watering, the cause is likely to be iron deficiency. This is more likely if the soil is either highly acid or alkaline.

Control: Have a soil test made and follow the directions in the report. If iron deficiency is the problem, apply 4 tablespoons of iron sulfate (sold as Copperas or Sulfasoil) in 5 to 10 gallons of water per 1,000 square feet. Sprinkle it in immediately. Repeat the treatment as necessary to maintain a normal green color. Avoid drifting spray, because iron sulfate will leave a brown stain on the grass blades.

Iron chelate materials also correct iron deficiency. When starting a new lawn, have the soil tested before planting. This can be done, usually for a small service charge, by your state university, county extension office, or a private soil-testing laboratory. The pH of the soil should be close to neutral (pH 6.0 to 7.0). If the pH is far outside this range (below pH 5.5 or above 7.3), treat it with iron.

Buried Debris—A thin layer of soil over buried rocks, lumber, bricks, plaster, concrete, and so forth dries out rapidly in dry summer weather and may resemble disease. Control by digging up suspicious areas, removing the cause, and adding good topsoil.

Moss—Moss occurs in lawn areas low in fertility, with poor drainage, high soil acidity, excess shade, compaction, or a combination of these factors.

Remove moss by hand raking. Have your soil tested and follow the instructions given in the report to correct the unfavorable conditions.

Dog Injury—Injuries caused by dog urine may resemble *Rhizoctonia* brown patch or *Sclerotinia* dollar spot. Affected areas are often more or less round and commonly up to a foot or more in diameter. These are usually bordered by a ring of lush, dark-green grass. Injured grass turns brown or straw-colored and usually dies. Heavy watering can help these spots to recover.

Inside & Outside Protection

Contact fungicides are sprayed onto the grass, form a protective shield around the grass blades, and keep the diesease from spreading. You must make sure that you spray every blade for contact fungicides to be effective. This group only protects your lawn for up to 2 weeks:

Anilazine
Cadmium compounds
Captan
Chlorothalonil
Chloroneb
Cycloheximide
Dinocap
Etridiazole (ethazole)
Iprodione
Mancozeb
Maneb
Mercury compounds
Thiram
Zineb

Systemic fungicides afford a much longer protection period of up to 6 weeks, with 3 to 4 weeks being normal. The systematic group is also much more expensive. Systemic fungicides enter the plant itself and protect it from the inside.

Contact controls prevent but don't cure; systemics cure. Contact protection should be applied to the turf area when the conditions are ideal for the disease and must be reapplied after cutting or heavy rain or watering. Systemic fungicides are applied at the first sign of damage and as a rule are not reapplied for 4 to 5 weeks:

Benomyl
Metalaxyl
Propamocarb
Thiophantate-ethyl
Thiophanate-methyl
Triadimefon (Bayleton)

How You Spray Does Make a Difference

Please, folks, read *all* of the directions before you mix and spray any of these chemicals. Safety is first and foremost, but waste is also a crime. This stuff costs an arm and a leg.

I don't care what kind of fungicide you are using (contact or systemic), I want you to spray the affected or infected area with 2 cups of liquid dish soap in 20 gallons of water (through a hose-end sprayer) first. Wait a half hour and then apply the chemical fungicide.

The soap itself is a type of prevention and cure, but its primary use is to open up the soil and root area for better penetration by the fungicide.

Common Lawn Diseases and Treatments	Anilazine	Cadmium Compounds	Captan	Chloroneb	Chlorothalonil	Dyrene	Cycloheximide	Dinocap	Etridiazol	Inprodione	Mancozeb	Maneb	Mercury	Thiram	Zineb	Benomyl	Metalaxyl	Propamocarb	Thiophanate-ethyl	Thiophanate-methyl	Triadimeton (Bayleton)
Pythium				x													x	x			
Dollar Spot	x				x	x	x			x						x					
Fusarium Blight																x					x
Fusarium Patch		x												x		x					
Fairy Ring	L	A	U	N	D	R	Y		S	O	A	P	+	N	I	T	R	O	G	E	N
Melting Out	x				x					x	x										
Leaf Spot	x				x					x	x										
Snow Mold		x		x			x														
Brown Patch	x				x					x	x					x					
Anthracnose					x						x					x			x	x	
Stripe Smut																x			x	x	x
Rust					x		x				x	x			x						
Mildew							x							x							x
Red Thread							x					x		x					x	x	x
Pink Patch										x	x	x		x			x		x	x	x
Slime Molds		x					x							x	x						

10

Pets and Varmints

If It Isn't the Mutts, It's the Moles

I've heard many of you complain that your entire garden looks, "like a dog." I assume you mean that it looks shaggy, unfed, mangy, and scroungy. Lawns often look like this because of a dog—your own or your neighbor's. On the other hand, squirrels, chipmunks, woodchucks, skunks, moles, weasels, cats, rats, voles, shrews, gophers, and a variety of other furry fellows could share the blame.

I am a firm believer in discouraging these guys and gals if at all possible, instead of destroying them—I trap them when it's possible. When all else fails, and it's between them or my garden, they lose. Here are a few hints on discouragement (and stronger) methods of animal controls.

Has Your Lawn Gone to the Dogs?

Dogs may be man's best friend, but the homeowner who is trying to have an attractive and healthy green lawn may sometimes doubt it.

If it isn't your own K-9 cutie "potty pocking" your front lawn, it is probably the work of an inconsiderate neighbor who fails to keep his or her pet under con-trol. Either way, it's a pain to your grass (not to mention you!).

If the problem is caused by your neighbor's dog, my advice is first to contact your neighbor, letting them know, in a pleasant way, what the problem is and that you would appreciate any help they can give you. If a second visit is necessary, tell them that the third call will be to the local animal-control department (or dogcatcher). Remember, never make threats, only promises—and then keep them.

I Hate to Shatter a Myth, But I Must . . .

Girl dogs always take the rap for being the cause of lawn damage, while the boys go scot-free. They shouldn't! There is no difference in the degree of potency of either dog gender's urine. It's their different potty habits that cause the problem. The female dog squats very close to the lawn surface—causing a quantity of highly acidic urine to be concentrated in one spot. The male, as a rule, lifts his leg and directs the urine onto a bush, pole, plug, or rock, causing less of a concentration in a given area of lawn. It's a good idea to have a urine acidity test taken when you have your dog in for its annual physical. Oftentimes, the vet tells me, a simple diet change is good for the animal's health—and can also improve the family lawn's health.

Land Plaster Builds a Protective Barrier

No construction is necessary to use this product. In the early spring (after you have cleaned up the lawn area) and again in the late fall, apply 50 pounds of lawn and garden gypsum to each 1,000 square feet of lawn area where your Rover rolls over most often. You will find that in most cases the severity of the damage will be reduced, if not eliminated.

"Grass is Good for Dogs" Is Another Myth!

According to my local veterinarian, there is absolutely nothing beneficial for dogs in eating grass. In fact, it can cause a great deal of harm. Dogs will be dogs and nibble on tender, new juicy grass in the early spring—it smells good and is sweet. It can also cause terrific cases of diarrhea—almost to the point where you'll have to take your dog to a vet for relief.

If your dog is eating grass later in the season, it's true that he probably has an upset stomach. All the grass will do is make him, ultimately, sick to the point of vomiting.

"Born Free" Is Not Very Practical

Some people think that their backyard is the best place for their dog to run. That's the worst thing you can do for your dog—and your lawn! Most parasitic insects mass on grass blades and pebbles. The only way to keep the area clean is to douse it with a salty, soapy solution (which means good-bye lawn). Home pets should be allowed to run on a cement slab with a carry-away trough along one side that runs into a sewer, so that the salty, acidic water will not contact your grass.

If You Insist on Dogs and Grass...

If you still want your dog to be able to run on grass, then I can make a few suggestions that will help you preserve your lawn: Check the chapter on soil (chapter 2), and prepare a good sand/loam base. Next, overseed with a combination of 50 percent Kentucky 31 tall fescue (it's coarse and ugly but tough as nails), 20 percent Rebel tall fescue, and 30 percent Hounddog tall fescue (I think this is the best combination).

Your pooch probably won't attempt to nibble on this stuff, since it's bitter and uncomfortably tough (both to chew and wear out). You can try to discourage the parasite egg masses from forming by spraying the turf area twice a month with a healthy solution of Fels Naptha soap and water. It's just a precaution, folks, not a cure.

Water Down the Damage

If your lawn is often visited by dogs, you must be very rigid about your watering techniques. There is less of a chance of severe damage to well-moistened soil (with a regular soap bath), than to a dry, stressed, poorly-cared-for lawn area. Water daily when dogs are a regular part of the landscape.

Cats May Get My Tongue

I have never been able to figure out why folks complain about dogs who run loose but don't make any fuss over cats. As far as I'm concerned, both should be kept under control in city or suburban areas.

As a rule, cats do no real damage to a turf area and should not be of any concern. Cats can, however, become very ill if they are allowed to eat grass soon after it has been sprayed with insecticide. (It is a natural instinct for cats to eat grass.) They can also be a nuisance when they dig their toilets into your flower, vegetable, or herb beds. Dip pieces of cotton clothesline in bone tar oil (a deer repellent) and stretch it across areas where cats tend to linger. This should do the trick.

On balance, cats are a helpful and friendly pet to have around since they will handle the mice, rabbits, and moles that tunnel and dig in the turf area.

This Subject Stinks!

You can usually tell when skunks have been in the area. The skunk's bad reputation is really unearned. He is a very gentle sort of fellow unless he gets upset—in most cases he sleeps all day and forages most of the night. The presence of skunks will usually cause mice and rats to move on, since skunks consider them a delicacy.

However, the skunk can try the patience of a person who is trying to have an attractive lawn, since at night they dig dozens upon dozens of holes in search of June bugs and grubs. This kind of skunk activity is really telling you that you have a bug problem. When you get rid of the insects in your lawn, he will move on.

Hickory, Dickory, Dock! I Hope the Mice Run Up the Block!

What we usually refer to as field mice—creatures that tunnel through our lawn winter and summer—are really voles. What they are doing is commuting from one bulb or young tree to another and making a mess of the lawn in the process.

Place D-Con traps or other mice bait under the shrubs and evergreens the voles seem to be coming from. In the very late fall, mix 2 ounces of bone tar oil (from Plantabbs Company*), 4 ounces of liquid dish soap and ½ cup of warm water in a bottle or jar and shake it—vigorously—for 5 minutes. Add the mixture to your

*Plantabbs Co.
16 West Aylesbury
Timonium, Maryland 21903

hose-end sprayer and spray the lawn area where you see the vole the most often; the smell will send him packing (maybe you, too!).

I Don't Know How Much Wood a Woodchuck Can Chuck...

But boy, would I ever like to chuck the woodchuck. In one night, these guys can dig a hole big enough and deep enough to lose a lawn mower or break a leg in. There are a couple of ways of getting them to move on:

First, throw a couple of handfuls of human hair and a ½ box of Paradichlorobenzene moth crystals into the openings they've dug. Or roll old tennis balls soaked in bone tar oil or drop gopher gassers (from your garden center) into the holes. As a last resort, trap them.

Opossums Really Do Play Dead!

Do not mess with these ugly, ugly, critters—they'll bite. They are not as smart as their cousin the raccoon. As a matter of fact, opossums are pretty stupid. They eat lots of junk, but are also fond of insects, and will really screw up your lawn if they get hungry enough.

Get rid of the bugs in your lawn and you will probably get rid of the opossum as well. While you are waiting for the insecticide to do its job, spray 2,500 square feet of grass with ¾ cup of ammonia and 1 cup of liquid soap from a hose-end sprayer of 15 to 20 gallon capacity. This spray will help the grass fill in faster where the opossum has been digging.

There Is Nothing Cute About a Raccoon

Raccoons are mean, nasty, and sneaky. As a rule, raccoons cause no damage to turf areas. They can cause havoc in the vegetable garden and with garbage cans. A raccoon can unlatch the can, take what he wants—and then the neighborhood dogs will come along and scatter the rest over the lawn.

Fill a window spray container with a little ammonia and squirt it into the weekly garbage supply to keep them away.

Birds of a Feather Flock Together

And it's always just after I have planted grass seed. I have found that if I spray the recently seeded area with a soap-and-bone-tar solution, I'll lose a lot less seed. By the way, the new blow-up plastic scarecrows with long colorful streamers really do scare away the birds. A mixture of ¼ teaspoon of turpentine and 3 tablespoons of liquid soap in 5 gallons of water, sprayed over the top of a newly seeded lawn, will also keep birds at bay.

Squirrel It Away

If there is anything that can make a lawn look like a battlefield, it's a squirrel digging it up—packing in food for the

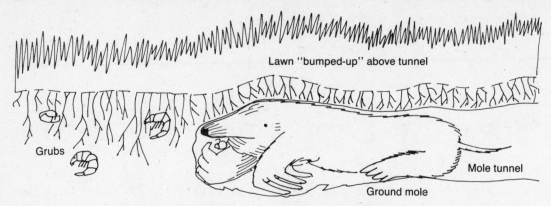

Lawn ''bumped-up'' above tunnel

Grubs

Mole tunnel

Ground mole

Moles in your lawn are a sure sign of insect trouble.

winter. Spraying with a bone-tar-and-soap solution (as above) is my only suggestion.

Moles Make a Mess!

What else can I say. Again, the presence of moles in your lawn is a signal that you also have a big grub problem. Get rid of the grubs, and the furry problem will move along as well. While you are waiting for the grubicide to work, place a wad of human hair and Paradichlorobenzene moth crystals in several of their runs—and watch them run.

Armadillos Aren't a Joke

No sir! This pest is no laughing matter. Armadillos do most of their damage to southern gardens, but they sometimes get overly energetic and dig up the grass.

Bone tar and soap will send them packing as well.

There Really Is a Snake in the Grass

There is nothing I know that will get your attention quicker than a snake slithering one wiggle ahead of your lawn mower. The obvious way to control snake is to speed up the mower. What a mess that will make in your grass catcher!

I find that if you fill your lawn spreader full of a mixture of sharp sand and diatomaceous earth and spread it over your lawn, you will discourage snakes, slugs, and snails. It gets on their bodies and cuts their flesh.

These are the most common troublemakers that lawn tenders run into and best-known methods of control.

11

Step-By-Step Lawn Program
Green Lawns Don't Just Happen—They're Caused!

Almost everyone who has a lawn dreams of it being the greenest on the block! And most of these dreamers also wish that their beautiful lawn would appear with little or no effort and certainly no financial expenditure on their part. My friend, I can guarantee that will never happen. I will, however, guarantee that you can have the greenest grass on the block, at the cost of a lot less time, effort, and money than you would expect—if you will just give Mother Nature a helping hand.

Golf course and park superintendents are grass-growing professionals. They are responsible for keeping the turf areas under their care picture-perfect at all times, even under some rather demanding and unusual conditions (tournaments, rallies, and parades, to name a few). No, you don't have these problems to contend with, but family barbecues and kids and dogs trampling all over the lawn surely qualify as demanding conditions.

The pro depends on proper timing—doing the right thing at the right time. He doesn't overreact, and he certainly never "overapplies." In order to have the lawn

you want, you're going to have to learn how to do that, too.

Sit back, relax, and follow along with me as I take you (by the numbers) through the steps that will guarantee you the greenest scene on the block. You will enjoy every step of the way.

Step 1. Crabgrass and Other Annual Weed Grass Control

The annual weed grasses can be a real pain in the grass! The most common varieties of annual weeds are known as crabgrass, foxtail, goose grass, barnyard grass, annual bluegrass, and sandbur.

To control this problem, apply a pre-emergence crabgrass control as early in the spring as you can walk out onto your lawn. I recommend that you apply pre-emerges with a small hand-held broadcast spreader (like the Ortho whirley spreader), or a chest-type broadcast spreader. I like these spreaders because you can walk through lingering snow patches and wet spots with them. Apply the product at half the recommended

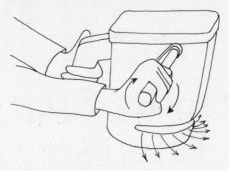

Apply preemerge crabgrass control in early spring.

rate, and then later apply the other half over the same area a week later.

(See chapter 7 for more information on weed control.)

Step 2. Early Lawn Cleanup

Most of you probably think that cleaning up your lawn before the growing season is a meaningless and unnecessary job. Let me set you straight right from the get-go (slang for start). Any turf superintendent worth his chewing tobacco will tell you what he tells his crew: The success or failure of your whole lawn-growing season depends on how well you perform your first lawn cleanup.

Heavy piles of snow should be spread out over the turf area to quicken the thaw. If they are allowed to linger until they melt on their own, they can cause diseases that are both difficult and expensive to control.

Fallen branches and trees should be removed as quickly as possible (before the grass begins to turn green). Plastic, paper, large areas of piled leaves, grass, or other trash must also be removed before the temperature gets to 50 degrees.

Remove accumulated dog waste from the turf and garden beds as soon as possible. This type of manure contains microorganisms that can be harmful to children and adults if left to incubate (they are transmitted by getting on the hands or feet while playing or working in the soil). Never put dog manure in a compost pile or a vegetable garden.

It is also an excellent idea to clean your evergreen and shrub beds out onto the lawn area before you begin your lawn cleanup, so that you won't have to do it while the tender new lawn grasses are just poking their heads aboveground.

Remove the old grass clippings, leaves, and evergreen needles to your compost pile. If you don't have one, start it with your current collection of lawn debris. Add a cup of household ammonia to a gallon of really warm water and pour the mixture over the top of the first batch to speed up the "cooking" (the breaking down of all this material into usable compost).

I suggest that you fill a hand or chest-type broadcaster spreader with ammonium sulfate and apply it over the top of the late patches of snow. This will speed up melting, while providing an early snack for the awakening lawn. In the mid-South and Northwest, apply the ammonium sulfate (at a number-3 spreader setting) mixed with 1 pound of Epsom salts per

Proper clean-up will get your lawn off to the right start.

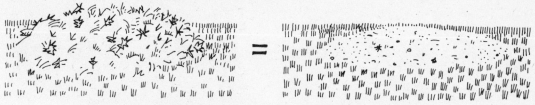

Remove piles of debris or clippings from the lawn before the temperature reaches 50 degrees.

Clean under shrubs first, then clear lawn before grass shoots appear.

Spread snow out evenly. Don't leave mounds of snow on lawn during spring thaw.

2,500 square feet (this will help the roots and color density).

If a salt-type material was used for road-ice control anywhere near your lawn, you should also apply gypsum, at a rate of 50 pounds per 1,500 square feet along the grass by walks, drives, and roadways to neutralize the salt damage. The same goes for lawn areas where dogs spent the winter.

The lawn should receive its first raking treatment each year with a push-or-pull lawn sweeper or a very flexible plastic or bamboo rake—never a heavy metal rake.

(See chapter 3 for more information on preparing your lawn.)

Step 3. A Wash Job and An Eye Opener

In most parts of the country (even the South and far West) your lawns have been asleep (dormant) all winter. Now it's time to wake them up. After you have finished

A quick ammonia and soap bath will perk up your lawn.

the first two steps above, I want you to fill the jar on your hose-end sprayer three-quarters full of household ammonia and one-quarter full of any liquid dish soap and spray this mixture over 2,500 square feet of lawn area.

Don't worry about spraying the trees, shrubs, evergreens, early flowers, or any other crops—they'll love it, too. The soap

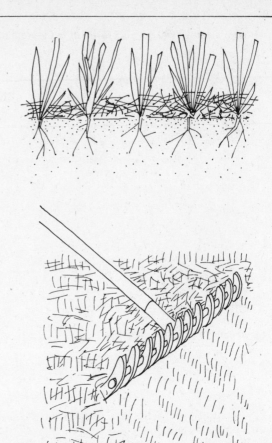

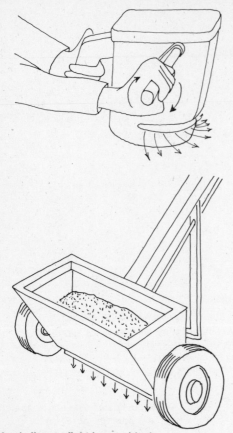

Apply lime to fight lawn acidosis.

Keep your lawn's thatch level low.

cleans and removes airborne pollution and acid rain (it's everywhere) from the leaves. The soap also softens the soil and shells of insects, disrupts the development cycle of diseases, and makes your yard look good. The household ammonia is "predigested" nitrogen which gives the new young shoots an early boost, acting the way a morning cup of coffee does for a human.

(See chapter 4 for more information on feeding your lawn.)

Step 4. Your Lawn Spells Relief—L.I.M.E.

Yes, my gardening friends, plants (like people) can get acid indigestion. Like you, they can get in trouble by overeating rich

foods. It's true that certain types of plants like rich, acid-type foods, but lawn grasses aren't one of them.

I recommend that you apply a good grade of pelletized limestone (like Neutra Nuggets) in the very early spring—before you fertilize the lawn for the first time. Neutra Nuggets are a super type of lime that spreads easier, cleaner and faster — and you won't need as much to do the job. Lime and gypsum can and should be used together, but lime and fertilizer should not be applied together. Wait a week in between applications of lime and fertilizer or apply the fertilizer a week earlier. Nitrogen is lost when the two treatments are applied at the same time.

(See chapter 2 for more information on lawn acidosis.)

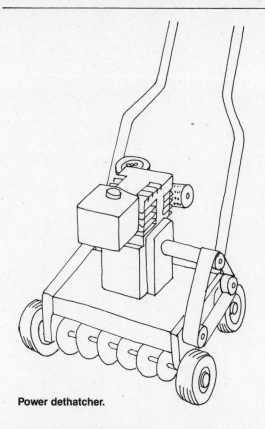

Power dethatcher.

Step 5. Raise the Roof on Lawn Problems—Dethatch!

Thatch is an accumulation of partially decomposed or undecomposed grass clippings, roots, and stems. It is a breeding place for insects, disease, and weed-seed germination.

Thatch is usually the result of several bad lawn care habits. The first bad habit is mowing your lawn without a proper catcher. The next is mowing infrequently, which allows the grass plants to crowd against each other.

Thatch should be removed in early fall. September is the best month to dethatch, since it allows for overseeding and accelerated fall growth. In the North, dethatching in late April or very early May can also provide some relief. You can rent a power rake (which makes for a fast and easy job), purchase a dethatching attach-ment for your lawn mowers (they're available for many models), or remove thatch by hand with a Cavex thatch rake.

Once the thatch is removed, mow the turf very low (just above the new green growth). Make sure that you pick up all of the dry grass clippings. Add these and the thatch to your compost pile.

On July 1 and August 1, spray your lawn with your hose-end jar filled two-thirds full of beer and the balance with household ammonia. Spray this mixture over 2,500 square feet of lawn, which will promote natural decomposition of the thatch and keep what little buildup there is down to acceptable levels.

(See chapter 5 for more information on turf maintenance.)

Step 6. Poking Holes in Lawn Care—Aeration

Aerating your lawn goes hand-in-hand with removing thatch. Foot traffic, improper watering, mowing, and feeding can all cause compacted lawns. Compacted soil will not let roots grow in their search for food, water, or air. Large patches of lawn can die out over a short period of time.

To reduce or prevent turf compaction, spray the turf area every 3 weeks with 1 cup of liquid dish soap per 10 gallons of water from a hose-end sprayer (over 2,500 square feet of lawn). You can also aerate your lawn with a rented power plugger, a turf plugger (that you step on), or a long, hollow pipe and a hammer. I have also

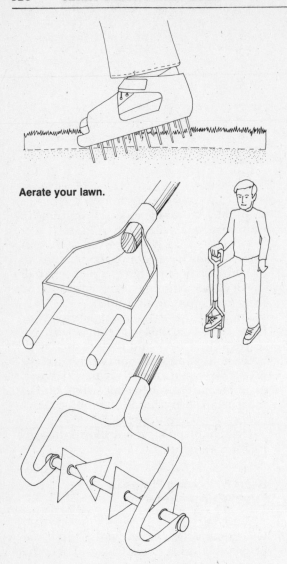

Aerate your lawn.

Overseed in fall or early spring.

used an ax blade, pick point, sharp sticks, and spiked sandals.

(See chapter 5 for more information on aeration.)

Step 7. Introduce a Tall Green Stranger—Overseed

Now that you have prepared the lawn area for the growing season, it's time to add the grow-with-all to green-up the scene. I lightly overseed every fall (with winter grass in the South and with a predominant variety of the current lawn grass in the North) or in the early spring—after I have taken care of the previous six steps. Use good, fresh, clean, high-quality seed that has spent at least a week in your refrigerator (to speed up germination). Do not broadcast more seed than is necessary—follow the instructions.

Now that the seed is down, top-dress the lawn very lightly with a mixture of 50 percent sharp sand or clean topsoil and 50 percent Hyponex Professional Planter Mix. This will ensure that the new seed stays moist. If you must roll the lawn,

Overseed: Seed, top-dress, roll, and spray.

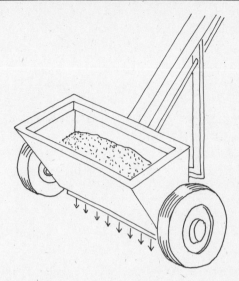

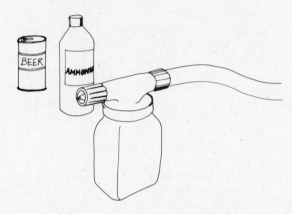

make sure the soil is not wet, and that the roller weighs no more than 30 pounds.

Now we are back to the eye-opener: fill your hose-end jar one-third full of household ammonia (for nitrogen), add 1 cup of liquid soap (a turf shampoo and seed softener), and fill the balance with beer (which keeps a tired lawn happy and also begins to decompose any new thatch buildup). Spray this mixture over 2,500 square feet of lawn.

You should also spray the lawn with 1 quart of beer (per 20 gallons of water over 2,500 square feet) on the Fourth of July—any place in the U.S.A.— if you know what's good for your thatch.

(See chapter 1 for more information on seeds and seeding.)

Step 8. Time for Dinner—Feeding

Here we go! In all of the steps up to now I have not once suggested that you feed your lawn with a regular fertilizer. Right? The reason for this was not out of neglect or memory loss but because the grass was not yet ready to eat. Now it is! But we're probably not going to feed it the way you've fed it in the past.

The secret to a long-lasting green lawn is to get the most out of both the fertilizer and the grass itself. As a rule, most homeowners feed their lawns in the spring and then not again until the following spring. That's a pity (for the lawn).

You see, there is no such thing as a lazy lawn. All lawns really want to grow healthy and green and manufacture oxygen. But if we don't do our part and give them a hand, they won't do their part either.

In the early spring (February in the South and West, March in the North and East), set any one of the broadcast spreaders (push, hand-held, or chest) at 25 percent of the recommended rate. Feed the entire lawn area at this rate. Two weeks later feed it again with the spreader set at 50 percent of the recommended rate.

Water the fertilizer into the lawn with your hose-end sprayer filled, as usual, three-quarters full of household ammonia plus 1 cup of any liquid dish-washing

Hose-end sprayer

Water hose

Liquid fertilizer mixture

soap (with 10 gallons of water over 2,500 square feet).

Always feed lawns before noon, and never at night. For the balance of the growing season, feed your lawn every 3 weeks with your hand-held whirley spreader set on the number-1 setting or with Super K-Gro Rapid Green liquid spray at half the recommended rate.

The results will absolutely amaze you and will make your lawn the envy of the neighborhood.

(See chapter 4 for more information on feeding your lawn.)

Step 9. Liquid Lunch—Liquid Fertilizer vs. Dry Application

If your lawn had its druthers it would take liquid lawn food over dry fertilizer any day of the week. Hold on, you haven't heard the whole story yet! If you want to use the liquid application method properly, you have to feed you lawn every 10 days.

If you follow the schedule in step 8, with dry applications in early spring, liquid feedings throughout the summer, followed with a half application of dry fertilizer in the fall, your lawn will be enviously green.

If you are using a major, reputable liquid lawn service, then you are also on the

right track. However, I suggest that you also apply half-rate applications of dry lawn food in early spring and again in fall.

Another important suggestion: Make sure to follow the service's recommendation of watering the lawn thoroughly the day before they apply the fertilizer and then water in after the application. Never feed a dry lawn with a liquid application and then not water it.

(See chapter 4 for more information on feeding your lawn.)

Step 10. Weed It or Feed It! Weed Control

Thousands upon thousands of you ask me, "Does your lawn have weeds?" You bet it does! Whether a lawn is professionally maintained or cared for by a conscientious homeowner, weeds will find their way into our turf.

Weed control is relatively simple if you approach it seriously and not haphazardly. My first bit of advice is to follow all of the steps preceding this one: Weeds are less apt to rear their ugly heads in a thick, healthy, well-tended lawn.

Next, in general weeds are easiest to kill when they are growing their best, which is during early spring and early fall. The best time of day to kill weeds is between 11:00 A.M. and 3:00 P.M. on a bright, sunny 65- to 70-degree day. It's best to kill weeds as quickly as possible. This means that liquid weed killers are more effective.

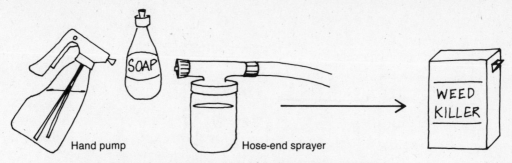

Spray your lawn with soapy water first, then apply weedkiller.

I would like to give you a little reminder about lawncare safety—for you, your lawn, and for the rest of your garden.

First, if you have a few stray weeds in your yard or along a fence, drive, or walkway, don't douse the entire lawn. (Don't use dry liquid weed-and-feed products just because they do two jobs at once or were on sale at the garden shop.) It's not necessary, safe, or economical. Spot-treat weeds with premixed or foam sprays.

Never use a weed killer on a windy day or when rain is forecast within 24 hours, and do not water for 24 hours after applications. Remember, weed killers will kill trees, shrubs, flowers, evergreens, and vegetable gardens if not properly used. Do not be sorry—be smart and safe.

Here are a couple of little tricks that will make the weeds that invaded your lawn wish they had stayed on the other side of the fence:

Before you apply any weed control, liquid or dry, spray the area with my soap-and-water mixture. Use 1 cup of liquid soap per 10 gallons of water (per 2,500 square feet) if the entire area is to be treated. (This includes turf where dry weed-and-feed is to be applied.) Otherwise, spot-spray only the infested areas. The soapy water acts as a wetting agent and opens up the soil, thatch, root cover, and foliage. Pouring it on and around the weeds will ensure a quick and effective kill.

Wait ½ hour after applying the soap solution, then apply the weed control of your choice.

(See chapter 7 for more information on controlling weeds.)

Step 11. Bugs, Bah Humbug—Insect Control

Insects, commonly referred to as bugs, cause home gardeners more aggravation than any other problem they face. It's too bad, because the aggravation is really not necessary.

You'll have to contend with twenty-four principal lawn grass insects. Twelve of the twenty-four are grubs, and the other twelve creep, crawl, fly, and hop across our yards. All twenty-four can be controlled and eradicated if you follow my recommendations and comply with steps 5 and 6 (Dethatch and Aerate) before you begin the battle.

First, spray the affected area with the soap-and-water solution recommended in step 10. Wait ½ hour and then apply your insecticide.

The best time to kill soil insects (grubs) is in April and May or in August and September. The best time to spray is between 7:00 P.M. and 8:00 P.M. I have found that adding a cup full of fresh tobacco-juice water to the insecticide mixture, coupled with the soap prespray, surprises the dickens out of most of the bugs.

The most common lawn insect controls that homeowners can use are diazinon

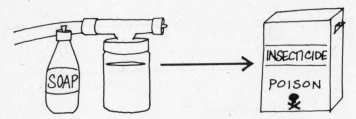

Spray your lawn with soapy water first, then apply insecticide.

and Dursban. If these are applied at the proper time and strength, they will get the job done. Recently, the EPA approved a new soil insect control called Oftanol (Mobay Chemical Company), which is almost as effective as chlordane was. My choices for dealing with aboveground insects are Sevin and methoxychlor—as well as the three I just mentioned. Most current insecticides are effective for only 2 weeks after spraying, but adding soap and tobacco juice seems to prolong the protection.

(See chapter 8 for more information on insect control.)

Step 12. In Sickness and in Health— Disease Control

There are seventeen grass diseases on my Most Unwanted List. And boy, oh boy, if ever one visits your lawn, you can really end up with your hands full and your wallet empty. The diseases are aggressive, and the cures are expensive.

The best defenses against lawn disease are what we call good cultural practices: clean turf, low thatch, good drainage, proper watering, balanced fertilization, noncompaction, and proper mowing. (See chapter 9 for more information on lawn diseases.)

Let's run through the cultural practices briefly:

Cultural Practices

• **Clean Your Turf Area.** Regularly remove any debris, trash, leaves, limbs, or piles of grass clippings left on the grass. (See step 2 above.) Edge beds, walks, drives, and curbs after each cutting to prevent the buildup of excess grass— where lawn diseases can breed. You may want to blow the lawn area clean or sweep it with a lawn sweeper. Finally, wash the turf area every 2 weeks with a mixture of 1 cup liquid soap and 1 cup mouthwash in your hose-end sprayer (per 10 gallons of water over 2,500 square feet).

• **Keep Thatch Buildup Low.** Thatch is an excellent breeding ground for lawn diseases. Never mow your lawn without the grass catcher in place and never use a mulching mower. Empty the bag before you begin to leave a trail of grass and stop and pick up any you do. Remove thatch buildup in early September. (See step 5 above and chapter 5 for more on thatch.)

• **Good Drainage.** Standing water or damp turf is an invitation to lawn diseases. Aerate the soil annually by applying gypsum in late fall or early spring. Build up any low spots. The soap-and-water spray will also help prevent problems from occurring.

• **Water Your Lawn Properly.** Lawn diseases need moisture and heat. Make sure that your lawn gets adequate water, but water it early enough in the day that the lawn goes to bed dry (the earlier in the day the better). On professionally tended turf, we wash the dew off to stop diseases from developing. (See also chapter 6).

• **Feed Your Lawn a Balanced Fertilizer.** If you feed your lawn too much nitrogen, which can happen if you use a great deal of ammonium sulfate or a slow-release source of nitrogen, you'll develop a lush, green, but weak stand of grass that will soon fall prey to lawn disease. You can prevent this problem by using a lawn food containing potassium. That's why I recommend that you use dry lawn food in the spring and fall with regular applications in between. (See step 8 above and chapter 4.)

● **Combat Compaction.** Compacted (packed down) soil can crush the roots and prevent water and food from reaching them. A compacted lawn is an unhealthy lawn, opening the door to developing diseases. To prevent soil compaction, remove plugs of soil by hand or mechanical means and spray every 3 weeks with soapy water. (See step 6 above and chapter 5.)

● **Mow Properly.** Use the sharpest blade possible each time you mow. Mow at the proper height (do not scalp the turf) and at the proper time (in the evening before sundown). Never let the grass grow too tall before mowing, and pick up your clippings. Always wash your mower off with soap and water and rinse it well. Make sure to scrape the grass buildup from under the deck often since it can spread disease. (See also chapter 5 on mowing.)

12

Questions and Answers
Have You Got Problems?

There's no way I could ever fit the answers to all of the questions I am asked on radio, TV, or in my mail into a book. They number in the millions.

But as I write these thoughts on how you should go about this garden chore or that lawn care job, I often wonder what goes through your minds. I can't help but put myself in your shoes (which is how I learned to solve most of your problems) and think of the questions you would ask me if I were right there in the room with you.

I can boil the questions I receive down into those that I'm asked most frequently, by lawn gardeners all over the country. The answers, given in this chapter, should help you solve most of your lawn problems.

Use the answers to these questions as a guide, but also read the chapters that cover your problem completely, to make sure that you understand both the problem and the solution.

FERTILIZING LAWNS

Q *Do the guys with the big trucks that come around to feed your lawn do a better job than I can?*

A The answer is no. They are just doing the job for you, for a price. Both liquid and dry applicators are, as a rule, very professional. The only problem arises if you don't do you share, which is to water properly.

Q *Which is the best type of fertilizer: dry or liquid?*

A They are equally good, especially when used in combination in a well-balanced lawn program. I use dry fertilizer at half the standard rate in early spring, K-Mart's Rapid Green liquid every 3 weeks throughout the summer, and dry at half rate again in the fall and I have a showcase lawn.

Q *If nitrogen is the most important ingredient in fertilizer, why do I need anything else?*

A Because otherwise your grass will die. It's true that nitrogen is the big shooter but you also need the other 10 guys on the team to make your lawn look good.
Nitrogen: Makes lawns green
Phosphorous: Promotes good roots
Potassium: Is a disease fighter
Calcium: Promotes root-hair growth
Magnesium: Is a big part of chlorophyll
Sulfur: Helps seeds form

Boron: Improves the yield
Copper: Makes enzymes work harder
Manganese: Stimulates germination
Molybdenum: Makes nitrogen enzymes work harder
Zinc: Needed for chlorophyll and growth

Q *When you look at the label on a bag, box, or bottle of fertilizer for the nitrogen content, it says "derived from" and then gives two or three different nitrogen names. What does this mean to me?*

A It tells you whether you are getting your money's worth and whether your lawn is getting its nitrogen's worth. The three numbers that appear are referred to as the *grade* or *formula*. I like to refer to it as the odds on your grass living or dying. The more varieties of nigrogen used, the better the product. Each source of nitrogen becomes available at different intervals. The faster it releases, the greater the chances of grass burn (the "hotter" it is). Here is a list of the most common nitrogen sources and their speed release:

Ammonium nitrate	33%	Fast-Fast
Ammonium sulfate	21%	Fast
Urea	45%	Fast
Isobutylidene (IBDU)	31%	Slow
Urea formaldehyde	38%	Slow
Methylene urea	38%	Slow
Sulfur-coated urea	32%	Slow

Q *How do you know how much fertilizer to buy for your lawn?*

A Do some arithmetic. Multiply the length of your property by the width, which gives you the total square footage. Divide that number by 10 and then the first number on the lawn-food bag. For example,

L 200′ × W 100′ = 20,000 sq. ft. ÷ 10 = 20,000, ÷ N(33) = 60.6 lbs.

In this example, I would have to buy 60.6 pounds of the fertilizer to apply 1 pound of nitrogen per 1,000 square feet to my lawn.

Q *My soil-test report says I need to add potash. Where do I get it?*

A From most garden centers. You can ask for muriated potash (potassium chloride). It's hot, so follow the directions carefully. Potassium sulfate is safer but more expensive.

Q *Our golf course superintendent applies sulfur-coated urea to our fairways late in the fall, and they get greener faster than any course in town. Can I spread it on my lawn?*

A You sure can, but don't forget that you must also put down a balanced food (at half rate in the spring because all the sulfur-coated urea provided was nitrogen). Oh, by the way, for a 5,000-square-foot lawn you should only need 10 pounds.

Q *How much per year should it cost for the materials to maintain a 1,000-square-foot lawn?*

A It's funny that you should ask, because I keep such a figure as a comparison from year to year. It's an old habit left over from my days as an estate and golf course gardener. Caring for a Kentucky bluegrass lawn of 20,000 square feet (not counting my labor—that's love) costs $12.78 (retail) per 1,000 square feet. I would think that most of you could have the greenest grass on the block for pretty close to $8.78 per 1,000 square feet. Before you gulp too hard, consider the maintenance budget for an average-to-better-than-average golf course: They figure $12,000 to $14,000 per green. Times 18 holes adds up to between $216,000 and $252,000 per course per year.

Q *I listen to you on the radio on Saturdays and catch you on TV occasionally, and you keep harping on the use of a household-ammonia-and-soap lawn soup. What's it do?*

A It makes my lawn a close personal friend of mine. Here is how it was explained to me. All of the nitrogen sources must turn into a gas before your grass can ingest and digest it. Household ammonia already is a gas, so the plant takes it in through its roots and foliage without waiting. The soap washes off dirt, soil, and wax from the foliage, and surface tension from soil and foliage, to let the gas pass. Try it, your lawn will love it.

Q *When you were at Lue Gardens in Orlando for the Annual Home Garden Show, you told a gentleman to mix 1 cup of clear corn syrup and 1 cup of liquid soap in 20 gallons of water and spray it on his lawn. What was it for?*

A It's an old formula for nematode control. What you may have missed was that I also told him to follow it up with a spray of 2 cups of chewing-tobacco juice, 2 cups of beer, and the balance of ammonia. It makes the nematodes drunk, sick, and blind while turning the grass green.

Q *What's potassium nitrate used for?*

A Bombs, gunpowder, controlling the sex drive of the U.S. Navy, removing stumps, and making grass green. If you plan to use it on the lawn, do it with extreme caution. It's even hotter than the nitrogens.

Q *Is poultry manure good for lawns?*

A Not right out of the henhouse, because it has wild straw and other junk mixed into it. Once it is processed and the nitogen content is determined, it's fine (but water, water, water it in).

Q *I have a bag of mine tailings from an iron ore pit, and it's a real find powder. Can I use it on my lawn to deepen the color?*

A Yes, but test it first on a small patch so that no one can see if you screw up. Mix it 50-50 with sharp sand, try it at 1 pound mixed per 1,000 square feet, which is a 2-pound actual. Oh, by the way, it's hot!

Q *Why do you always wear spikes when you fertilize?*

A That way, the fertilizer gets where it belongs quicker. Another trick is to hook up your hose to a hot-water outlet, adjust it to warm, and water quickly.

This is also a kick in the fertilizer's pants.

Q *When is the best time to apply fertilizer?*
A If it's liquid, from sunup to 11:00 A.M. If it's dry, wait until the dew is gone but before 11:00 A.M. Then water it all in.

Q *What's the best-brand lawn food available on the market today?*
A Whichever one gives you the results you are looking for and fits your budget. I use Super K-Gro from K-mart, the largest national brand by volume. It does what I want it to do when I want it to do it.

GRASS SELECTIONS

Q *What is the toughest grass there is?*
A Artificial! But then you have to clean the carpet and that's more work than real grass. Tall fescue, Rebel, Falcon, Hounddog, Mustang, Olympic, Jaguar, Galway, and Adventure are all tough grasses. Kentucky 31 was the old standby, but it's really too clumpy, and has screwed up an ankle or two.

Q *I just can't seem to get grass seed to sprout on my poor soil, and I have tried them all. Help!*
A This is more of a plea than a question. Try a seed mixture of 40 percent Falcon tall fescue, 20 percent Ruby fine fescue, and 40 percent Derby perennial rye. Place the seed in a cloth bag and soak it overnight; change the water and soak it for 24 hours more. Now drain, dry, broadcast, cover it lightly with topsoil, roll it with a roller, dampen with a quart of household ammonia to 20 gallons of water (with a hose-end jar) to cover 3,500 square feet. Keep it damp and pray. I've put the cart before the horse, but don't forget to test your soil.

Q *What kind of grass seed will grow where it's damp and shady?*
A A rough bluegrass called Sabre. It won't do well where it's hot and dry, even with shade.

Q *What is the best grass for a dog run?*
A The vet says that concrete is best, because you can keep it clean and free of parasites. If you insist on grass, Kentucky 31 tall fescue.

Q *When you buy sod, should you have all one variety, or a mixture of several varieties? I am interested in Kentucky bluegrass.*
A A blend, by all means. My favorite is the one Lofts Seed, Inc.* recommends to sod growers: 50 percent Nassau Kentucky bluegrass combined with any two of the following: Ram I, Barons, Mystic, or Georgetown Kentucky bluegrass. The reason for a blend is that each variety has its own strengths; some grow faster, some take drought better, and so on.

Q *I am in charge of a Little League field. In the past it has looked terrible and played the same. What's the best blend?*

*Lofts Seed, Inc.
11417 Somerset Rd.
Beltsville, Maryland 20705

A Ask Arnold Palmer to help you out. Mix 80 percent Nassau Kentucky bluegrass with 20 percent Palmer perennial ryegrass (named after Arnold, by Lofts). You'll need 4 pounds per 1,000 square feet or 170 pounds per acre.

Q *How can I make my winter lawn in Florida as green as my lawn up north?*
A Overseed in November with a blend of Cowboy, Palmer, and Prelude perennial ryegrass. You'll need 6 pounds per 1,000 square feet.

Q *How do I keep my ditch from washing out?*
A I begin by placing boulders in piles 10 to 12 feet apart to slow up the flow. Next, I try to hold the seed in place until it germinates, by raking crosswise of the ditch. Third, I sow a mix of 50 percent Houndog tall fescue, 20 percent Palmer perennial ryegrass, 20 percent alkali grass and 10 percent Sabre rough bluegrass, at 6 pounds per 1,000 square foot, or 200 pounds per acre.

Q *Is it true that you can speed up the sprouting time of grass seed?*
A Yep! It's called pre-germinating. Place small amounts of grass seed (for spot-seeding) in a closed plastic bag or refrigerator container (covered) with a cup of weak tea (the ordinary kind) per pound of seed. Refrigerate for 24 hours, dry, sow, cover, roll, moisten, and keep it damp. Larger amounts should be soaked in a cloth bag or nylon stocking in water for 24 hours. Then change the water, soak again for 24 hours, and follow the other steps as mentioned above.

Q *What are ornamental grasses used for? And what are they?*
A You *really* want to get more bang for your buck, don't you? These grass species are utilized in plantings for visual effects only and are usually found in more modern building complexes. You can use them around your home to accent shrubs and evergreens in place of flowering material. Sheep fescue, Chinese silvergrass, maiden grass, plume grass, pampas grass, weeping love grass, and fountain grass are a few of those available.

Q *I have a summer home (cabin) near a river, but we don't spend all summer up there. What kind of grass seed will I need to buy to get a halfway-decent-looking lawn when we are there?*
A What I refer to as the Indian River blend is 50 percent Baron Kentucky bluegrass, 20 percent orchard grass, 20 percent Derby perennial rye, 5 percent timothy, and 5 percent Landino clover. To mow it, have a local farmer run his sheep on it; 8 sheep to the acre. Oh, by the way, 4 pounds per 1,000 square feet or 150 pounds per acre should be enough. And seed it on September 1.

Q *Can you buy wildflower mixes for rural properties?*
A Sure you can. My favorite for your neck of the woods can be purchased from Lofts Seed, Inc., Bound Brook, New Jersey 00805. It's called Pinto Wild-

flower Mix and contains bachelor's buttons, lance-leaved coreopsis, baby's breath, baby snapdragon, scarlet flax, Lewis flax, evening primrose, corn poppy, catchfly, black-eyed Susan, calendula, purple coneflower, and oxeye daisy. It's best to sow this in the fall, at 5 pounds per acre. What a beautiful sight this will be all spring, summer, and early fall.

Q *How do you keep birds from eating your grass seed?*
A Test this on a small batch and patch first; it worked for me: Mix 1 ounce of turpentine with 2 ounces of liquid soap, then add to a hose-end jar of 10 gallons of water and spray quick and light.

Q *What's the best all-around variety of Bermuda grass?*
A Tufcote, Midiron, or Vamont all make good-looking lawns. Sod from April to October and plant sprigs from April to August.

Q *Is St. Augustine grass good for shady areas?*
A Sure is and, if properly taken care of, will make a nice lawn. Try Floratam. You can plant year-round in southern Florida and southern California. Plant sprigs from May to August and sod through October 15.

Q *Where do you recommend centipede grass?*
A In someone else's yard. It's not that great-looking a lawn and won't take the pitter-patter of grandchildren's feet or grandma or grandpa's feet, either. If you must have it, though, you can get seed, sod, or sprigs and plant from April through August.

Q *What's the best way to store grass seed?*
A In the refrigerator, in its bag, box, bottle, or can. Keep it dry and cool, but don't freeze it.

Q *What does hot water do to seed?*
A If it's too hot, it makes a dead mess out of it. Warm water softens the shell or husk and speeds up germination.

Q *Zoysia grass lawns are beautiful. Can I grow zoysia in Michigan?*
A You can, but I wouldn't. Zoysia turns a terrible straw-brown with the first frost and is the last grass to green up in the spring. Zoysia is best grown in southeastern Virginia, southeastern North Carolina, most of South Carolina, Georgia, Florida, Alabama, Mississippi, Louisiana, Texas, Oklahoma, southern New Mexico, most of Arizona, southern Nevada, southeastern California, southern Kansas, southern Missouri, southern Illinois, southern Indiana, and western Kentucky. I do not believe in borderline lawning. It's not fair to the grass and a waste of time and money to you.

Q *Should you always mix a nurse grass in with the grass seed variety you are interested in?*
A Not if you want a good lawn. Nurse grasses actually set good varieties back, because they eat up all the food

and take up all the space that the permanent variety needs for growing. Pregerminate, cover the seed, roll, and keep damp. Your new grass should do well.

Q *Is it a good idea to cover new seed with straw?*
A I try to avoid it if I can, because the loose seed it contains blows around. Du Pont Company now produces a lawn-and-garden blanket made of a strong, lightweight polyester that lets water and light through but holds in the heat and slows down evaporation. I love it.

Q *Should you mix clover into a lawn?*
A Not if you want a good-looking lawn. The white flowers look as bad as yellow dandelions. Clover is also dangerous in areas where people walk and play. It is slippery and can cause spills.

Q *What is really meant by dormant seeding?*
A Dormant seeding is the broadcast of grass seed onto frozen or snow-covered earth. We use this method if we have large areas to cover or if we were too late in the fall. It works, but it's not a good practice because you sometimes lose a great deal of seed to the spring runoff.

Q *How long does turf dye last?*
A It depends on the amount of rainfall, irrigation, or snow. To tell the truth, I think it looks like heck. Where you can, overseed with winter rye. In the North, leave it be. The exception to this advice

is where disease, dogs, gasoline, or other problems have caused injury. Try to match the natural color.

Q *Everything that I read, your books included, tells me not to start a lawn in June or July. We just moved into a new home on June 10 and I can't stand the dirt. What can I do?*
A Plant a lawn—that's what I said! But, and this is a big but ... don't buy your main choice. Try to level the grade and remove any objects that will tear up the mower. Scuff up the soil, pregerminate rye (common) grass spread, cover lightly, water, and mow when it grows. On September 30, till your lawn under, green grass and all, and start a new lawn properly.

Q *What's the best kind of grass to grow on a really steep embankment?*
A None. Oh sure, we can grow grass on darn near any soil terrain if we can hold it, but how do you safely mow it? Why not try crown vetch or some other ground cover?

Q *We have an acid-soil problem all of the time because of our evergreens. What kind of grass will take this?*
A Canada bluegrass (Revbens), perennial rye, colonial bent grass, creeping bentgrass, hard fescue, chewings fescue, red fescue, or Bermuda grass will all do well.

Q *What kind of grass can we grow to keep our beach from blowing away?*
A There are several. Your feed or seed

store will have to order them from Lofts Seeds for you. Here are a few:

Beach grass
Blowout grass
Indian ricegrass
Needle and thread
Prairie Sandried
Sand bluestem
Sandhill Muhly
Sand lovegrass
Switch grass

SOIL

Q *How do you lower the soil pH?*
A This problem is called alkaline soil. It is corrected with sulfur at 25 pounds per 1,000 square feet. Ammonium sulfate can also help.

Q *How do you correct the damage done by salts?*
A Spread gypsum at 50 pounds per 1,000 square feet.

Q *Water just runs off the garden, out from under our new sod, and won't go into the dirt. What can be done?*
A Spray with a wetting agent (liquid dish soap), at 1 ounce to the gallon, at 1-week intervals for three applications—that should do the trick.

Q *Is the stuff they pick up from the curbs when the street sweeper comes by good backfill?*
A Not on your grass, garden, hands, or feet. That "stuff," a you refer to it, contains many, many parasites that can in-

jure your, your children's, and your pets' health. Don't you dare!

Q *I can get free sludge from the sewage-process plant, is it safe to use?*
A If it's processed, it's great. If it's raw, it's dangerous. Call your local board of health and your county extension agent before you collect a large quantity.

Q *I think I got took. There was a man in our neighborhood selling black topsoil by the bushel. His price included spreading it. I bought it. Now I have dead spots on my lawn and more weeds than I ever believed there were in the world. Was it the soil and what can I do?*
A You hit the nail on the head. Your problems came from the so-called black dirt, which was probably taken from the edge of a river. If it is still early summer, kill the weeds. In the fall, power-rake and reseed and don't ever, ever let anyone put anything on your lawn again.

Q *Can I mix my lime and fertilizer together in the spreader?*
A No. Lime would neutralize the effect of the nitrogen. Lime should not be applied within 2 weeks on either side of lawn feeding.

Q *How much sand must I add to my clay soil to break it up?*
A The bottom of Lake Michigan. Sand just makes matters worse—you end up with brick clay. You should add leaves, grass, sawdust, manure, shredded wood, hair, garbage, and a pinch of

sharp sand plus peat moss—mix well.

Q *Is mushroom compost good to work into the soil for a new sod lawn?*

A Wow! I wish you had not asked me that question. Mushroom compost is, as a rule, hot stuff when it's fresh, but after a year it's great. I still don't trust it!

Q *You will probably think I am nuts, but here goes. I can get large quantities of animal manure from our local zoo. You name it and we got it. Have you ever had tomatoes grown in elephant or giraffe manure?*

A I have probably seen them all used, safely and successfully, but I suggest that you talk to the veterinarian at the zoo (concerning parasites), as well as to the grounds superintendent to see what his experience has been with the day's latrine collection.

Q *I have approximately 6 to 8 feet of fill to bring in to raise the grade of my lawn. They are tearing up a nearby interstate and replacing the concrete. The truck driver will dump this broken-up concrete at my place, and the dozer operator said he would grade it for me and then they'll cover it up with about 3 feet of darn nice topsoil. Will I have any problems?*

A You will have several . . . problems, that is. First will be washdown. When it rains or you water the soil well, it will work down through the millions of cracks in the concrete chunks. Second, most big trees will be stunted. Third, if you decide to add on to the house or build a garage, you can't get footings

down. Advertise in your local want ads for clean fill dirt.

Q *We bought a piece of property that used to have an oil well (which went dry) on it. Nothing will grow there now. What can we do?*

A Contact the Department of Natural Resources (or similar organization) in your neighborhood. It is the responsibility of a drilling company to put back the topsoil when they leave a location. Believe me, you need new topsoil—and lots of it.

Q *Do I have to take out stumps that will be at least a foot under my finished grade?*

A Not if you don't mind putting up with millions of toadstools and other fungus diseases (such as fairy ring) in your turf that thrive on a good organic diet. You would be amazed at what you can get done if you ask. I asked a dozer operator how much he charged to pull stumps and he did it for a few bucks. Ask!

Q *I can have all of the renderings from a brewery. Is this organic? And can I use this in the soil for my new sod lawn?*

A By all means, but you must really work it into the soil. I mean down to a good foot deep. You must also add other organics, and then do a pH test plus an N-P-K test to make sure it's not too hot a spot for the sod roots.

Q *Can or should fertilizer be worked into raw soil?*

A I have always stuck to an organic fertilizer like milorganite, when I am adding to raw soil; it's a processed sludge, unlike the one we talked about (above). There is now, however, a warning on the bag not to use milorganite in a vegetable garden, so if part of the lawn area is to be used as a garden, do not use the milorganite in that area.

Q *How effective is a soil sterilizer?*
A In most cases that I have seen, totally. Vapam, used according to directions in the very early spring, kills about everything I have seen and gets everything off to a good start.

Q *How often should you take a soil test? And do they work?*
A As often as your own health checkup— once a year. A professional soil test will cost twelve to fifteen dollars. You can do it yourself for one dollar with the home soil-test kit—and they really do work.

BUILDING NEW LAWNS

Q *Give me your opinion as to whether it is best to start a new lawn from seed or sod?*
A You must consider several factors. The first and most important is your budget. If money is no object, by all means sod should be your choice. If you must stay within a budget or you have the patience to wait, seeding will be just as rewarding. Just remember that even the sod you lay out started from seed. The difference is that someone else did the work. The soil and grading must all

be done the same for sod, seed, sprigging, or plugging.

Q *When is the best time for sprigging a lawn with Bermuda?*
A Late winter or very early spring, when the plants are dormant. One square yard of Bermuda sod should produce 3,000 sprigs. Plant on 1-foot centers and leave just a small part of each sprig above the ground.

Q *Which grasses can be planted by plugs?*
A Bermuda, centipede, St. Augustine, carpet grass, and zoysia. Plugs should be 3 inches in diameter and planted 1 inch apart.

Q *When is the best time to start a new lawn?*
A From August 15 to September 20, and never after October 1. The second best time is between April 15 and May 15 and never in June or July.

Q *What are the absolutely necessary steps in rebuilding a good, long-lasting lawn?*
A You underlined *absolutely* in your letter, so I did the same thing, because you must *absolutely* do it this way:
1. Test your soil or send it away.
2. Remove all rocks, glass, wood, or metal. If a piece is partially buried, dig it out.
3. Check the want ads for someone to plow and disc your new turf area.
4. Level it to shed water away from the house.
5. Respond to the results of the soil test and add the needed nutrients.
6. Plant.

Q *Are do-it-yourself soil-test kits reliable?*

A You bet your grass they're reliable. If they aren't, that's what you lose—your grass. The professional tests are more extensive and should be used at least every 2 years. But as a check, you can use the same one I do: Luster Leaf Soil Test Kit, from Luster Leaf Products, Box 1067, Crystal Lake, Illinois 60014. With this kit I can test for pH, nitrogen, phosphate, and potash. For $12.95 you can get the tube, syringe, filter paper, measuring scoop, and enough solution for twelve tests. This is no toy, it works.

Q *Should you add lime before you seed?*

A If a soil test indicates it, yes. If you don't test and you live east of the Mississippi, no. West of the Mississippi, use lime at 50 pounds per 1,000 square feet. If you can get Nutra Nuggets or Pelletized Lime, you will only need 25 pounds per 1,000 square feet.

Q *Should you use fertilizer before you seed or sod or wait until after?*

A Newly-built-on soil will require fertilizer added to the soil at a rate of 25 pounds of 4-12-4, 5-10-5, or 6-10-4 per 1,000 square feet. You must work both lime and the fertilizer into the top 8 to 10 inches of soil.

Q *There seems to be a best time for everything, how about seeding?*

A Why should grass seed be any exception? Seeding is best done after 6:00 P.M., unless you're drilling the seed in. Between your watering the seed in and the dew, cool evening, and darkness the seed will have a chance to get comfortable.

Q *How do you know how much seed you will need to buy for good thick grass?*

A The smaller the seed, the less you will need. The larger the seed, the more you'll need.

	Seed per 1,000 Square Feet (in pounds)	Seeds per Pound (approximately)
Bahia grass	5	175,000–250,000
Bent grasses	1	8 million
Bermuda grass	2	2 million
Bluegrasses, Kentucky	1½	2 million
Carpet grass	3½	1 million
Centipede grass	2	800,000
Fescue, Fine	4	500,000
Fescue, Tall	6	250,000
Ryegrasses	6	200,000
Zoysia grass	2	1 million

Just remember that if every seed germinated, you would have that many plants!

Q *What should your spreader setting be for grass seed, or should you spread it by hand?*

A Again, I must answer by saying that it depends on the size of the seed. You can tell from the number of seeds per pound about how thick the seed should be. If you had the patience to plant seed by hand and could place each seed ½ inch apart, you would have a whopper of a lawn. When broadcasting seed, divide the quantity in half and cover the area with seed twice, in crosswise patterns.

Q *Is hydroseeding practical?*
A Hydroseeding is used to seed large areas and steep slopes. In hydroseeding the seed is mixed with a fiber mulch, mixed with water, and blown on to the earth. As a rule these companies do not do home lawns.

Q *When should you begin to fertilize a newly seeded lawn?*
A I do it after the seed is planted. I mix 1 cup of liquid soap with 1 quart of household ammonia in my hose-end sprayer and apply with 20 gallons of water to 3,000 square feet. My first dry-fertilizer application is after the third mowing.

Q *What kind of mulch should you use to cover the new seed?*
A Straw is what you see used the most. I don't like it because it blows around the neighborhood and some wild grasses show up. Redwood mulch and a mixture of peat moss and light topsoil should work well. Burlap is an excellent seed cover and can be used for other jobs later.

Q *When do you mow the new grass?*
A Before it looks like it needs it. Don't let it fall over. Cut it in the evening and water it early the next morning.

Q *When should new sod be mowed?*
A If you are watering it as you should, it will grow just as though it were still in the sod field—and should be cut 7 days after it was put down.

Q *How do you keep sod on banks?*

A I cut the long, straight piece out of old hangers, bend them in half like a hair pin, and pin the sod down. I can mow without removing them. Later on, when the roots are established, I remove them.

Q *When do you feed new sod?*
A Two weeks after it has been laid I feed it with Super K-Gro Rapid Green liquid lawn food—and every 2 weeks after that.

Q *How long do you mow a new lawn in the fall?*
A Until it stops growing.

Q *Should you spray a weed killer on the weeds that grow in newly seeded lawns?*
A No. Not until the next proper cycle. Fall lawn: kill the weeds in the spring. Spring lawn: kill the weeds in the fall. Same goes for sod.

Q *Should you roll a newly sodded lawn?*
A By all means, but not with more than 9 gallons of water for ballast in the roller (9 gallons of water is 72 pounds of weight). You only roll it to make sure that the roots come in contact with the soil.

Q *Should you feed a fall-planted lawn with fertilizer in the late fall?*
A Yes, if you started a new lawn in the August-September range, you should feed it in early November at half the rate recommended on your lawn fertilizer bag.

Q *Should you overseed or dormant-seed a fall-planted lawn?*

A You will know before the snow flies whether you have some bare spots, so you will know where to overseed. If the new stand is attractive, I don't believe its necessary to dormant-seed.

Q *Why do you recommend a late-late application of milorganite sludge fertilizer on new lawns?*

A When I worked on a golf course, the superintendents always applied this type of fertilizer to the greens to protect them from the fungus diseases that develop in the early spring and late winter. I find the same to be true.

Q *Does a fall application of bonemeal help grass?*

A Yes, but as a rule it is too light to spread and smells bad. I mix it with Epsom salts. Use 75 percent bonemeal and 25 percent regular Epsom salts.

Q *Should you spray an insect spray on a new lawn in fall?*

A I have a question for you—what for? If you have bugs, yes. If not, no. Don't use insecticides unnecessarily.

REBUILDING OLD LAWNS

Q *Should all yards be rebuilt every year?*

A *Rebuilt* is the wrong word. How about *revitalized* annually? It depends on how good and conscientious a yardkeeper you were. As a rule, you should give your lawn a face-lift every second fall.

Q *Should you remove thatch every year?*

A If the buildup exceeds ¼ inch, you will

have to. If you are spraying in May with the half-beer/half-ammonia mix, you are feeding your lawn dry lawn food at half the recommended rate in the spring and again in the fall, if you are feeding your lawn with a liquid lawn food every 3 weeks all season, and if you spray the lawn with a quart of beer mixed with 20 gallons of water on the Fourth of July, you probably won't have to worry about thatch for 3 to 4 years. If not, you'll have to dethatch every year.

Q *How low should you go with the mower before you begin to rebuild?*

A The University of New Hampshire says to cut to ¾ inch or lower, removing all clippings and other debris.

Q *When is the best time and what is the best way to remove thatch?*

A Fall is the best time, and a power rake is the fastest and most effective method. Hand rakes are the very best, but you wouldn't live through the job. Mower attachments work well on some mowers.

Q *I used a power rake and still had thatch when I was done. What did I do wrong?*

A You weren't finished. Power-rake the area in two directions—as often as needed to get up all the thatch. Thoroughness is the most important factor, because the new seed has to come in contact with the soil beneath.

Q *After I dethatched, the grass was long again. Should I mow it low again?*

A You bet, and make sure you remove those clippings.

Q *Do you top-dress first and seed second, or vice versa?*

A Reseed first with a blend or mix of several different strains of the same variety for a tougher, more attractive lawn. Use a little hand-held Ortho whirley spreader set on "Seed." Now use a light half-soil/half-seed mix to cover the seed.

Q *Do you roll a reseeded lawn just like a newly seed lawn?*

A Heck yes, the seed you put down is new, isn't it. Don't make the roller too heavy.

Q *Should you spread fertilizer on an over-seeded lawn?*

A I mix half lawn food and half Epsom salts, set my little spreader on a number-2 setting, and go to it.

Q *What is verticutting?*

A It is really called vertical thinning and is done with a machine of the same name. You can rent them. Vertical thinning is done when the thatch is over an inch thick. This machine cuts slits of turf out and encourages thicker grass.

Q *If you had an insect problem before you started rebuilding a lawn, when do you tackle it?*

A As soon as you finish the other jobs. The best investment you can make is to buy a pair of lawn spike sandals. These heavy-duty plastic soles have 2-inch steel spikes through them and strap on over your shoes. They poke dozens of holes in the soil as you walk to let the insect-control chemicals down to where the bugs hide.

Q *What's the best soil-insect control?*

A Soap and water and either diazinon liquid or Dursban liquid. Spray the area with 1 cup of liquid soap to 10 gallons of water over 1,500 square feet. Wait a ½ hour and then apply the diazinon or Dursban.

Q *How often do you feed the renovated lawn in the fall?*

A I already fed it with Epsom salts and fertilizer. Two weeks later I feed it with K-Mart's Rapid Green and then in November, I feed it with milorganite or other processed-sluge fertilizer.

Q *When should you apply lime?*

A When a soil test indicates the lawn needs it.

Q *My lawn was bothered by a disease called fusarium blight. That's why I renovated. What do I do to prevent a reoccurrence?*

A All of the steps we have talked about, but with a couple of differences. Dissolve a bar of old-fashioned Fels Naptha soap in a pan of boiling water (instead of the standard liquid dish soap) and in May spray the area with Bayleton and in June with Benomyl. Feed and water well all summer.

Q *What do I do with all the weeds I have this fall?*

A Since you have just renovated, *nothing*—until early next spring.

Q *When can I overseed with winter grass on my rejuvenated Bermuda lawn?*

A From September 15 to November 30—with a mixture of turf-type perennial ryegrasses, such as Cowboy, Prelude, and Palmer.

Q *Should I plug my lawn area as well as spike and dethatch it?*

A No. Plugging is best done in midspring where the grass is really growing and developing roots. I bought a two-hole step plugger from the Brookstone catalog, where I also get my spike sandals and whirley spreader (with a hopper). Send for their catalog, and ask for the one with all the garden stuff. Write: Brookstone, Peterborough, New Hampshire 03458.

Q *Is it true that you can spray grass with cow-manure/water in the fall and not have to feed it again until next fall?*

A I wish I could say it was true, but no, it's not quite true. You've been reading the ground-maintenance magazines. They were talking about Bov-a-Mura, which is a specially processed cow manure. When sprayed on turf (home lawns) at 2 gallons per acre in spring and fall, it cuts down thatch, improves water penetration and rooting, makes the turf less susceptible to diseases, and deepens the color. P.S. It does not have a bad smell. P.B.I. Gordon Company, manufacturers of Acme Lawn and Garden Chemicals, sells the product to golf courses, ballparks, and parks. They now make it for the consumer.

Q *If your old lawn was pale and yellow, should you use iron in the fall?*

A Nope! Let's see how the new fall growth turns out first. If you follow my recommendations for regular care, you won't have an anemic lawn.

Q *Should you mulch a newly renovated lawn?*

A I know fellows who do, but none of them are award winners. It makes a mess to clean up.

MOWING

Q *I do everything you suggest, exactly as you suggest, when you suggest I do it, and my grass is the greenest on the block until the morning after I mow. Now what do you suggest?*

A Sharpen your blade. It's that simple, folks. If your blade is dull or even close to dull, you shatter the head of the grass. If you are feeding the professional way, the ragged edge turns white. I have three blades for my machines, and one is always razor-sharp. (I slit pieces of rubber hose to protect the sharp edges.)

Q *When is the best time to mow grass?*

A The height depends on your preference. I run my bluegrass at 2½ inches. It looks its best the second day after I cut it and must be cut again on the fourth. The best time of day to cut grass is after 7:00 P.M.

Q *How often can you mow grass without interfering with its performance?*

A It depends on the type of grass and on how much stress and strain your lawn has suffered. I don't like to see grass cut more often than every other day, but I have—for show purposes—mowed every day for 3 weeks with no negative results.

Q *I love the bluegrasses, but I also like a low tight-looking turf, and I can't find a bluegrass that mows low. Is there one?*

A I don't know how low you want to go, but here are a few good improved varieties of Kentucky bluegrass that are suitable for close mowing:

Adelphi
Aquilla
Baron
Bonnieblue
Continental
Fylking
Galaxy
Glade
Majestic
Nugget
Parade
Pennstar
Ram I
Touchdown

Q *I was told you should not pick up your grass clippings, so I bought a mulching mower. Now they say you must pick them up. Who is right?*

A The guys who dreamed up the mulching mower, I believe, did it for a selfish reason: to avoid having to develop a safe mower—and that's a shame. Pick it up.

Q *If you had your choice of types of mowers—reel or rotary—which would you pick as the best?*

A I won't even hesitate. A reel mower is my hands-down favorite. Here is a quote from the Mallinckrodt Company of Saint Louis, Missouri: "It has been found that a good well-maintained reel-type mower cuts more cleanly than the best well-maintained rotary mowers, and therefore bruise and damage turf less severely." I concur.

Q *Why are reel mowers more expensive than rotary?*

A There are fewer made, the engines are more powerful, and the blades more expensive. They are the top of the line.

Q *How do you sharpen a reel mower?*

A Carefully. Take it into the mower shop to have the job done right. Always clean a reel up after each use to keep it like new. Oil and scrape the shoe.

Q *I ruin my rotary mower every time I use it up at the lake on my meadow lawn. I have even bought used ones—they die, too. What do you suggest?*

A A high-wheel rotary mower! These machines are designed to cut dense or rough growths of grasses or weeds. If you have several neighbors up there, why not go in together on a mower?

Q *Is an electric starter better than a pull starter?*

A I have had less problems with the pull start, unless your health won't permit it.

Q *Okay, Mr. Answer Man, what's going on with the mower people? Why are we back to the two-cycle engine?*

A They need less service, the machines don't break down as much, and they cut on a side angle without oil spilling to one side. The pros love it.

Q *Will gum-out hurt mower engines?*

A I haven't found it to be a problem, but I use it sparingly.

Q *Can you use ether to start a mower engine in the spring?*

A Don't be dumb! I'm sorry, I didn't mean to lose my temper, but your wife was right to tell you to ask me first. That stuff is dangerous to have around, let alone use it in a mower or an auto.

Q *Why do mowers seem to run so rough shortly after they are serviced?*

A In most cases the air filter is clogged. It takes very little time to remove the sponge filter after you mow and wash it out with warm soap and water. Plugged air intake causes most of the rough running.

Q *Why do you get so much drag on a rotary mower?*

A If the underdeck is mottled with gobs of grass crud (buildup of fresh, soft, damp grass), hose it out after each mowing.

Q *Why won't the grass blow into the bag?*

A Grass crud (as above) is also the culprit here.

Q *How do the ballparks on TV get such beautiful patterns when they mow?*

A They use reel mowers and cross-mow. I think a well-defined mowing pattern makes the difference between a good-looking lawn and a perfect one.

Q *I am a new landscaper, and I was told that I need more than one type of mower. Is it true?*

A I am afraid so. Here are the most popular grasses and the mowers you should use:

Bahia grass	Rotary
Bent grass	Reel
Bermuda grass, common	Reel or rotary
Bermuda grass, hybrids	Reel
Carpet grass	Rotary
Centipede grass	Reel or rotary
Fescue	Reel or rotary
Field grasses	High-wheel or flail
Kentucky bluegrass	Reel or rotary
Rye	Reel or rotary
St. Augustine grass	Rotary
Zoysia grass	Reel

Q *Is it true that the bigger the riding mower the better?*

A Sounds like an ad for riding mowers, but it's the truth. Make sure the tires are big and soft, that the throttle kills if you fall off, and that everything that covers the blade is made out of steel.

INSECT CONTROL

Q *How effective are most of today's soil-insect controls?*

A Not very. At least not for very long. However, there are one or two that have a longer soil life. Most soil-insect controls last 2 weeks.

Q *How long after you apply a soil chemical can you safely play on the lawn or let your pet run on it?*

A If liquid is used, when it is dry; if granular soil-insect control is used, waiting a full day or two is better.

Q *When is the best time to apply insect controls?*

A If the insect eats the foliage, I suggest after 7:00 P.M. in the evening. If its grubs are the problem then in the morning, around 10:00 A.M.

Q *How can you be sure the insect control will work?*

A If the insect lives above the ground, spray with soap and water, wait ½ hour, and then spray. If the bug lives in the soil, spike-spray with soap and water, then apply the insecticide.

Q *How can you speed up dry insect control?*

A I always spike, apply, and then water it in with soap and water.

Q *What does soap and tobacco juice do to bugs?*

A Makes them sick as hell. The soap causes them to dehydrate, while the tobacco acts as a contact killer. I use 1 cup of each mixed with my liquid insect controls.

Q *What are the safest soil insecticides?*

A I would say diazinon and Dursban are the two most popular, are easily available, and are safe when used as directed.

DISEASE CONTROL

Q *It seems the harder I work at keeping my lawn healthy, the more problems seem to pop up in the form of leaf spot, powdery mildew, and so forth. What am I doing wrong?*

A Worrying too much. All of you should memorize these basic steps:
Control thatch, spike often, wash with soap and water at least twice a week, feed on a regular basis, mow when necessary, pick up clippings, water early in the morning, keep your equipment clean, and do not let a lot of strange feet tread on front lawns.

Q *When should you apply lawn-disease chemicals?*

A I spray after 7:00 P.M., but first I spike, spray with soap and water, and then apply the chemical.

Q *Is there one chemical that you can use to prevent lawn diseases?*

A I wish I could say yes, but I can't. Lawn diseases are just like people diseases— no one antibiotic cures all our ills. In lawn cases we have twenty-four different lawn medicines to help save our lawns.

Q *Is it true that you can't cure fusarium blight?*

A No, it's not true. Expensive, but not

true. This fall I want you to remove the thatch, spike, rough up the soil, seed with a mixture of bluegrass and 15 percent Derby perennial rye, cover, roll, water, and feed with milorganite. In the spring, feed normally and spray with Bayleton in May, continue to feed, and in late June spray with benomyl.

Q *Is there a preventive fungicide?*
A Not one you can buy! But here is what Sid True Heart taught me to do when I was a kid: Cut up a bar of Fels Naptha soap and dissolve it in a gallon of boiling water. Let it set and cool. Once a month take a cup of this soapy water and a cup of mouth wash, shake them together, and dissolve the mixture in water until it will go through a hose-end sprayer. Spray with 10 gallons of water for 1,500 square feet of lawn.

Q *Do the dry lawn-disease products work?*
A Many of the major lawn-food manufacturing companies make these products, and yes, they do a great deal of good. They are expensive, so don't waste them. If you have a problem, use them; if not, save your money.

Q *Does plugging the turf help control lawn diseases?*
A Any method of aerating the soil helps. Always wear some type of spikes when on the lawn.

WATERING

Q *I let the water run for an hour in one spot on my lawn. When I dig down, the dirt is hardly wet at all. Why?*
A Water has to fight two things before it can even get to the soil. Water must first get all of the grass wet. Then the extra water begins to drip down into the thatch layer underneath. If this thatch buildup is too thick or just too dry, it will shed water, like the roof it is named after. You have got to get rid of the thatch!

Q *I removed the thatch from my lawn the hard way (by hand) with a lawn groom rake, but I still have trouble with my grass drying out too quickly. What can I do?*
A Simply spike the turf area with turf spike sandals, or even golf shoes. Next, fill your hose-end jar with water and add a cup of liquid soap per each 10 gallons. In your case the lawn has a surface-tension condition caused by wind, heat, and static electricity. The soap will remove this.

Q *The experts all refer to well-drained lawns and then you say I need 4 inches of penetration, but don't make it soggy. How can I have one but not the other?*
A Once water begins to drip off the foliage and drop onto the soil, it fills the soil pores, which are connected tubes of different sizes and shapes. Water also moves down through cracks, worm holes, and decayed root holes. When

enough water comes from your sprinkler to fill all of these openings in a well-drained yard, the soil is said to be saturated. If the grade and texture of the soil are as we have discussed in the soil section, then the saturation will be temporary. If water lays close to the surface or in pools on the surface, your lawn will have a problem breathing and eating. Plug the lawn with a two-hole step plugger, purchased from the garden shop. Cut trenches and lay plastic drainpipe from wet spots.

Q *How deep do you really have to keep moisture for a good lawn?*
A As a general rule, 5 to 6 inches is considered to be excellent for the comfort of most lawns. It may surprise you to know that some roots will go down to 5 feet. Shallow-rooted grass dies easily and is the result of light watering with a cheap sprinkler.

Q *How often should you water your lawn?*
A If you have prepared the turf area properly, removed thatch, spiked, removed surface tension with a surfactant (liquid dish soap), and watered to a depth of 4 to 5 inches, I would say water every 3 days—until 1 inch of water collects in a jar three-quarters of the way out into the sprinkler pattern.

Q *I would like to have an in-ground sprinkler system, but I can't afford to have it installed. Can I get a good one that I can put in myself?*
A No doubt about it. Nelson* or Rainbird** both have systems that you can install yourself. The nice part about this kind of a system is that you can install one station (section) at a time—as you can afford it. Second, both of these companies distribute through thousands of outlets nationally.

Q *What's the most efficient lawn sprinkler?*
A For the homeowner it's just got to be the impulse-type sprinkler, because it gives a uniform distribution of water over a rather large (they're adjustable) pattern. The nozzle capacity of these types are from 3 to 9 gallons of water a minute, depending on the size. If you can possibly afford it, buy a brass head and a heavy base.

Q *I have heard that oscillating sprinklers are no good. Is this true? And if it is, why do big stores sell them?*
A It is true. They are not very efficient and do little to help your lawn—or your water bill. They are sold because the average homeowner does not recognize the value of a good sprinkler.

Q *I see grounds keepers watering the greens of the golf course with a hose and nozzle. Is this the best way to water?*
A If you have a fireplug and hose at your disposal, it is. They are cooling the greens, not watering. If you were to

*L.R. Nelson Co.
7719 N. Pioneer
Peoria, Illinois 61615

**Rainbird National
Sales
145 N. Grand
Glendore, California
91740

hand-water with a ⅝-inch hose at typical city water pressure it would take 2½ hours and 600 gallons to get down an inch of water. You don't seem the type.

Q *How do you check the rate of discharge of your sprinkler?*
A The specific water pressure of your town, well, or pump, plus the length and size of your hose, as well as the kind of sprinkler, will determine the amount of water being discharged. Reduced rates can be caused by a longer hose, a small diameter, or reduced water pressure. To check the rate of discharge, place three straight-sided soup cans in a line out from your sprinkler. The nearest can't be closer than 8 feet and the farthest one should be within the spill zone. Let the water run for 1 hour. Now you can figure how long it takes to get down 1 inch.

Q *What's the best diameter of hose to use for lawnwork?*
A A big one! I use a ¾-inch heavy-duty rubber hose because I get lots of water fast, it doesn't kink, and it's a snap to repair. The small-diameter, cheap plastic hoses are a waste of time and money.

Q *I always end up with hot spots, even after I water. How do you correct this?*
A Move the sprinkler to the edge of the area you just watered. This gives you an overlap. If you follow this pattern throughout the entire lawn, you will eliminate hot spots.

Q *When is the best time to water a lawn?*
A Plant pathologists advise against evening watering unless you are applying insect or disease controls. From sunup to 11:00 A.M. is best—never water after 2:00 P.M.

Q *What happens to the water rule when the city says no watering until after 10:00 P.M. and not after 6:00 A.M.?*
A Comply! And either set your alarm for sunup or purchase a battery-operated computer that screws onto your faucet and automatically turns on the water—they cost under fifty dollars.

Q *You can inject fertilizer and chemicals into a sprinkler system safely, but if you do it with a garden hose you contaminate the hose. What's the alternative?*
A Use a Syfonex Brass Hozon Siphon Mixer, but instead of hooking it up at the top, get a 1-foot section of hose and screw it into the sprinkler, then connect it to the siphon mixer, then connect your hose. Now place the mixed material in a bucket set next to the sprinkler and siphon. Only the 1-foot piece of hose is contaminated.

Q *Is irrigating good or bad?*
A It's terrible! It carries weed seed, disease, and bugs. It also weighs 8 pounds per gallon. But then, in the Southwest you have no choice. I spike my lawn the morning after and spray it with a cup of soap water (Fels Naptha) plus 1 cup of mouth wash and 2 cups of chewing-tobacco juice per 10 gallons of water. I make any disease or bug think twice.

Q *Can you overwater, but not drown the lawn exactly?*

A What you are asking is whether I can do all the other lawn care jobs right but overwater. The answer is yes. The grass will turn yellow because you washed all the food away before the grass can eat it.

WEED CONTROL

Q *Why can't all weeds be killed with one kind of weed killer?*

A Because of the different types of roots. We do have a weed killer available that will destroy just about any weed around, but it will also destroy grass if it touches it. The chemical is glyphosate (also known as Roundup, Shootout, and Kleenup).

Q *How do you most effectively kill the grassy weeds?*

A These are known as annual grasses. The most effective treatment is a preemergence herbicide. This type of weed control should be applied 2 weeks before the seed should ordinarily germinate. The most common grassy weeds are:

Annual bluegrass
Barnyard grass
Crabgrass
Foxtail
Goose grass
Rescue grass
Sandbur

Timing is the key here. If you miss, you can use a postemergence before they go to seed.

Q *Won't rock salt, oil, kerosene, and gasoline do a more permanent job of killing weeds on drives and roads than weed killers—and be a lot cheaper?*

A In most cases, yes. But consider the danger to both you and the surrounding vegetation before you resort to this type of weed control.

Q *Can't you burn off weeds when you have a large open area?*

A I believe the Department of Natural Resources in my own home state of Michigan could give you an answer to that one. They tried it, but the fire got away from them and burned several thousand acres. Oh, yes! The weeds grew back heavier than ever.

Q *We have some large stands of sumac that we want to get rid of. I am told that a chemical called Dybar will really do the trick. Where can you buy it?*

A I will answer the last question first. You can't! Buy it, I mean. Dybar is used to kill full-grown trees! If you used it and the watershed carried it to another area, it could cause a disaster.

Q *How late in the spring can you kill weeds?*

A You can effectively kill weeds anytime they grow. It is not a good idea to spray large areas on hot summer days. Spot-treat late in the summer.

Q *I have used a popular-brand weed-and-feed in the spring for the last two years with disappointing results. I use it just like they say, so what am I doing wrong?*

A Thatch can slow it up or rain can reduce its effectiveness, just to mention a couple of things. Before you apply any weed killers (dry or wet), spray the weed-infested area with a soap-and-water solution (1 cup liquid soap per 10 gallons of water) while it's still damp. Then apply the dry weed-and-feed. If you're using a liquid, wait ½ hour and then spray.

Q *Spot weed killers are a rip-off, aren't they?*

A You are mixing up premix with the foam spot killers. Neither one is a rip-off. If you only have a few weeds, why buy a pint of concentrate? To make any of them work better, add a capful of liquid soap to the mix.

Q *How come when you dig out weeds, you end up with more?*

A Because you are doing them a favor by pruning them, which encourages branching. Pulling has the same effect.

Q *What's the best brand of broadleaf weed killer—I mean the one that kills the most weeds?*

A Any of the broadleaf weed killers that contain a combination of 2, 4-D, MCPP, and Banvel. This combination is sold as Super K-Gro broadleaf weed killer or Acme Super Weed-No-More.

Q *How do you wash out sprayers to make sure all of the weed killer is out?*

A Three times. I do it four times, and then I'm still afraid someone will use it on flowers or the garden. I use laundry soap and rinse and then mix a strong solution of 4 tablespoons of baking soda in a gallon of water. Spray to clear and wash again. I use my weed-control equipment only for weed control—they are clearly marked with red paint.

Q *Can Roundup be used safely around trees and shrubs?*

A Yes, but be careful how you use it. Keep the spray down and use it only on a calm day. I use Shootout from K-Mart—it's the same material.

Q *How do you destroy nut grass?*

A I paint the foliage with Shootout when it gets higher than my good grass. I do the same with other types of weed grass that are scattered here and there. I use a sponge paintbrush.

Q *When is the best time to kill weeds?*

A One o'clock in the afternoon; that's when they are most vulnerable.

Q *Is it better to try to control weeds in the spring or the fall?*

A If you are going to overseed or renovate your lawn, wait until spring. The spring (when they are growing) is the best time to control weeds. The next best time is in the fall.

Q *Is it true that weed killers can destroy other plants even if they don't touch them?*

A You are talking about bag goods or spilled liquids. Yes, the fumes can do it, so watch where you store them.

Q *What's the best way to prevent weeds?*

A Control the buildup of thatch, spike,

water well, feed regularly, mow properly, keep your equipment clean, and avoid foreign topsoils.

Q *Are there weeds we can't destroy?*
A As a rule, the answer is no. If I want it gone, I can get it—and safely—with the chemicals I have available at the garden center.

Q *I saw a man using a weed torch. Do they work?*
A This tool is from H. D. Hudson Sprayer Company.* It works, but chemicals do a better job.

*H. D. Hudson
500 N. Michigan Ave.
Chicago, Illinois 60611

13

State-By-State Lawn Care
Helpful Publications

I am, like you, a home gardener. Don't raise your eyebrow, it's true. I do not own or operate a garden center, greenhouse, sod field, or golf course. It's true that I have, over the years, been involved with all of these industries, all over the world. I am a garden writer, author, broadcaster, marketing consultant, product spokesman, inventor, storyteller, and homebody who has, like you, limited time in which to enjoy my hobby. With my reputation on the line, I may put just a little more effort into my lawning than do most of my neighbors.

Performance and results depend on quality information. When my neighbors have a problem, they wander over, and we discuss it. I wish I could do the same for you folks, but I have a suggestion for what to do when you have a problem. Go to your phone book and look up the telephone number of the cooperative extension service for your state and county. There is an agricultural extension agent in every county in this country. These agents, both women and men, are extremely bright, dedicated, sincere, and hardworking and will be glad to help you find a solution to your lawn or garden problem.

Another suggestion is to write to the cooperative extension service at one of the addresses included in the table that follows and request a full directory of their publications and prices. You will be amazed at the variety of subjects they cover. Under each state I have listed those booklets that I think might be helpful as a source of additional information directed specifically toward your state. I have found that in many cases, sending a self-addressed, business-size stamped envelope gets you a quicker reply.

A Weather Word to the Wise

I am not a meteorologist. I have been a weekend weatherman on WXYZ-TV in Detroit. As a result of this training, I've learned a great deal about weather and what to look for in order to be prepared. Below, I have outlined a few of the weather facts that will help you take the best care of your yard.

Code
A = Number of growing days
B = Last frost of spring
C = First frost of fall
D = Average inches of rain during grow-
      ing period
E = Best growing months
F = Number of rainy growing days
G = Number of days over 90 degrees in
      July
H = Number of days over 90 degrees in
      August

1 = Kentucky bluegrass
2 = Fine fescue
3 = Bent grass
4 = Tall fescue
5 = Ryegrass
6 = Bermuda grass
7 = Zoysia grass
8 = Dichondra
9 = St. Augustine grass
10 = Centipede grass
11 = Carpet grass
12 = Bahia grass

State: Alabama

Code	Birmingham	Montgomery	Mobile
A	241	279	298
B	3/19	2/27	2/17
C	11/14	12/3	12/12
D	33	38	58
E	3/15–11/15	3/1–12/1	2/15–12/15
F	75	77	90
G	13	20	23
H	11	17	20

Grass: 4, 6, 7, and 10

The following publications are available from: U.S. Cooperative Extension Service, Auburn University, Auburn, Alabama 36849.

Number	Title
ANR-22	Weed Control in Turfgrass
29	Bermudagrass Lawn
47	Alabama Gardeners Calendar
73	Centipedegrass
74	Zoysiagrass
91	Control of Turfgrass Diseases
92	Selecting Turfgrass for Your Lawn
170	Two-lined Spittle Bug Control
171	Sod Webworm Control
172	Fall Armyworm
173	Southern Chinch Bug
175	Control of Fire Ants
176	Mole Cricket Control
177	White Grub Control
231	Tall Fescue Lawns
239	Lawn Maintenance in Alabama
262	St. Augustinegrass
324	Lawn Insect and Disease Control Guide

State: Alaska

Code	Anchorage	Fairbanks	Juneau
A	124	100	181
B	5/15	5/21	4/22
C	9/16	8/30	10/21
D	8	4	15
E	5/17–9/14	5/23–8/28	4/24–10/19
F	49	51	92
G	8	21	7
H	3	10	5

Grass: 1, 2, 4, and 5

The following publications are available from: U.S. Cooperative Extension Service, U.S. Department of Agriculture, University of Alaska, Fairbanks, Alaska 99701

Number	Title
P-239	Establishing a Lawn in Interior Alaska
11	Establishing a Lawn in Alaska

State: Arizona

Code	Tucson	Phoenix	
A	245	304	
B	3/19	2/5	
C	11/19	12/6	
D	11	7	
E	3/15–11/15	2/7–12/7	
F	38	24	
G	29	31	
H	28	31	

Grass: 1, 2, 3, 4, 5, 6, 7, and 10

The following publications are available from: U.S. Cooperative Extension Service, University of Arizona, College of Agriculture, Tucson, Arizona 85721

Number	Title
8310	Kentucky Bluegrass
8387	Zoysia Grasses
Q46	Bermuda Grass
0391	Overseeding Bermuda Grass
8539	Seeded Bermuda Grass
A-6	Lawns for Arizona

State: Arkansas

Code	Texarkana	Fort Smith	Little Rock
A	233	234	241
B	3/21	3/21	3/17
C	11/19	11/10	11/13
D	28	29	31
E	3/20–11/7	3/20–11/7	3/15–11/10
F	64	60	66
G		22	21
H		21	19

Grass: 6, 7, 9, 10, and 11

State: California

Code	Santa Rosa	Fresno	Eureka
A	207	250	253
B	4/10	3/14	3/10
C	11/3	11/19	11/18
D	30	10	40
E	4/12–11/1	3/16–11/17	3/12–11/16
F		22	71
G		29	
H		26	

State: California

Code	Riverside	Marysville	Red Bluff
A	265	273	274
B	3/6	2/21	3/6
C	11/26	11/21	12/5
D	10	21	22
E	3/8–11/24	2/24–11/20	3/7–12/3

State: California

Code	Bakersfield	San Jose	Sacramento
A	277	299	307
B	2/21	2/10	2/6
C	11/25	1/6	12/10
D	6	14	17
E	2/21–11/21	2/12–1/8	2/7–12/8
F			
G	29		23
H	26		21

State: California

Code	Pasadena	Santa Barbara	Palm Springs
A	313	331	334
B	2/3	1/22	1/8
C	12/13	12/19	12/18
D	19	17	31
E	2/5–12/15	1/21–12/17	1/18–12/16

Grasses: 1, 2, 3, 4, 5, 6, 7, 8, 9, and 10

State: California (continued)

Code	San Francisco	Los Angeles	San Diego
A	356	359	365
B	1/7	1/3	
C	12/29	12/28	
D	21	14	9
E	1/7	1/3	1/2
F	66	33	42
G	1		
H	0		

The following publications are available from: U.S. Cooperative Extension Service, University of California, 2200 University Avenue, Berkeley, California 94720

Number	Title
2983	Dichondra
21269	Fusarium Blight Control
2540	Insect and Mite Control on Lawns
2585	Know Your Turfgrasses
2586	Lawn Aeration and Thatch Control
2587	Mow Your Lawn
21250	Practical Lawn Fertilization
21347	Water Your Lawn
2209	Pest Control in Lawns
2619	Disease Control in Lawns

State: Colorado

Code	Denver	Pueblo	
A	171	174	
B	4/26	4/23	
C	10/14	10/14	
D	15	12	
E	4/28–10/12	4/25–10/12	
F	42		
G	15	22	
H	10	18	

Grasses: 1, 2, 3, 4, and 5

The following publications are available from: U.S. Cooperative Extension Service, Colorado State University, Fort Collins, Colorado 80521

Number	Title
7202	Lawn Care
7203	Seeding a Bluegrass Lawn
7215	Kentucky Bluegrasses for Colorado Lawns

State: Connecticut

Code	Bridgeport	Hartford	New Haven
A	174	180	195
B	4/6	4/22	4/15
C	10/16	10/19	10/27
D	18	21	21
E	4/28–10/14	4/24–10/17	4/17–10/25
F	49	59	54
G	4	8	
H	2	5	

Grasses: 1, 2, 3, 4, and 5

The following publications are available from: U.S. Cooperative Extension Service, University of Connecticut, Storrs, Connecticut 06268

Number	Title
81-6	Lawn and Shade Problems
70-30	Lime for Lawns
70-32	Lawn Soils and Seedbed Preparation
79-71	Lime, Fertilizers and Manure
71-22	Watering Lawns
73-31	Mowing Lawns

State: Delaware

Code	Wilmington		
A	191		
B	4/18		
C	10/26		
D	23		
E	4/20–10/24		
F	56		
G	7		
H	5		

Grasses: 1, 2, 3, 4, and 5

The following publication is available from: U.S. Cooperative Extension Service, University of Delaware, Newark, Delaware 19711

Number	Title
97	The Art of Lawn Care

State: Florida

Code	Jacksonville	Tampa	Miami
A	313	349	365
B	2/16	1/10	
C	12/16	12/26	
D	48	51	60
E	2/18–12/24	1/12–12/24	
F	103	105	127
G	23	20	8
H	21	20	8

Grasses: 5, 6, 7, 9, 10, 11, and 12

State: Georgia

Code	Atlanta	Augusta	Savannah
A	242	249	274
B	3/21	3/14	2/27
C	11/18	11/1	11/29
D	29	34	41
E	3/23–11/16	3/16–10/30	2/29–11/27
F	72	74	89
G	7		19
H	5		15

Grasses: 4, 6, 7, 9, 10, and 11

State: Hawaii

Code	Hilo	Honolulu	
A	365	365	
B			
C			
D	119	25	
E			
F	282	101	
G			
H		4	

The following publications are available from: U.S. Cooperative Extension Service, University of Hawaii, Honolulu, Hawaii 96822

Number	Title
TM-1	Sun Turf Bermudagrass
TM-2	Turf Weed Control
TM-3	Soil Preparation
C-495	Turfgrass Fertilization

State: Idaho

Code	Pocatello	Boise	
A	1 1	7 7	
B	4/28	4/23	
C	10/6	10/17	
D	23	11	
E	4/30–10/4	4/25–10/15	
F		23	
G		19	
H		15	

Grasses: 1, 2, 3, 4, and 5

The following publications are available from: U.S. Cooperative Extension Service, University of Idaho, Morrill Hall, Moscow, Idaho 83843

Number	Title
CIS-150	Yard and Garden Weed Control
CIS-340	Lawn Pest Control
CIS-374	Bluegrass Billbug in Idaho Lawns
CIS-583	Selecting Turfgrasses for Idaho Lawns
CIS-731	Thatch in Lawns
EXP-565	Establishing and Maintaining Idaho Lawns

State: Illinois

Code	Peoria	Springfield	Chicago
A	181	186	192
B	4/22	4/20	4/19
C	10/20	10/23	10/28
D	21	21	21
E	4/24–10/18	4/22–10/21	4/21–10/26
F	55	59	61
G	6	8	5
H	4	10	4

Grasses: 1, 2, 3, 4, 5, 6, and 7

The following publications are available from: U.S. Cooperative Extension Service, U.S. Department of Agriculture, University of Illinois, Urbana, Illinois 61801

Number	Title
C-1076	Turfgrass Pest Control
C-1082	Illinois Lawn Care
C-1105	Turfgrasses of Illinois
NC-12	Lawn Diseases
NC-26	Lawn Weeds

State: Indiana

Code	Fort Wayne	Indianapolis	Evansville
A	179	193	216
B	4/24	4/17	4/2
C	10/20	10/27	11/4
D	20	22	24
E	4/26–10/18	4/19–10/25	4/4–11/2
F	59	60	73
G	5	6	15
H	4	3	10

Grasses: 1, 2, 3, 4, 5, 6, and 7

The following publications are available from: U.S. Cooperative Extension Service, Purdue University, Lafayette, Indiana 47907

Number	Title
AY-1	Ten Steps to a Good Lawn
AY-2	Lawn Care Programs
AY-3	Starting a Lawn
AY-4	Fertilizing Lawns
AY-5	Varieties and Mixtures for Lawns
AY-6	Zoysia and Bermuda Grass
AY-7	Watering Lawns
AY-8	Mowing, Thatching and Aerifying
AY-9	Broadleaf and Viney Weed Control
AY-10	Crabgrass and Other Grass Control
AY-11	Control of Creeping Weed Grasses
AY-12	Tall Fescue and Bench Grass
AY-13	Sodding and Renovation
AY-14	Improving Lawns in Shade
AY-15	Maintenance of Bentgrass
AY-16	Athletic Field Care
AY-231	Determining Spring and Fall Frost-Freeze Risks

State: Iowa

Code	Sioux City	Des Moines	
A	169	175	
B	4/27	4/24	
C	10/13	10/16	
D	18	20	
E	4/29–10/10	4/26–10/14	
F	52	55	
G	9	9	
H	6	6	

Grasses: 1, 2, 3, 4, and 5

The following publications are available from: U.S. Cooperative Extension Service, Iowa State University, Ames, Iowa 50011

Number	Title
PM-1113	Calibrating a Fertilizer Spreader
NCR-12	Chemical Control of Turfgrass Diseases
PM-1072	Establishing a Lawn from Seed
FG-450	Iowa Turfgrass Research
PM-930	Lawn Weed Control
PM-1053	Renovation of Lawns Damaged by Fusarium Blight
PM-491	Sodding a New Lawn
PM-1127	Thatch Control in the Home Lawn
PM-1063	Turfgrass Management Calendar—Kentucky Bluegrass Lawns
PM-1055	Turfgrass Renovating
PM-1067	Which Grass Is Best for Your Lawn

State: Kansas

Code	Topeka	Wichita	
A	200	210	
B	4/9	4/5	
C	10/26	11/1	
D	26	24	
E	4/11–10/24	4/7–10/30	
F	57	56	
G	14	21	
H	12	19	

Grasses: 1, 2, 3, 4, 5, 6, and 7

The following publications are available from: U.S. Cooperative Extension Service, Kansas State University, Manhattan, Kansas 66506

Number	Title
C-647	Turf Disease Control
NCR-12	Lawn Diseases in the Midwest
NCR-26	Lawn Weeds and Their Control
L-694	Recommended Turfgrass Varieties
MF-658	Buffalo Grass Lawns
MF-628	Fall Lawn Fertilizing Program
MF-544	Fertilizing Your Lawn
MF-652	Keys to a Good Lawn
MF-534	Overseeding Your Lawn
MF-438	Mowing Your Lawn
MF-608	Planting Your Lawn
MF-353	Selecting a Grass for Your Lawn
MF-736	Fescue Lawns
MF-440	Watering Your Lawn
MF-683	Zoysia Lawns
AF-106	Webworm, Cutworm, Armyworm, Chinchbug and Ant
AF-105	White Grubs

State: Kentucky

Code	Lexington	Louisville	
A	198	220	
B	4/13	4/1	
C	10/28	11/7	
D	24	25	
E	4/16–10/26	4/3–11/5	
F	66	68	
G	5	9	
H	5	7	

Grasses: 1, 2, 3, 4, 5, 6, and 7

State: Louisiana

Code	Shreveport	New Orleans	
A	262	292	
B	3/8	2/10	
C	11/15	12/9	
D	29	47	
E	3/10–11/13	2/22–12/7	
F	67	93	
G	25	20	
H	24	19	

Grasses: 1, 2, 3, 4, 5, 6, and 7

State: Maine

Code	Greenville	Caribou	Bangor
A	116	125	156
B	5/27	5/19	5/1
C	9/20	9/21	10/4
D	14	15	17
E	5/29–9/18	5/21–9/18	5/3–10/2
F	43	54	47
G		1	
H		1	

State: Maine

Code	Portland		
A	169		
B	4/29		
C	10/15		
D	16		
E	4/31–10/13		
F	54		
G	2		
H	2		

Grasses: 1, 2, 3, 4 and 5

The following publication is available from: U.S. Cooperative Extension Service, University of Maine, Orono, Maine 04423

Number	Title
D-12	Home Lawn Maintenance

State: Maryland

Code	Baltimore		
A	238		
B	3/28		
C	11/19		
D	26		
E	3/30–11/17		
F	68		
G	11		
H	8		

Grasses: 1, 2, 3, 4, 5, 6, 7, and 10

The following publication is available from: U.S. Cooperative Extension Service, University of Maryland, College Park, Maryland 20742

Number	Title
171	Lawn Care in Maryland

State: Massachusetts

Code	Pittsfield	Worcester	Boston
A	138	148	217
B	5/12	5/7	4/5
C	9/27	10/2	11/8
D	19	18	23
E	5/14–9/25	5/9–9/30	4/7–11/6
F	4/9	50	73
G		1	5
H		1	3

Grasses: 1, 2, 3, 4, and 5

State: Michigan

Code	Marquette	Detroit	Grand Rapids
A	159	182	190
B	5/13	4/21	4/23
C	10/19	10/20	10/30
D	16	18	16
E	5/15–10/17	4/23–10/18	4/25–10/28
F	60	58	52
G	2	6	5
H	2	4	3

Grasses: 1, 2, 3, 4, and 5

The following publications are available from: U.S. Cooperative Extension Service, Michigan State University, East Lansing, Michigan 48823

Number	Title
E-1480	Sod Web Worm Contract
E-1485	Chinch Bug Control
E-1484	Bill Bug Control
E-1489	Lawn Grasses for Michigan
E-1509	Crabgrass Control
E-1452	Dandelion Control
E-653	Lawn Weed Control
E-1488	Watering a Lawn
E-1487	Lawn Mowing
E-1329	Smut on Turfgrass

State: Minnesota

Code	Duluth	Minneapolis	St. Paul
A	125	166	166
B	5/22	4/30	4/30
C	9/24	10/13	10/13
D	15	17	17
E	5/24–9/22	5/4–10/11	5/1–10/11
F	47	55	55
G	1	6	6
H	1	4	4

Grasses: 1, 2, 3, 4, and 5

The following publications are available from: U.S. Cooperative Extension Service, University of Minnesota, St. Paul, 55101

Number	Title
AGBU-0488	Home Lawn
AGBU-0541	Computer Programmed Soil Test Recommendations for Lawns, Turf and Garden
AGBU-0818	Chemical Guide to Insect, Disease and Weed Control on Turf
AGFS-1008	Controlling Lawn and Turf Insects
AGFS-1123	Thatch Control in Lawns and Turf
AGFS-1137	Weed Control in Lawns and Other Turf
AGFS-1429	Fertilizing Home Lawn and Landscape Materials
AGBU-1513	Lawn Disease in Midwest

State: Mississippi

Code	Jackson	Biloxi	
A	235	298	
B	3/18	2/17	
C	10/8	12/12	
D	27	58	
E	3/20–10/6	2/15–12/15	
F	80	90	
G	24	23	
H	21	20	

Grasses: 6, 7, 9, 10, and 11

State: Missouri

Code	Springfield	St. Louis	Kansas City
A	201	206	207
B	4/12	4/9	4/6
C	10/30	11/1	10/30
D	26	23	28
E	4/14–10/28	4/11–10/30	4/8–10/28
F	59	60	61
G	16	14	19
H	14	11	12

Grasses: 1, 2, 3, 4, 5, 6, and 7

The following publications are available from: U.S. Cooperative Extension Service, University of Missouri, 309 University Hall, Columbia, Missouri 65201

Number	Title
G06700	Bluegrass and Fescue Lawns: Establishment
G06705	Bluegrass and Fescue Lawns: Maintenance Calendar
G06708	Thatch: Enemy of Lawns
C06750	Lawn and Turf Weed Control
G06955	Improving Lawn and Landscape Soils
G07201	Sod Worms as Pests of Lawns

State: Montana

Code	Great Falls		
A	139		
B	5/9		
C	9/25		
D	15		
E	5/11–9/23		
F	38		
G	9		
H	9		

Grasses: 1, 2, 3, 4, and 5

The following publication is available from: U.S. Cooperative Extension Service, U.S. Department of Agriculture, Montana State University, Bozeman, Montana 59715

Number	Title
1097	Lawns, New and Old

State: Nebraska

Code	North Platte	Omaha	
A	160	189	
B	4/30	4/14	
C	10/7	10/20	
D	14	23	
E	5/1–10/5	4/16–10/18	
F	45	58	
G	12	14	
H	11	9	

Grasses: 1, 2, 3, 4, and 5

State: Nevada

Code	Reno	Las Vegas	
A	155	239	
B	5/8	3/16	
C	10/10	11/10	
D	7	4	
E	5/10–10/8	3/18–11/18	
F		19	
G	22	31	
H	18	30	

Grasses: 1, 2, 3, 4, 5, 6, 7, and 10

The following publications are available from: U.S. Cooperative Extension Service, U.S. Department of Agriculture, University of Nevada, Reno, Nevada 89507

Number	Title
73-2	Which Lawn Is Best?
73-4	How to Water Your Lawn
73-6	What Should You Know About Mowing Your Lawn
73-9	Lawn Fertilization—How Often and With What?
73-10	Removing Thatch
73-14	Brown Spots in Your Lawn

State: New Hampshire

Code	Berlin	Concord	
A	109	142	
B	5/29	5/11	
C	9/15	9/30	
D	12	14	
E	5/31–9/13	5/13–9/28	
F	41	48	
G		5	
H		3	

Grasses: 1, 2, 3, 4, and 5

The following publications are available from: U.S. Cooperative Extension Service, University of New Hampshire, Taylor Hall, Durham, New Hampshire 03824

Number	Title
	Liming Acid Soils Under Turf
	Yearly Guide for Home Lawn Maintenance
	Renovation of Turfgrass Areas
	Installation and Maintenance of Sod

State: New Jersey

Code	Trenton	Newark	Atlantic City
A	218	219	225
B	4/4	4/3	3/31
C	11/8	11/8	11/11
D	25	24	27
E	4/6–11/6	4/5–11/6	4/2–11/9
F	67	69	65
G	7	8	5
H	4	6	5

Grasses: 1, 2, 3, 4, and 5

The following publications are available from: U.S. Cooperative Extension Service, Rutgers State University, P.O. Box 231, New Brunswick, New Jersey 08903

Number	Title
FS-102	Your Lawn and Its Care
FS-103	Establishing Your Lawn
FS-104	Steps to an Instant Lawn
FS-108	Renovating Your Lawn

State: New Mexico

Code	Santa Fe	Albuquerque	
A	178	198	
B	4/24	4/13	
C	10/19	10/28	
D	13	8	
E	4/26–10/17	4/11–10/26	
F		23	
G		16	
H			

Grasses: 1, 2, 3, 4, 5, 6, 7, and 10

The following publications are available from: U.S. Cooperative Extension Service, U.S. Department of Agriculture, New Mexico State University, Las Cruces, New Mexico 88001

Number	Title
481	Turfgrass in New Mexico

State: New York

Code	Watertown	Binghamton	Syracuse
A	151	154	168
B	5/7	5/4	4/30
C	10/4	10/6	10/15
D	16	18	17
E	5/9–10/2	5/6–10/4	5/2–10/13
F	50	56	60
G		4	
H		2	

State: New York

Code	Albany	Buffalo	New York City
A	169	179	219
B	4/27	4/30	4/7
C	10/13	10/25	10/12
D	17	17	24
E	4/29–10/11	5/1–10/23	4/9–11/10
F	58	60	69
G		1	6
H		1	4

Grasses: 1, 2, 3, 4 and 5

The following publications are available from: U.S. Cooperative Extension Service, U.S. Department of Agriculture, New York State College of Agriculture, Ithaca, New York 14853

Number	Title
185	Home Lawns
IB-190	Home Lawns: Varieties and Pest Control Guide
127	Turfgrass Disease List and Identification Key for New York State

State: North Carolina

Code	Ashville	Raleigh	Wilmington
A	195	237	262
B	4/12	3/24	3/8
C	10/24	11/16	11/24
D	26	30	40
E	4/14–10/22	3/26–11/14	3/10–11/22
F	69	71	79
G	3	10	15
H	1	8	13

Grasses: 1, 2, 3, 4, 5, 6, 7, and 10

The following publication is available from: U.S. Cooperative Extension Service, North Carolina State University, Raleigh, North Carolina 27607

Number	Title
AG-69	Carolina Lawns

State: North Dakota

Code	Bismarck		
A	136		
B	5/11		
C	9/24		
D	10		
E	5/13–9/22		
F	42		
G	8		
H	9		

Grasses: 1, 2, 3, 4, and 5

The following publications are available from: U.S. Cooperative Extension Service, U.S. Department of Agriculture, North Dakota State University, Fargo, North Dakota 58102

Number	Title
H-244	Your Lawn: It Can Be Beautiful
W-432	Chemical Weed Control in Lawns
PP-653	Lawn Diseases

State: Ohio

Code	Cincinnati	Cleveland	Columbus
A	192	195	192
B	4/15	4/21	4/17
C	10/25	11/2	10/30
D	21	20	21
E	4/17–10/23	4/23–10/31	4/19–10/28
F	65	68	64
G	10	3	6
H	8	2	3

Grasses: 1, 2, 3, 4, and 5

The following publications are available from: U.S. Cooperative Extension Service, Ohio State University, 2120 Fyffe Road, Columbus, Ohio 43210

Number	Title
4001	Broadleaf Weed Control in Lawns
4006	Fetilization of Lawns
4008	Thatch—A Problem in Lawns
4011	Turfgrass Selection
4012	Lawn Renovation
4014	Sodding the Home Lawn
4015	Renovation of Perennial Grasses
4019	Soil Preparation for Lawn Establishment
4020	Lawn Mowing
4023	Lawn Watering

State: Oklahoma

Code	Tulsa	Oklahoma City	
A	221	224	
B	3/25	3/28	
C	11/1	11/7	
D	27	25	
E	3/27–10/30	3/30–11/5	
F	56	56	
G	23	22	
H	21	21	

Grasses: 1, 2, 3, 4, 5, 6, 7, and 10

The following publications are available from: U.S. Cooperative Extension Service, Oklahoma State University, Stillwater, Oklahoma 74074

Number	Title
F-2654	Broadleaf Weed Control in Home Lawns
F-2655	Grassyweed Control in Home Lawns
F-2656	Thatch Removal in Lawns
F-2657	Dollar Spot of Turfgrass
F-7306	Ornamental and Lawn Pest Control
AF-7637	Home Lawn Disease Control Guide

State: Oregon

Code	Bend	Eugene	Portland
A	91	205	263
B	6/8	4/13	3/6
C	9/7	11/4	11/24
D	12	43	34
E	6/10–9/5	4/15–11/12	3/8–11/22
F			
G		6	4
H		5	3

Grasses: 1, 2, 3, 4, and 5

The following publications are available from: U.S. Cooperative Extension Service, U.S. Department of Agriculture, Oregon State University, Corvallis, Oregon 97331

Number	Title
EC-966	Establishing Lawns by Sodding
EC-967	Fertilizing Home Lawns
EC-968	Controlling Weeds in Home Lawns
EC-969	Establishing and Maintaining a Seeded Lawn in Eastern Oregon
EC-970	Grasses for Oregon Lawns
EC-1018	Removing Thatch and Aerating Lawns
EC-1021	Establishing New Lawns by Seeding

State: Pennsylvania

Code	Altoona	Williamsport	Scranton
A	151	164	174
B	5/6	5/3	4/24
C	10/4	10/13	10/14
D	22	19	19
E	5/8–10/2	5/5–10/11	4/28–10/12
F	62	61	63

State: Pennsylvania

Code	Harrisburg	Philadelphia	
A	204	232	
B	4/9	3/30	
C	10/30	11/17	
D	21	26	
E	4/11–10/28	4/1–11/15	
F	68	70	
G	9	7	
H	6	5	

Grasses: 1, 2, 3, 4 and 5

The following publications are available from: U.S. Cooperative Extension Service, Pennsylvania State University, University Park, Pennsylvania 16802

Number	Title
S-147	Mowing Turfgrasses
S-149	Growing Turf Under Shaded Conditions
S-150	Crabgrass Can Be Controlled
S-158	Principles of Turfgrass Irrigation
S-159	Aeration of Turfgrass Areas
S-160	Thatch and Its Control
S-162	Tall Fescue for Turfgrass Use
S-163	Turfgrass Seed Mixtures
S-195	Zoysia in Pennsylvania
S-198	Turfgrass Maintenance Fertilization
S-200	Turfgrass Species and Varieties
S-201	Lawn Management Through the Seasons

State: Rhode Island

Code	Providence		
A	197		
B	4/13		
C	10/27		
D	21		
E	4/15–10/25		
F	62		
G	3		
H	2		

Grasses: 1, 2, 3, 4, and 5

State: South Carolina

Code	Columbia	Charleston	
A	262	294	
B	3/14	2/19	
C	11/21	12/10	
D	34	44	
E			
F	74	94	
G	20	15	
H	16	13	

Grasses: 1, 2, 3, 4, 5, 6, 7, and 10

The following publications are available from: U.S. Cooperative Extension Service, U.S. Department of Agriculture, Clemson University, Clemson, South Carolina 29631

Number	Title
EC-528	Cool Season Grasses in South Carolina
EC-547	Warm Season Grasses in South Carolina
EC-580	Irrigating Your Lawn
EC-582	Prevent Lawn Mower Accidents
EC-583	Centipedegrass Problems
EC-592	Chemical Weed Control for Turfgrass
IC-122	Turfgrass Disease Control Guide

State: South Dakota

Code	Huron	Rapid City	Sioux Falls
A	149	150	152
B	5/4	5/7	5/5
C	9/30	10/4	10/3
D	12	11	16
E	5/6–9/28	5/9–10/1	5/7–10/1
F	44	44	45
G	12	11	12
H	11	12	9

Grasses: 1, 2, 3, 4, and 5

The following publication is available from: U.S. Cooperative Extension Service, South Dakota State University, Brookings, South Dakota 57006

Number	Title
FS-715	Lawn Care

State: Tennessee

Code	Knoxville	Nashville	
A	220	224	
B	3/31	3/28	
C	11/6	11/7	
D	25	24	
E	4/2–11/4	4/31–11/9	
F	73	68	
G	7	15	
H	6	10	

Grasses: 1, 2, 3, 4, 5, 6, 7, and 10

The following publications are available from: U.S. Cooperative Extension Service, U.S. Department of Agriculture, University of Tennessee, Knoxville, Tennessee 37901

Number	Title
837	Selecting of Lawngrasses for Tennessee
838	Establishing a Lawn in Tennessee
956	Lawns, Weeds and Their Control

State: Texas

Code	Lubbock	El Paso	Dallas
A	205	238	244
B	4/1	3/26	3/18
C	11/9	11/14	11/17
D	15	6	23
E	4/3–11/7	3/28–11/12	3/20–11/15
F	40	33	51
G			27
H			26

State: Texas

Code	Houston	Corpus Christi	
A	262	335	
B	3/14	1/26	
C	11/21	12/27	
D	38	27	
E	3/16–11/23	1/28–12/25	
F	80	73	
G	26	27	
H	24	26	

Grasses: 1, 2, 3, 4, 5, 6, 7, 9, 10 and 11

State: Utah

Code	Ogden	Salt Lake City	
A	155	192	
B	5/6	4/13	
C	10/8	10/22	
D	16	15	
E	5/8–10/6	4/15–10/20	
F			
G		26	
H		20	

Grasses: 1, 2, 3, 4, 5, 6, 7, and 10

The following publication is available from: U.S. Cooperative Extension Service, U.S. Department of Agriculture, Utah State University, Logan, Utah 84321

Number	Title
EL-86	Home Lawns for Utah

State: Vermont

Code	St. Johnsbury	Burlington	
A	127	148	
B	5/22	5/8	
C	9/23	10/3	
D	14	16	
E	5/24–9/21	5/10–10/1	
F	46	58	
G		3	
H		1	

Grasses: 1, 2, 3, 4, and 5

The following publications are available from: U.S. Cooperative Extension Service, U.S. Department of Agriculture, University of Vermont, Burlington, Vermont 05901

Number	Title
C-146	Lawn Care
BR-1214	Building a New Lawn
GD-13	Lawn Disease
GD-14	Lawn Problems

State: Virginia

Code	Roanoke	Richmond	Norfolk
A	165	218	242
B	4/14	3/29	3/19
C	10/26	11/2	11/16
D	25	29	34
E	4/16–10/24	3/31–10/31	3/21–11/14
F	66	68	79
G	9	13	11
H	6	11	8

Grasses: 1, 2, 3, 4, 5, 6,7, and 10

State: Washington

Code	Centralia	Yakima	Seattle
A	173	190	255
B	4/27	4/15	3/14
C	10/17	10/22	11/24
D	46	8	36
E	4/29–10/15	4/17–10/20	3/16–11/22
F			
G		14	1
H		11	1

Grasses: 1, 2, 3, 4, and 5

The following publications are available from: U.S. Cooperative Extension Service, Washington State University, Pullman, Washington 99163

Number	Title
EB-0482	Home Lawns
EB-0607	Lawn Weed Control
EB-0924	Lawn Renovation
EB-0938	Disease Control in Lawns
EB-1108	Furarium Patch in Turf
EB-1117	Thatch Control
EB-1280	Turfgrass Soil-Water
FG-0041	Fertilize Guide, Home Lawns

State: West Virginia

Code	Parkersburg	Charleston	
A	159	193	
B	4/16	4/18	
C	10/21	10/28	
D	21	22	
E	4/18–9/31	4/20–10/26	
F	66	71	
G	8	7	
H	6	5	

Grasses: 1, 2, 3, 4, and 5

The following publications are available from: U.S. Cooperative Extension Service, West Virginia University, 294 Coliseur, Morgantown, West Virginia 26505

Number	Title
427	Lawn Care Calendar
322	Wild Onion and Garlic in Lawns
82	Lawn Problems
330	Dandelion Control
334	Lawn Mower Safety
406	Lawn Care
502	Liming the Lawn
752	Maintain Turfgrass in Shade

State: Wisconsin

Code	La Crosse	Green Bay	Milwaukee
A	161	161	188
B	5/1	5/6	4/20
C	10/8	10/13	10/25
D	19	16	18
E	5/3–10/6	5/6–10/10	4/22–10/23
F	54	55	61
G		3	4
H		2	3

Grasses: 1, 2, 3, 4, and 5

The following publications are available from: U.S. Cooperative Extension Service, University of Wisconsin, 1420 Washington Avenue, Slurlevant, Wisconsin 53177

Number	Title
A9NYT012	Lawn Diseases from the Midwest
A9NYT-026	Lawn Weed Identification
A-1990	Lawn Weed Control
A-2303	Fertilizing Your Lawn

State: Wyoming

Code	Cheyene		
A	141		
B	5/14		
C	10/2		
D	15		
E	5/16–9/30		
F	50		
G	6		
H	3		

Grasses: 1, 2, 3, 4, and 5

The following publications are available from: U.S. Cooperative Extension Service, University of Wyoming, Box 3354 University Station, Laramie, Wyoming 82070

Number	Title
B-682	Keeping Ahead of Lawn Drought
B-682.2	Seeding New Lawns
B-682.3	Sodding New Lawns
MP-39	Watering Lawns

State: Puerto Rico

Code	San Juan		
A	365		
B			
C			
D	70		
E			
F	219		
G	4		
H	5		

Grasses: 5, 6, 7, 9, 10, 11, and 12

State: Virgin Islands

Code	St. Croix	St. John	St. Thomas
A	365	365	365
B			
C			
D	50	50	50
E			
F	180	180	180
G			
H			

Grasses: 5, 6, 7, 9, 10, 11, and 12

Parting Thoughts

Of all the books and articles I have written over the years, the ones I have enjoyed writing the most are those that deal with lawn care. It should come as no surprise to you folks, therefore, when I say that writing *this* book has been the most fun. I enjoy anything and everything to do with home gardening, but like anything else, we all have favorites (commonly known as druthers). There is nothing I would *druther* do than work on my lawn.

Lawning—as I affectionately refer to the time I put into grass care—may not be the most popular area of home gardening, but it is the one that you, your neighbors, and the other 81 million Americans spend the most time and money on.

A recent homeowner survey conducted by Dr. Hale N. Tongren (Department of Marketing, George Mason University, Fairfax, Virginia) for the American Seed Trade Association revealed that:

61.9 percent wanted a lawn as nice as most in the neighborhood

18.0 percent wanted the prettiest, best-kept lawn in the neighborhood

18.7 percent wanted to keep their lawn mowed regularly and reasonably green

This indicates to me that most of you have a lot of pride in how your property looks but think you lack the knowledge to have a better-than-average lawn.

I am telling you that with no more time and effort, those of you in the 61.9 percent bracket can join those of us in the "American Turf Clubs" (18.0 percent), while the 18.7 percent of you in the "reasonably green" department can really surprise your neighbors and go for and attain the greenest grass on your side of the fence.

Yes, you will have to put some physical labor into it, and yes, you still have to spend a few bucks—but a lot less of either than you think, if you will just try the steps I have outlined in this book.

There are those who will tell you that some of my suggestions are crazy. It won't be a turf pro, it will be someone who has never had his job or reputation depend on the appearance, quality, or health of the turf. Try it my way. The results will amaze you, and save your money, time, and effort.

Thank you for inviting me into your green scene. I hope I have helped you better understand just how important your lawn is to your own health, and the pride in accomplishment that you derive from it.

Index

About the Author

Jerry Baker is *America's Master Gardener*. Millions of readers know him through the success of his best-selling books—*The Impatient Gardener, Plants Are Like People* and *Talk To Your Plants*—and through his frequent radio and TV appearances.